INTERACTIONS

Perspectives on the Global Past

Jerry H. Bentley and Anand A. Yang
SERIES EDITORS

Interactions: Transregional Perspectives on World History
Edited by Jerry H. Bentley, Renate Bridenthal, and Anand A. Yang

Contact and Exchange in the Ancient World
Edited by Victor H. Mair

Interactions

Transregional Perspectives
on World History

EDITED BY
Jerry H. Bentley, Renate Bridenthal,
and
Anand A. Yang

University of Hawai'i Press
Honolulu

Library of Congress Cataloging-in-Publication Data

Interactions : transregional perspectives on world history / edited by
Jerry H. Bentley, Renate Bridenthal, and Anand A. Yang.
  p. cm. — (Perspectives on the global past)
 Essays from the conference Interactions, Regional Studies,
Global Processes, and Historical Analysis held in Feb. 2001 at
the Library of Congress.
 Includes bibliographical references and index.
 ISBN-13: 978-0-8248-2867-7 (alk. paper)
 ISBN-10: 0-8248-2867-4 (alk. paper)
 1. Area studies—Congresses. 2. Intercultural communication—
Congresses. 3. Intercultural communication—Case studies—Congresses.
I. Title: Transregional perspectives on world history. II. Bentley, Jerry H.
III. Bridenthal, Renate. IV. Yang, Anand A. V. Series.
 D16.25.I527 2005
 901—dc22

         2005010033

Designed by Elsa Carl, Clarence Lee Design

Printed by The Maple-Vail Book Manufacturing Group

Contents

Acknowledgments

The essays in this volume originated at a research conference, "Interactions: Regional Studies, Global Processes, and Historical Analysis," held in February 2001 at the Library of Congress, in Washington, D.C. The conference represented part of a larger effort to build bridges between the various fields of area studies scholarship that focus on well-defined world regions by accentuating the links between them, thereby contributing to the development of transregional and global historical analysis. The idea of drawing area studies associations into dialogue emerged in 1995 as a project of the American Historical Association (AHA). Conceived by Sandria B. Freitag (then executive director of the AHA) and the program committee planning the AHA annual meeting of 1996 (cochaired by Renate Bridenthal and Patrick Manning), it was later developed as a series of grant proposals for two research conferences and three summer seminars for community college instructors, all held at the Library of Congress.

It would have been impossible for this family of projects to succeed without the intense collaboration of educational institutions, funding agencies, scholarly associations, and energetic individuals. The AHA and the Library of Congress provided an institutional home for the projects in Washington. Both Freitag and Arnita Jones (who succeeded Freitag as executive director of the AHA) generously supported the projects with their time and AHA staff resources. Apart from Freitag and Jones, particular thanks go to AHA staffers Linn Shapiro, Debbie Doyle, and Brandon Schneider, all of whom devoted enormous time and energy to the projects. At the Library of Congress, Carolyn Brown, Prosser Gifford, and Les Vogel offered gracious hospitality in making the library's incomparable resources and facilities available to project participants. Under the leadership of executive director David Berry, the Community College Humanities Association provided essential logistical support. Funding for the projects came principally from the Ford Foundation. Thanks go especially to the Foundation's enterprising program officer, Toby Alice Volkman, and its visionary vice president, Alison Bernstein, both of whom supported the projects as efforts to build constructively on the legacy of area studies scholarship, which the Ford Foundation itself had generously sponsored for more than fifty years.

Planning for the research conference was the work of a steering committee chaired by Jerry H. Bentley representing the World History Association and Renate Bridenthal representing the AHA. Other members of the steering committee representing area studies associations and other constituencies included Sandra Greene from the African Studies Association; Nadine Ishitani Hata, Arnita Jones, and Stanley Katz from the AHA; Anand A. Yang from the Association for Asian Studies; David Berry from the Community College Humanities Association; Ann Twinam from the Conference on Latin American History; Saul Sosnowski from the Latin American Studies Association; Prosser Gifford and Carolyn Brown from the Library of Congress; and Leila Fawaz from the Middle East Studies Association.

ONE

Regional Histories, Global Processes, Cross-Cultural Interactions

Jerry H. Bentley

The 1990s were not kind to area studies. After the collapse of the Berlin Wall, area studies came under attack from several different directions. Some critics charged that not only had cold war interests tainted area studies from their inception and influenced scholars' conceptions of the larger world, but further that both the institutional structures and the substantive content of area studies were expressions of U.S. hegemony in the larger world.[1] Others argued that area studies perpetuated orientalist constructs deriving from European and Euro-American colonialism.[2] A few questioned the scientific status of area studies, characterizing them as purely descriptive exercises with no theoretical or explanatory power.[3] Yet others charged that area specialists focused so intently on their own regions that they lost sight of the comparative and global contexts of regional experiences, with the result that the area studies project in general was becoming a fruitless and ingrown enterprise.[4] Combined with threats of dwindling financial support, these critiques brought area studies to a point of crisis. Because area studies have been the principal filters through which scholars, policy makers, journalists, and the general public alike have produced and organized knowledge about the larger world since World War II, this was—and remains—a very important development.

By the late 1990s, scholars and funding agencies alike had launched a series of initiatives seeking variously to revive area studies and restore them to their former glory, to transform area studies and encourage them to address comparative and global issues, or to move beyond area studies altogether and develop new ways of organizing knowledge about the larger world.[5] In this atmosphere of reevaluation and experimentation, the American Historical Association (AHA) took the lead in organizing a series of programs funded by the Ford Foundation to promote fresh thought about historical analysis of world regions and large-scale processes. Partners of the AHA in developing these programs were the Library of Congress and a group of professional societies, including the African Studies Association, the Association for Asian Studies, the Community College Humanities Association, the Council on Latin American History, the Latin American Studies Association, the Middle East Studies Association, and the World History Association. Between 1999 and 2003, representatives of these groups organized three summer seminars for community college faculty and two research conferences, all held in Washington, D.C., at the Library of Congress.[6]

This volume presents essays from the first research conference on "Interactions: Regional Studies, Global Processes, and Historical Analysis" (February 2001). The purpose of this conference, as well as the larger series of programs as a whole, was not to extend the critique of area studies, but rather to promote scholarship that would build constructively on area studies by crossing the political, geographical, and cultural boundary lines conventionally observed by area specialists and indeed by historians and most other scholars as well. The conference did not focus on a specific issue such as industrialization in Japan or decolonization in Africa or international diplomacy during the cold war. Rather, it addressed the very general theme of cross-cultural interactions, featuring presentations that explored processes of cross-cultural interactions and their significance from area studies and historical perspectives. By focusing on processes that trespassed the conventionally observed boundary lines, so the organizers hoped, the conference would promote fresh ways of deploying area studies scholarship and encourage the emergence of scholarly approaches to explore some pertinent historical contexts of the contemporary globalizing world.

Meanwhile, by focusing on a very general theme rather than a specific issue, the conference organizers sought also to place questions of conception and method on the agenda of historians and area studies scholars. Indeed, a particular concern of the conference was to establish cross-cultural interactions as a category of analysis for historians and area specialists. The term *cross-cultural interaction* is of course quite problematic, and, as a relative newcomer to scholarly vocabularies, it no doubt harbors unusually good potential to generate miscommunication and misunderstanding.[7] Yet the conference organizers took it as self-evident that numerous historical processes of enormous significance have worked their effects across the boundary lines that historians and area specialists commonly draw to delimit the geographical scope of their analyses. These processes include climatic changes, biological diffusions, the spread of infectious and contagious diseases, mass migrations, transfers of technology, campaigns of imperial expansion, cross-cultural trade, the spread of ideas and ideals, the expansion of religious faiths and cultural traditions, and perhaps others as well.[8] Granting that there are multiple alternative ways to conceive and analyze processes of cross-cultural interaction, organizers of the conference neither assumed nor imposed any rigid construction. Rather, they sought to recruit presentations that would put empirical flesh on conceptual bones, thereby contributing to a larger effort to anatomize processes of cross-cultural interaction as they have unfolded at particular times, in specific lands, through individual and collective experiences. The concern, in other words, was less to seek some general or abstract understanding of these processes than to analyze their workings as inflected by particular conditions of specific times, places, societies, and cultural traditions.

The following essays represent some of the fruits generated by the Interactions conference. As such, they serve as a sampler of recent scholarly reflection on processes of cross-cultural interaction, and they exemplify several distinct and promising approaches to the analysis of these processes. The essays range widely over historical time and geographical space. Indeed, at first blush, there might seem little to link discussions of the postclassical Naqshbandiyyah sufi order, the formation of an African diaspora consciousness, the role of the Red Cross movement in China, and the emergence of contemporary regimes of world order. It would certainly be possible to explore any of these topics with little if any reference to the others.

Because of themes that wend their ways through these essays, however, the collection forms a whole greater than the sum of its individual parts. One theme that links many of the following essays is the issue of agency and structure. When scholarly attention tacks between individual experiences and large-scale processes, as is frequently the case in studies of cross-cultural interactions, questions of the relationships between human agency and historical structures inevitably arise and demand attention—or else they lurk beneath the surface and threaten the integrity and coherence of studies that ignore them. Historians and area specialists alike have strong professional interests pushing them to emphasize and even maximize the role of human agency in human affairs—including the agency of individuals as well as that of groups acting collectively—yet a scholarly focus on large-scale processes categorically confirms the point that neither individually nor collectively do men and women make their own history under conditions of their own choosing. Might it be possible to resolve or at least relax the tension between these two positions? On a spectrum of possibilities, ranging from absolute, effective human free will on the one hand to totally deterministic structure(s) on the other, the balance point between agency and structure will naturally shift dramatically from one situation to another, and indeed even in the cases of individual situations, depending on the perspective taken. There can be no question or pretense here of fashioning general principles or historical laws, but several of the essays offer useful guidance toward the striking of a balance between human agency and historical structures.

Quite apart from the issue of agency and structure, another theme that surfaces frequently in these essays has to do with the roles of states in processes of cross-cultural interaction. In many essays, a tension is noticeable between the historical dynamics unleashed by transregional or global processes on the one hand and the efforts of states to control or influence those processes in their own interests on the other. Yet although they acknowledge that states do not entirely control their own destinies, the essays agree strongly on one fundamental point: states still matter. Some essays attribute more influence to the workings of large-scale processes, while others emphasize the effectiveness of state actions, and several point to the roles of states in organizing and sustaining large-scale processes themselves. In all cases, however, the effort to understand the workings of large-scale processes requires close attention to state actors. Even when states have experienced limited success in advancing their specific goals, they have nevertheless influenced the development and operation of transregional and global processes.

Yet another theme that emerges clearly in several of the following essays is the reciprocal influence of global and local developments. All of the essays deal with large-scale historical processes, or at least with cases that represent important aspects or dimensions of large-scale processes. The authors, however, recognize clearly that a sophisticated understanding of these processes requires close attention to the ways human actors have sought to take advantage of opportunities presented by large-scale processes while at the same time adapting to the circumstances of particular times and specific places. For some purposes it might well be valuable to analyze large-scale processes on very general or abstract levels, just as for some purposes it might well be meaningful to study local developments on a small scale from purely local perspectives. The authors of these essays do not deny the value of either abstract or closely focused analyses, but they would agree that the richest understanding emerges from studies that take account of both the dynamics that have driven large-scale processes and the inflections they have undergone in specific historical settings.

Finally, and most generally, all of the essays collected here establish the theme of cross-cultural interactions as one crucial to the understanding of the world and its development through time. During the past half century, both history and area studies have achieved considerable intellectual power as projects to understand the world in time. They have fostered expertise in world languages and cultural traditions, and they have generated libraries of information about individual lands and peoples. In some cases, they have pushed beyond the development of information and the production of knowledge to the formulation of understanding, insight, and even wisdom about the larger world. In doing so, both history and area studies have focused their gaze almost exclusively on the experiences of individual societies (indeed mostly on modern national states) and largely ignored transregional and global processes that have profoundly influenced the development of both individual societies themselves and the world as a whole. This concentration on individual societies has enabled historians and area specialists to bring clear focus to their work, and it has provided them with appropriate contexts for the analysis of many important issues. At the same time, however, it has also inspired them to emphasize themes such as cultural differences, exclusive identities, and local knowledge, while discouraging them from considering larger contexts that go a long way toward explaining the experiences of individual societies themselves. By exploring processes of cross-cultural interaction, the essays in this volume offer some promising ways to understand the larger world through comparative, cross-cultural, transregional, hemispheric, oceanic, systematic, and otherwise global approaches to the past. In doing so, the essays do not abandon history and area studies so much as build on them and move beyond them by crossing the geographical and cultural boundary lines conventionally observed in history and area studies scholarship. They undermine the notion that the conventionally recognized world regions are natural or coherent areas. In place of such facile assumptions, they suggest that there is neither a single conceptual grid nor any set of stable, nailed-down categories that is universally applicable for purposes of understanding the larger world. Instead, the construction of world regions and human geography must take into account shifting patterns of cross-cultural interactions that shape the development of individual societies and the world as a whole.

C. A. Bayly establishes a context for the following studies in his essay on premodern globalization and its elaboration through time into the international networks that are the primary avenues of contemporary globalization. Bayly's globalization has deep historical roots. His periodization envisions an era of archaic globalization beginning about 1600 C.E., followed by an age of protocapitalist globalization extending from 1760 to 1830 and a period characterized by European-dominated internationalism after 1830. Notwithstanding the prominence of industry and empire in his later eras,

Bayly sees considerable continuing influence of the principles that drove his archaic globalization. By Bayly's account, this archaic globalization arose from universalizing kingship, the expansion of universalizing religious traditions, and widely shared understandings of bodily health that placed a premium on exotic medicines and potions. These three principles encouraged vigorous global exchanges of commodities, peoples, and ideas in the early modern world, Bayly argues, and moreover established patterns that continued to influence global exchanges in his later eras of protocapitalist globalization and European internationalism. Although the three principles of archaic globalization did not necessarily manifest themselves in the specific forms of the earlier era, Bayly sees their general influence persisting in the ages of protocapitalist globalization and European internationalism, which saw considerable continuity and intensification of links established earlier (by rapid expansion of slave trading in the late eighteenth century, for example, and the survival into the twentieth century of cultural and social values that drove efforts to consume exotic products).

By virtue of its emphasis on cultural and social values rather than finance, transport, mobility, and communications, Bayly's vision of globalization history differs markedly from the dominant views of contemporary globalization. Yet Bayly has clearly fingered some important dimensions of globalization, even if they are somewhat obscure and certainly undernoticed in most studies. Indeed, his understanding of globalization history wins implicit endorsement in many of the studies that follow. The next three contributions address his themes quite directly through the exploration of various globalizing processes.

John Voll's essay on the Naqshbandiyyah sufi brotherhood, for example, offers a case study on the workings of Bayly's archaic globalization by examining the effects of an expansive religious tradition. Organized in the thirteenth century as a local expression of Turkish devotion in central Asia, by the fifteenth century the Naqshbandiyyah had spread to northern India, eastern Turkestan, and southwest Asia. By the eighteenth century, the group was active in western China, and in the twentieth century it established a presence in North America. Throughout the centuries of its existence as a large transstate organization, the Naqshbandiyyah promoted Muslim renewal and Islamic identity, often benefiting from the patronage of ruling elites who aided the group's representatives with an eye toward enhancing the cultural unity of their lands and acquiring merit for themselves. Relations between the Naqshbandiyyah and states became more complicated in the nineteenth century, when the group played a prominent role in the mobilization of resistance to European imperialism. On balance, though, Voll holds that the organization does not reflect a world of clashing civilizations, but rather has demonstrated the possibility of cross-cultural dialogue in the interests of "a renewal of human society based on moral values."

If Voll's essay helps to develop the notion of archaic globalization, Sven Beckert's contribution on the global significance of cotton delves into Bayly's era of protocapitalist globalization. In the nineteenth century, the empire of cotton embraced Europe, Asia, and the Americas. Cotton integrated the lives of merchants, manufacturers, skilled workers, manual laborers, slaves, bureaucrats, and consumers around the world. It inspired technological and organizational innovations in the forms of new machinery and the factory system. It launched global migrations of workers. It linked plantations to factories, capitalism to industry, and wage labor to indentured labor and slavery. Only in global context is it possible to comprehend the role of cotton in the nineteenth century. Yet only in light of specific state policies is it possible to understand the emergence of cotton as the world's most important economic product of the early nineteenth century. Beckert argues that the global cotton market was not a natural phenomenon, but rather was a conscious construction of state policies reflecting public and private interests. Policies regulating labor, land use, and tariffs—not to mention episodes of imperial expansion—were crucial in ordering an environment that favored the rise of cotton. Thus, Beckert makes it clear through the example of his study that the understanding of large-scale processes calls for approaches that keep both global and local developments in view, integrating them in sophisticated analyses that are attentive to the influences of the global on the local and vice versa.

The state comes into clear focus once again in Caroline Reeves's essay on the experiences of the International Committee of the Red Cross (ICRC) in China. As Reeves points out, the ICRC is a prominent globalizing agency that is particularly keen to promote a global moral order. It does so by extending its recognition and services only to member states that subscribe to certain treaties and conventions. Yet the experiences of the ICRC in China during the late Qing dynasty show that local political interests profoundly influence the effects of globalizing agencies and globalizing processes in particular lands. Reeves argues that Chinese diplomats manifested considerable interest in ICRC membership principally because they sought recognition as a sovereign member of the civilized international community. The benefits and responsibilities that flowed from ICRC membership were less important than the symbolic significance and international diplomatic status conveyed by ICRC membership. In the event, however, before Chinese diplomats were able to establish a relationship with the ICRC, domestic turmoil flowing from the Boxer Rebellion and international military intervention threw their campaign off its track. Internationalism fell out of favor, at least temporarily, and as Reeves points out, the only Red Cross activity in China during the early years of the twentieth century was the effort of the Japanese Red Cross to care for Europeans wounded in the bloody campaign to suppress the Boxer Rebellion. By 1904 the campaign to establish a Chinese Red Cross had resumed, but the ICRC did not recognize a Chinese chapter until 1912, the year after revolution had put an end to the Qing dynasty.

The next three essays complement Voll's, Beckert's, and Reeves's studies of globalizing processes by focusing attention on specific issues arising from movements of peoples and commodities. Colin Palmer takes up the question of identity formation in the African diaspora. The latter-day term *African diaspora* implies a much stronger sense of community than was possible for involuntary migrants recruited from different societies, delivered to different regions, and subjected to different influences, whose descendants had little conception of their ancestral homelands. Under conditions of slavery and pseudoscientific racism, Palmer finds that the formation of African American identities reflected considerable influence of European and Euro-American thought. Palmer notices several distinct patterns in voices that represented the emergence of African American identities: they characterized Africa in Eurocentric terms, emphasizing African achievements that resembled those of European peoples and their Euro-American cousins; they accounted for contemporary African weakness by reference to innate barbarism, the absence of Christianity, European exploitation, and slave trading; and they reflected the development of a strong missionary impulse—sometimes a religious impulse that sought to Christianize the African continent but occasionally also a secular drive to bring enlightenment and modernity to a benighted ancestral homeland. In all these cases, it is clear that African American thinkers drew heavily on European and Euro-American constructs—although they sometimes reacted strongly against them—in their efforts to determine the significance of Africa for African American identities. In this light, there is deep resonance to Palmer's call for new constructs and fresh comparative approaches to the study of Africa.

Adam McKeown turns attention to the more recent movement of Chinese migrants to the United States, and he brings unusually clear focus to the role of the state and its bureaucracies in regulating the migratory flow. By the late nineteenth and early twentieth centuries, the institution of passports, visas, and official policies regulating migration offered government agencies scope for controlling functions that formerly had fallen to networks of lawyers and private businessmen. Despite the elaboration of ever more clear and precise rules, and despite the building of a large bureaucracy to oversee migration, individuals who did not meet the criteria for legal migration nevertheless found ways to obtain false papers allowing them to enter the United States. In McKeown's story, unqualified migrants pursuing their own individual interests won numerous battles and skirmishes, but the bureaucrats representing state interests largely won the war, although it took them some time to bring the migration process under reasonably effective control. Yet tensions between the desires of individuals to move and the obligations of government officials to control movement in the perceived interests of the state persist to the present day. Thus, McKeown's essay makes clear once again that the study of large-scale processes calls for sensitive analysis that takes proper account of both global and local developments.

If McKeown shows that movements of peoples are messy processes that resist official supervision, Alan L. Karras confirms that movements of goods and commodities also offer abundant scope for irregularity. Karras's study focuses on state efforts to regulate and control trade, which he finds have historically been only sporadically effective. As in the case of migration, states have long sought to control trade through bureaucratic and administrative measures, but they have not prevented enormous volumes of smuggled goods from flowing alongside legal trade. Karras attributes the limited effectiveness of regulatory efforts to the fact that states have been unable to detect most smuggled merchandise and further that they have been unwilling to punish most smugglers severely even when they have detected illegal trade. In fact, Karras holds that state options are not entirely open when it comes to the matter of controlling trade. Quite apart from informal collusion between local officials and smugglers pursuing their individual interests, strict enforcement of laws and regulations sometimes runs the risk of damaging local economies in which production, brokering, marketing, and transport all revolve around smuggling. Thus, as long as trade flows between lands and peoples, it is safe to predict that smuggling will survive alongside legal commerce. Karras notes a frequent pattern according to which individuals serving their own interests rewrite the laws and regulations by evading them.

The final three essays of the volume turn from the study of processes proper to considerations of conceptual issues that recent scholarship has placed on the agenda of historians and area studies scholars. Kären Wigen notes that, as historians have shifted their analytical focus from states to historical processes, they have created the need for fresh historical and geographical conceptions. States simply do not make the best containers for the study of many historical processes. With an eye toward priming the pump for a new round of rethinking historical and geographical conceptions, Wigen reviews four earlier projects to reconsider received constructs by fashioning fresh understandings of the world's oceans. She highlights four distinctive conceptions of the world's oceans articulated by historians, geographers, and other scholars between about 1450 and 1950. One conception viewed maritime space as an extension of national territory, while another posited oceanic arcs or bands that facilitated the flow of peoples and goods across the waters. A third conception took whole ocean basins as large zones of interaction and exchange, and the fourth viewed all the world's seas as parts of a single global ocean that served as the highway of globalization. Wigen's point is neither that one of these conceptions is right and the others wrong nor that later conceptions have superseded their predecessors. Rather, she sees at least some limited merit in all of them, suggesting that in the lack of permanent or stable constructs a flexible approach to historical geography is most useful for purposes of analyzing processes that cross the national and cultural boundary lines conventionally observed by historians and area specialists.

Stephen H. Rapp, Jr.'s essay moves Wigen's principles from the waters onto terra firma and applies them to the case of the Caucasus, the mountainous isthmus linking the Black and Caspian Seas. Rapp points out that geographies of world areas that reflect modern and contemporary times will inevitably distort the understanding of premodern experiences. This point holds especially true for regions like the Caucasus that had few large and strong states of their own but conducted intense dealings with several powerful neighbors. To highlight its distinctiveness, Rapp proposes to construe this region as Caucasia. At various times from deep antiquity to the present, Caucasia had close historical and cultural relations with Persia, Byzantium, the Greco-Roman Mediterranean basin, Muslim southwest Asia, Russia, the Ottoman Empire, and Christian Europe. In Rapp's view, it makes little sense to lump Caucasia with one or another of these admittedly larger and more powerful neighbors. Rather, he suggests that Caucasia participated in several different overlapping cultural communities, often simultaneously, although it frequently engaged more fully with the community whose political, military, economic, and cultural power was dominant at any given moment. Thus, while readily acknowledging Caucasia's close links with neighboring communities, Rapp seeks to establish it as a distinctive space of considerable historical importance. Even without large or strong states of its own, Caucasia has nevertheless been a perennially influential region because it has bridged different neighboring cultural communities and served as a major hemispheric crossroads of peoples, products, and ideas.

Charles Bright and Michael Geyer conclude this volume with their own contribution to fresh historical and geographical conceptions—the notion of the regime of world order in the twentieth century. Bright and Geyer view the regime of world order as a new organizing principle that helps bring the significance of twentieth-century history into clearer focus. The authors take the role of the state seriously: the regime of world order concept explicitly seeks to understand the dominance of two hegemonic states—namely, imperial Britain and corporate America—that built regimes of world order in the twentieth century. While making a prominent place for states, however, Bright and Geyer place the development of British and American hegemony in the context of global financial, commercial, and cultural flows. The authors clearly recognize that British and American regimes of world order reflected the hegemons' political, military, and economic power. Going beyond that, however, they argue that dominance through regimes of world order depended crucially on British and American ability to secure compliance and the consent of many peoples to participation in world orders that brought disproportionate economic benefits to the hegemonic powers themselves. Thus, Bright and Geyer build a cultural dimension into their regime of world order concept, thereby acknowledging the agency of all parties to historical regimes of world order while also deepening and enriching the understanding of processes sometimes treated more mechanically as macroeconomic operations or developments in international relations.

The essays presented here do not pretend to establish new sets of fixed analytical categories for history and area studies. Both individually and collectively they raise more questions than they answer concerning the construction of useful temporal and spatial categories for historical and area studies analyses. Nor do the essays in this volume seek to displace earlier modes of historical and area studies scholarship. Rather, they recognize that the local, regional, and national frameworks conventionally employed by most historians and area specialists are useful, meaningful, and entirely appropriate for the analysis of many issues. Accordingly, they seek to complement and build constructively on earlier studies and scholarly approaches by focusing attention on problems and processes that local, regional, and national frameworks often do not bring into clear view. Indeed, a later volume of essays (flowing from the conference on "Seascapes, Littoral Cultures, and Trans-Oceanic Exchanges") will continue this effort by considering patterns that emerge when historians and area specialists take bodies of water as sites of human activity. After all, historical development takes place simultaneously on many different spatial registers—individual, local, regional, national, continental, hemispheric, oceanic, global, and perhaps others as well. Attention to processes that unfold on the multiple registers of historical development and to the different faces that these processes present from different perspectives can only lead to enriched understanding of human experience.

NOTES

1. Ravi Arvind Palat, "Fragmented Visions: Excavating the Future of Area Studies in a Post-American World," *Review* 19 (1996): 269–315; Immanuel Wallerstein, "The Unintended Consequences of Cold War Area Studies," in *The Cold War and the University: Toward an Intellectual History of the Postwar Years* (New York: New Press, 1997), pp. 195–231; Bruce Cumings, "Boundary Displacement: Area Studies and International Studies during and after the Cold War," in Christopher Simpson, ed., *Universities and Empire: Money and Politics in the Social Sciences during the Cold War* (New York: New Press, 1998), pp. 159–188; and Martin W. Lewis and Kären E. Wigen, *The Myth of Continents: A Critique of Metageography* (Berkeley: University of California Press, 1997), esp. pp. 163–169.

2. Vicente L. Rafael, "The Cultures of Area Studies in the United States," *Social Text* 12 (1994): 91–111.

3. Robert H. Bates, "Area Studies and the Discipline," *APSA-CP: Newsletter of the APSA Organized Section in Comparative Politics* 7:1 (winter 1996): 1–2. Bates later softened his position somewhat in seeking a synthesis of area studies and social science; see "Area Studies and Political Science: Rupture and Possible Synthesis," *Africa Today* 44 (1997): 123–132, and "Area Studies and the Discipline: A Useful Controversy?" *PS: Political Science and Politics* 30:2 (1997): 166–169. See also the reactions to this and other critiques of area studies in *APSA-CP: Newsletter of the APSA Organized Section in Comparative Politics* 8:2 (summer 1997) and in the newsletter of the Association for Asian Studies, *Asian Studies Newsletter* 42:3 (summer 1997) and 42:5 (October 1997).

4. Andre Gunder Frank, "A Plea for World System History," *Journal of World History* 2 (1991): 1–28.

5. Itty Abraham and Ronald Kassimir, "Internationalization of the Social Sciences and Humanities," *Items* 51 (1997): 23–30; Globalization Project, University of Chicago, *Area Studies, Regional Worlds: A White Paper for the Ford Foundation* (Chicago: Globalization Project, 1997); Toby Alice Volkman, "Crossing Borders: The Case for Area Studies," *Ford Foundation Report* (winter 1998): 28–29; Ford Foundation, *Crossing Borders: Revitalizing Area Studies* (New York: Ford Foundation, 1999); Martin W. Lewis and Kären E. Wigen, "A Maritime Response to the Crisis in Area Studies," *Geographical Review* 89 (1999): 161–168; and Neil L. Waters, ed., *Beyond the Area Studies Wars: Toward a New International Studies* (Hanover, N.H.: University Press of New England, 2000). For an account exploring

the apprehension generated by new initiatives, see Jacob Heilbrunn, "The News from Everywhere," *Lingua Franca* 6:4 (May/June 1996): 48–56.

6. Themes of the summer seminars were "Globalizing Regional Histories" (July 1999), "Explorations in Empire" (July 2001), and "Seascapes, Littoral Cultures, and Trans-Oceanic Exchanges" (July 2003). Themes of the research conferences were "Interactions: Regional Studies, Global Processes, and Historical Analysis" (February 2001) and "Seascapes, Littoral Cultures, and Trans-Oceanic Exchanges" (February 2003).

7. See Patrick Manning, "The Problem of Interactions in World History," *American Historical Review* 101 (1996): 771–782, responding to Jerry H. Bentley, "Cross-Cultural Interaction and Periodization in World History," *American Historical Review* 101 (1996): 749–770.

8. Jerry H. Bentley, "The New World History," in Lloyd Kramer and Sarah Maza, eds., *A Companion to Western Historical Thought* (Oxford: Blackwell, 2002), pp. 393–416.

Two

From Archaic Globalization to International Networks, circa 1600–2000

C. A. Bayly

This chapter traces the nationalization of interactions across the emerging modern world. The dominant trend in the history of the global order from the later eighteenth century was the growing influence of the nation-state and its alter ego, the colonial state. For this, above all, was the period of the "internationalization of nationalism," when the discourses and practices of the nation-state became rooted among the elites in all major world cultures. This chapter considers the apparent paradox of international connections, which were themselves generated by the emerging order of competitive nationalism. But, to understand the significance of this shift, we first need to consider the nature of globalization before the high point of the nation-state. The networks of what will be called "archaic globalization" persisted under the umbrella of the nineteenth-century international system. At times they empowered it; at other times they challenged it.

I use the term "archaic globalization" to describe the links created by geographical expansion of ideologies and social forces from the local and regional level to the interregional and intercontinental level.[1] Archaic globalization was multicentric. In its early stages, the "expansion of Europe" itself was simply one among several contemporary examples of globalization, rather than an incipient "world system." We can detect a continuity of form and underlying principles in these patterns from classical antiquity through to the early modern period. Vast political and economic changes occurred during this era, of course. By the seventeenth century, the new cultural and economic network of the slave-plantation system and New World silver had ushered in the era of protocapitalist globalization in part of the Atlantic region. Nevertheless, the rationale underlying global networks for much of the population of Mediterranean Europe, Asia, and Africa in 1750 bore some similarities to those that had existed five or even ten centuries earlier. Of course, the concept of archaic globalization is an ideal type, a deliberate academic stereotype. It is a heuristic device that can help to make clearer the fundamental changes brought by global modernity by contrasting it with the modern order. To some extent, though, the global elites of the old world themselves understood their beliefs and activities to be continuations of the world picture and practices of the Ancients, the Companions of the Prophet, or the Early Christian Fathers. So the concept does strike some resonance with the ideologies of people in the old world.

Three principles underlay archaic globalization: first, universalizing kingship; second, the expansive urge of cosmic religion; and, third, humoral or biomoral understandings of bodily health. These forces patterned the global exchange of ideas, personnel, and commodities. The idea of universal kingship drove monarchs, their soldiers, and administrators over vast distances in search of honor, whether in the service of the Most Christian Empire or of Manchu supremacy. The courts of these world conquerors "cherished men from afar" and acted as magnets for honorific commodities drawn from distant lands.[2] These were not protonational states, as nationalists later came to argue. They were global polities that nurtured the exotic at their core long after the period of initial empire building. The Qing spoke Manchu within their court and camp. The Indian Mughals continued to speak Chagtai Turkish even after they adopted the outward form of Persian culture or the deportment of their Hindu subjects. The Chinese emperor Qian Long, who dominated the eighteenth century, continued to draw ritual specialists, nomad generals, and foodstuffs from deep central Asia in a characteristic Manchurian form of globalization. He is reputed personally to have learned not Portuguese or Dutch, but the nomadic Uighur language to communicate with his most distant feudatories.[3] For their part, the emperors of all the Russias and the Ottoman sultans laid claim to the legitimacy of Rome. Beijing and Rome were the political archetypes for most of the world's population. The tsars brought Greek priests, German administrators, and Siberian shamans into their courts.

The intelligentsias of the archaic globe subscribed to mythologies and ethical systems that complemented these political ideologies. Along with the charisma of Rome, or "Rum," the story of Alexander was encountered widely across Eurasia and Africa. Seventeenth-century Mughal kings modeled their meetings with Hindu renouncers on the reported deportment of Alexander before the cynics and Indian Brahmins.[4] Even in the nineteenth century, British travelers penetrating into the high passes of Afghanistan looked for Greeks, throwbacks to Alexander's army, among the tribal peoples.[5] The philosophy of Alexander's teacher, Aristotle, also retained its potency across a vast area of Christendom and Islam even in the eighteenth century. Aristotelian ethics had passed through the hands of medieval Islamic writers into the everyday moral language of the Indo-Islamic world. Works of *akhlaq*, Aristotelian-*cum*-Islamic ethics, were read daily at the courts of many Islamic rulers. They informed the judgments of local juris-consults.[6] New translations of Aristotle into Ottoman Turkish were made in the seventeenth century. Meanwhile, Aristotle and his followers remained an important influence on the intellectual landscape of Europe and its colonies. Until as late as 1860, churchmen in Spanish America were using these texts to justify slavery.

The idea of the civic republican tradition has informed European and early American intellectual historiography since John Pocock's seminal work in the 1960s. But perhaps we can also glimpse another, wider civic republican tradition that mitigated the autocracy of kings in Asia and in North Africa. These common elements in the world "mythoscape" provided discursive openings between Europeans, Asians, and Africans up to the mid-nineteenth century, even in situations otherwise characterized by ruthless exploitation and religious conflict.

Even after the growth of Atlantic slavery and migration, many of the greatest global movements of people remained pilgrimages and the wanderings of seers in search of traces of God. They reflected the imperatives of cosmic religion. Jerusalem and Rome retained their magnetic attraction for Christians in the Age of Enlightenment. For example, both Napoleon and the Irish revolutionary Wolfe Tone took time off more pressing engagements to consider how to bring the Jewish people back to Jerusalem.[7] For Muslim rulers from Sumatra to Nigeria, the organization of the Hajj remained the prime duty of relations with the wider world. Again, the expansion of sufi "mystical" orders within Islam orders provided a religious analogy to the globalizing of great kings. Even in the Atlantic world, Christian belief established patterns of long-distance godly migration. One need only think of the diaspora of the Franciscans and Jesuits, the origin of the Mormons, or the regular wanderings of English and Irish Quakers across the Atlantic in the eighteenth century.

Finally, bodily practice helped to structure archaic globalization. The world's biomedical systems—from the Greek, Islamic, and Hindu through to Daoist and Confucian—overlapped. Specialists read each other's texts. They sought out similar spices, precious stones, and animal products that were thought to enhance reproduction, sex, and bodily health. These prized commodities, drawn from across the world, were believed to have the magical property of transforming human substance, health, and fortune. To this extent, they can be called "biomoral" products. They were not simply items of consumption, which marked the outward status and wealth of individuals, as in modern "trophy" consumption. Along with markers of royalty, such as precious metals, weapons, and horses, the search for prized "medicines" —biomoral products—imposed deep patterns on world trade and the movement of peoples.[8] They helped create the archaic "ethnoscape," to borrow a term from Arjun Appadurai.[9] Even in the eighteenth century, for example, much of China's overseas trade was designed to capture biomoral products and tokens of kingship. It was as medicines that tea, then tobacco, and finally opium entered China. Each of these commodities became in time tokens of leisure and then, in the nineteenth century, items of pathological mass consumption. To a lesser degree this was also true for Western Europe and the Atlantic world.

Archaic globalization worked, then, in several different and mutually reinforcing registers. At the broadest level, we have the ideoscape—the *imaginaire*—of the old world constructed by universal kingship and cosmic religion. In the intermediate register lay the ethnoscape, the uneven patterns of diasporic trading, military, and specialist communities generated by these ideological predispositions. These were the links that scattered Armenian merchants from the kingdom of Hungary to the south China seas. Finally, in the register of bodily practice, the human being constructed global linkages through acts of biomoral transformation of substances and goods. The logic of such consumption was strategically to consume diversity. This pattern of collecting charismatic goods and substances differed substantially from the market driven uniformity of today's world.

The mention of tea, tobacco, and opium directs our attention to a second historical phase in which archaic globalization was supplemented by, but not replaced by, protocapitalist globalization. This began in the Atlantic system in the seventeenth century and spread to much of the rest of the world by 1830. This phase was associated with the growth of Atlantic slavery. It also saw the rise of the European chartered companies, arms of mercantilist state power, and the royal trading entities created in the Asian world to handle and control these burgeoning trades. Protocapitalist globalization developed by filling out and becoming parasitic on—"cannibalizing," to use another of Appadurai's phrases—the earlier links created by archaic globalization. For instance, the capture of slaves, once a strategy in the building of the archaic great household in Africa and the Ottoman world, became a brutal protocapitalist industry at the behest of European entrepreneurs.

These new globalizing entities, the chartered companies and early modern navies, tried methodically to subordinate and redistribute labor on a vaster scale, but the change was uneven. In the register of bodily practice and personal deportment, the transformation was particularly slow. In Europe and outside, the trading companies carefully maintained the cultural repute of what were originally biomoral products intended to transform the spirit and substance of the recipient and convey the beneficence of the exotic. So, for instance, tobacco was—and in some quarters is still—seen as a stimulant to mental capacity. Aristocratic and burgher taste preserved the rituals of sociability and the aura of rarity surrounding what were now industrial products if production alone is considered.

The first great age of truly global imperialism between about 1760 and 1830 was, therefore, thoroughly "hybrid" when viewed from the perspective of the underlying principles of its globalization. There were elements of novelty emanating especially from the European Atlantic economy. Here for the first time changes in the Americas directly affected Asia. For example, the American Revolution significantly altered trading patterns in Asia by forcing the English East India Company to redouble its purchases of tea in China and eventually to introduce Indian opium into Qing territory. Later, the French invasion of Spain and the consequent Latin American revolutions drastically curtailed the supply of New World silver to Europe, the Ottoman Empire, and Asia. Indirectly, these huge variations in specie supply fostered social conflicts within the Chinese Empire. They helped impel the British push for conquest and revenue resources in India. They sped the bureaucratic reforms of the Ottoman Empire. Yet, during this same period, the instruments of international statecraft and the ideoscapes that informed them retained archaic features. Thus, for example, a dynasty from near Alexander's birthplace became rulers in Egypt. Cossack-style raiders from beyond the borders remained central to the building of the British Indian and Russian Central Asian empires even when "gentlemanly capitalists" had already transformed the principles of accountancy underlying the East India Company or the Russian state.

At the ideological level, hybridity also characterized the period 1760–1830. On the one hand, Captain Cook and Admiral Bougainville, who explored the Pacific, used rationalistic and methodical methods of survey. The learned men of the British and French royal and oriental societies sought to make a map of all mankind by which all species of peoples and products could be categorized.[10] On the other hand, archaic ideologies still prevailed. For instance, travelers in Egypt set themselves to tap the cosmic power of the pyramids. What modern Egyptologists call "Pyramidiocy" has a very ancient pedigree. In the 1790s an Anglo-German official in India believed he had found descriptions of the ancient British Isles of the days of Joseph of Arimethea in the Sanskrit texts.[11] At this time, too, a Scotsman became an Amerindian king in Honduras and a British Indian officer carried floats of the Hindu deities around in his retinue. Religious practice remained both ritualized and syncretic. In the British and American world, neither belief nor race, but simple baptism, widely remained the qualifier for public office. Even in the central lands of Islam, sultans made prestations to Christian monasteries and synagogues.

In the register of bodily practice, the boundaries of the ethnic nation-state were not yet hard and fast. Officers in North America married the daughters of Amerindian chiefs. Large Eurasian and Afro-Asian communities developed across the world. Despite the beginning of a separate medical profession, most people still opted for a portfolio of different types of medical treatment, reinforced with prayer and magic. The consumption of exotic and charismatic herbs and other products continued the exchange of biomoral information at the global level. The cowpox vaccine traveled from Persia to England. From there it was disseminated by direct bodily contact back to European trading posts in India and the China coast and on to the royal centers of the interior.

How were honor and value assigned to people in these patterns of global interconnection? We must reject the view that either race or nationality as understood at the end of the nineteenth century was yet dominant. What we see instead is a global system of caste loosely linking the discrete ranking systems of the Americas, Africa, and Eurasia. I do not mean by this the intricate pollution-based caste system of nineteenth-century India, but the notion of *casta,* or caste, that was common across the whole Iberian Atlantic, Pacific, and Indian Ocean world. In this scheme, European aristocratic blood purity provided one pole of embodied status and slave origins the other. As in the eighteenth-century Mexican manual of pedigree, *Las Castas Mexicanas,* all other human groups could be intricately distinguished in a hierarchy stretching between these poles.[12] This archaic notion of caste, *casta,* or race, *raza,* prevailed in the Caribbean, Iberian, and English American worlds.

European *casta* was generally compatible with the biomoral divisions of the Hindu system of *jati.* Muslims could loosely identify it with their own forms of status discrimination. These were based on humoral principles and historic closeness to the family of the Prophet. In turn, Chinese merchants in port cities adapted such Eurasian and Islamic categories to their own concepts of refinement and barbarity. As Frank Dikotter has shown in his book on race in modern China, classical Chinese biomoral rankings assigned highest value to yellow races. Whites were associated with mental dullness and blacks with uncontrolled passions.[13] Caste as a global integrator of embodied status remained the key discriminator of the ethnoscape of the archaic and protocapitalist diasporas. It operated at a deeper level than nationality, which itself remained a flexible and porous category. The "Dutch" of the Dutch East India Company were a polyglot group of Germans, Scandinavians, Swiss, and French Huguenots, characterized by their recruitment by the Dutch Company. The "French" in India included many Catholic Irish adventurers.

After about 1815, the European state and Western colonialism undoubtedly began to impose a new pattern of internationalism on the archaic world order. The nation-state increasingly dominated global networks. It imposed its system of more rigidly bounded territories, languages, and religious conventions on all international networks. But it is important to keep in mind that patterns of archaic globalization persisted strongly under the surface of this new international order. More than that, they both empowered and subverted it.

When we consider how international networks were structured in the nineteenth century, the unintended consequences of older-style links as much as the policies of the leaders of the national states remain crucial. Why for instance, after two savage and destructive wars, and despite widespread British support for the Confederacy during the Civil War, did the United States and Britain drift together in the course of the nineteenth century? International relations specialists have usually viewed this question from the perspective of "reason of state." But prevailing archaic connections were equally, if not more, important. Even after the events of 1783 and 1812, lawyers on both sides of the Atlantic continued to cling to the old lineages of common law. Old Protestant churches renegotiated their links and mounted an evangelical offensive across the globe. Before 1848, transAtlantic links of marriage and emigration remained very similar to what they had been during the "peopling of America" in the seventeenth and eighteenth centuries.

Archaic links of religion, economy, and bodily practice also continued to underpin the new international order of the nineteenth century in the economic sphere. Classic Marxist and liberal theories of the international economy have generally emphasized the economic rationality of expanding capitalism. In this theory, the aim of Western expansion was to seize resources and subordinate labor. This is true in great measure. In the early nineteenth century, much of the globe became a vast agricultural hinterland for Western Europe. This occurred before mass industrialization, even in Britain. Still, many features of archaic global economic links persisted and remained formative in these new systems. Archaic globalization had been partly driven by the desire to acquire the exotic, to collect rarities, and to transform biomoral substance. That desire did not abate in the nineteenth century. Fans and exotic spices had proved lucrative items of global trade in the seventeenth century. Yet ostrich feathers and Japanese pottery for Europe and rhinoceros horns and birds-nests and a variety of aphrodisiacs for the Chinese markets proved to be some of the most enduring trades at the end of the nineteenth century.

One particular item of international trade is greatly resistant to Smithian analyses of supply and demand. After 1860 gold may well have been manufactured through capitalist forms of production and labor control in Australia, California, and South Africa. Its markets, however, responded to quite different rationales of prestige and familial consumption. Throughout the nineteenth century and even up to the 1980s, gold consumption in India and the Middle East has been highly price inelastic. Indians, Arabs, and others continued to import huge quantities of gold for adornment and family saving, regardless of its price on the international market. Anthropologists have shown how gold operates as a universal, honorific currency in India, independently of the market.[14] Until recently, the accumulation of gold bangles and other ornaments was preeminently a tactic for preserving the financial viability of women in their husbands' families. Gold was also believed to exert beneficial biomoral on the body of the wearer. These archaic principles of consumption continued to bulk heavily in the ledgers of the gentlemanly capitalists of the modern world for whom gold acted as a kind of reserve currency.

Another aspect of this persistence of the archaic was explored some years ago by Avner Offer. Offer noted that a key strength of the British and American worlds in 1914–1918, compared with the Central Powers, was their massive endowment of horsepower. Even at the height of the industrial age and even as the military significance of cavalry declined, horsepower remained the key form of power on the battlefields of the 1910s and 1920s.[15] The Western Allies of the First World War benefited from aristocratic patterns of horse ownership and horse sports, whose origins lay in the feudal age but had been spread overseas by empire.

The global marriage patterns of the nineteenth century also preserved some archaic features. In general, anthropologists have examined the structure of marriage patterns within small societies. Social historians have tended to consider the marriage practices of particular national nobilities. What happened in the nineteenth century, though, was a massive expansion of global hypogamy—down-marriage, often by younger sons—which often entailed marriage between distinct cultural or assumed racial groups. It is often said that by the 1830s sexual relations between European and Asian women were a thing of the past. There is indeed evidence of a slow imposition of racial boundaries in marriage and sex in the course of the nineteenth century. But this should not be overstated. The Anglo-Indian community may generally have been formed before 1850, but large Anglo-Chinese and Anglo-Burman communities came into existence after this date. They played a dominant role in commerce and the service economies of much of southern and eastern Asia. The ancient practice of Muslim out-marriage with foreigners continued to pin together the Arab, Indian, and Muslim East throughout the nineteenth century. It later became important as a network of sentiment that helped link the Pan-Islamic movements worldwide. Mixed-race community formation remained common in the Americas, even though what became known as "miscegenation" was gradually limited by bourgeois racist ideas in English-speaking North America.

Archaic conceptions of kinship continued to act as powerful formative influences on the European and American worlds themselves. The global links of European royal families—the Bourbons, Hohenzollems, Saxe-Coburgs, and others—became a strategic network for the prosecution of private diplomacy in the later nineteenth century.[16] At the same time, the practice of aristocratic hypogamy in northern Europe was to provide a vital resource for declining estate owners after the onset of the great agricultural depression of the 1870s. British aristocratic families welcomed American heiresses. The case of the Churchills and the Curzons, whose families both acquired "new" blood and new wealth by bringing in American heiresses, are only the best-known examples of this practice. Old Spanish, Portuguese, and French property owners kept their estates solvent by bringing over women from wealthy colonial backgrounds in Brazil, Cuba, and Mexico. All of these archaic connections were transformed within the new capitalist structures of the world economy. Yet all of them reflected the traditions and strategies of an earlier period. Modern eugenic theory merely validated older conceptions of bloodlines.

This chapter now considers how global connections did slowly become international connections. Much work has been done on the growth of the nation-state and its alter ego, the imperial state, after 1850. Less attention has been paid to the process by which global links were themselves reconstructed by the system of nation-states. Archaic patterns of global interactions persisted, but they were increasingly represented in terms of national essences and taken cognizance of by national governments. This change took place in all the different registers in which we have understood the working of archaic globalization.

At the first level, that of ideology, the critical point was the international appropriation of theories of individual and states' rights. Intellectual history remains very Eurocentric and American-centered. We need to look at how Asia and Africa took up and used rights theories. Imperial expansion was obviously a key determinant of this. The apparatus of the European state and its territorial rights over space and citizens was exported to the fluid, segmented world of Asia and Africa. The idea of a universal Chinese, Ottoman, or even Catholic Christian empire became redundant, but colonial patriots also began to assert their rights as individuals or representatives of cultures in the language of these appropriated theories. In the 1830s, Ram Mohan Roy, the Bengali reformer, argued in London that the rights of the Mughal Empire, which was now perceived as a state rather than as a universal polity, had been violated by the English East India Company. The defeat of China during the opium wars ultimately forced the Middle Kingdom to claim merely equal territorial and economic rights under the law of nations. The "ideoscape" of the modern international world was envisioned as a dialogue or concert of equal political entities that claimed uniform rights. Equally, the universalizing tendency inherent in newly diffused theories of individual and group rights began to create networks beyond the nation-state. These constituted an incipient international civil society.

Other aspects of the global pattern of ideologies—the ideoscape—were also transformed. At one level, religions still remained global in their aspirations. Increasingly, though, they tailored their activities, forms of bureaucracy, and appeal to the nation-state. Later-nineteenth-century Christian missions were national missions. The revived Catholic Church of the late nineteenth century spoke a universalizing language, of course, but it took the form of a parastatal organization. Its appeal was heavily directed to submerged nationalities in Catholic France and Ireland, for instance. Pan-Islamism likewise dreamed of a universal *khilafat*, but its actual method was to empower submerged or embattled Muslim nations. Race theory, which became dominant at the end of the nineteenth century, purported to be a global historical theory. Its discursive implications, however, were almost everywhere worked out in the language of the nation-state. In this it differed significantly from the archaic, tactile, and embodied system of *casta*.

Second, the ethnoscape—the international movement of peoples—of the late nineteenth and twentieth centuries was increasingly regulated by state surveillance and by the control of flows of migration. From the regulation of trans-Atlantic emigrants shipping by the British and American governments in the 1820s through the quarantine regulations of the great cholera epidemics of the 1830s and 1840s, states acted more and more insistently to control international traffic. The doctrine of free trade struggled for some decades with this urge to state regulation, but, by the later nineteenth century, fears of racial decline and the internationalization of crime had handed victory to state surveillance. The imposition after 1900 of rigid control in the United States, culminating in the National Origins legislation of 1924, was simply one aspect of this phenomenon. Such interventions defined more clearly the "essence" of the state, but they also formed the context for international connections.

Looser links of global commerce gave way to formal international conventions. This was true even in the days of free trade before the 1870s. But as the ideology of "national political economy" became more current, the economic interests of nations had to be presented internationally. This led to an increasing bureaucratization of international trading links. The old system of honorary consuls or consultation with headmen of guest merchant communities was replaced with commercial consulates and international economic treaties. During the Anglo-Boer War, British politicians panicked over the way in which international firms were supposedly perverting the course of international relations. International stock markets and capital flows were strengthening, though national controls on the location and use of capital became more stringent with the development of the national patent and the idea of the national head office.

Third, at the level of bodily practice, international links were conducted in a different way from the earlier hierarchical cosmopolitanism. Assumed racial groups were increasingly physically separated. Europeans in the East gave up the practice of using Indian and Chinese wet nurses for their children. In the course of the nineteenth century, they eschewed non-European dress and foods.[17] The process, never complete, also affected Asians and Africans. By the 1920s and 1930s, Hindu nationalists were mounting campaigns to expel Muslim body servants from their households and prohibit their women from visiting Muslim charismatics and healers. This is a good example of the way in which archaic boundaries of pollution were "nationalized," as it were. Yet more rigid nationalization demanded a complementary internationalization at the level of the body. In the international public sphere, males were more and more constrained to wear English topcoats and hats while they spoke, ate, drank, and deported themselves in a French style.

To chart this process of the nationalization of erstwhile global connections, this chapter takes three case studies. The first is a state institution, the passport. Second, this chapter considers an international voluntary association, the Red Cross. Finally, it examines a critical international conference, the World Parliament of Religions, held in Chicago in 1893.

Until recently little work has been done on that preeminent tool of the microsurveillance of international boundaries, the passport. The history of the passport, however, clearly indicates the transition between global cosmopolitan networks and the internationalism of the nation-state. A recent book by John Torpey, *The Invention of the Passport*, lucidly fills a great gap in our knowledge as far as Europe is concerned.[18] In the eighteenth century, elite traders and nobles moved readily across much of Europe. It was the poor and the peasantry who were tied to the land and needed papers to move around. The external passport was a royal letter, a boon that conferred on great nobles, clerics, and others royal protection and a request that they would not be hindered by the petty officials of another king's realm.

In Europe and the Americas, the passport became a tool of external political surveillance only during the French Revolution, when governments sought to control the movement across their borders of political agitators or, in the case of the French Republic, reactionaries and royalists. Fear of revolution continued to spur the development of passport offices and agencies throughout the nineteenth century. The 1848 revolutions and the aftermath of the 1870 Paris Commune saw panic attempts to extend the system even to ordinary people. But there was a general move to relax controls over both internal movement and emigration beyond states' borders. It was during the later nineteenth century, in response to fears about the consequences of labor mobility, that further, more rigid controls on movement across national boundaries were imposed.

The Asian world saw a similar process, but its roots were somewhat different. In Asia, too, great kings had given subjects charters for travel—in India they were called *parwanas*, leaves to pass. At the local level, movement was controlled through recognized leaders and headmen. Villagers on the move do not seem to have been forced to carry papers as they were in Europe and China, but the books of the village accountant gave elites an indirect control over the labor movement. In India, the expansion of the passport system to encompass ordinary merchants and travelers was at first a consequence of monopoly building by the European companies, which were deeply jealous of their European rivals. The Dutch and English East India companies kept meticulous records of all foreign European subjects in their territories, fearing that they would institute competitive commerce. Asian states faced with this aggressive imperialism of monopoly instituted countermeasures, limiting foreign merchants and personnel to particular points and controlling their own subjects' relations with them. The eighteenth-century Chinese state-trading corporation, the Cohong, was a good example of this. All foreigners in Canton were forced to carry accreditations from their assigned merchants.

Political fear rapidly replaced commercial jealousy after 1800. By 1830, the authorities in south India were arresting merchants from the Middle East "who were traveling without passports."[19] They feared purist Muslim teachers and other religious emissaries would spread anti-British messages in volatile port cities. In turn, however, the imposition of passports opened up queries about who was and who was not a British Indian subject.[20] Willy-nilly, European imperial governments asserted their rights to protect or control the external movement of their subjects. Indian merchants overseas became subjects of British India rather than guest foreigners. This was a critical point in their transformation into subjects of a nation. By contrast, some contemporary merchants of the Arab and Chinese diasporas were able to secure foreign nationality in European enclaves in order to avoid Chinese or Ottoman taxation or land law.[21] In this case, the passport as an international device was being used to subvert, rather than to strengthen, the emerging modern state. In either case, however, the state became the single most important determinant of global diaspora.

The Red Cross, my second case study, provides an example of the way in which an urge to provide humanitarian aid outside the state was later nationalized, as Caroline Reeves's analysis of the Chinese case in this volume shows. Global humanitarianism drawing on the Christian and humanist traditions became a strand in the international public sphere. Originally a response by Henri Dunant to the horrors of the battlefield of Solferino, the Red Cross organization soon became associated with Switzerland as a nation-state.[22] The red cross itself was not so much a Christian symbol as the obverse of the Swiss flag. Since 1880, the central organization has been heavily Swiss. Its subordinate bodies were built around different national committees of the Red Cross. This quasi-international national organization has pressed national governments to create international conventions on the laws of war, but the tension between the national and the international has always remained latent. In the 1880s and 1890s, the symbolic unity of the organization was breached when enraged Ottoman Muslims attacked Red Cross volunteer doctors serving on battlefields because they were wearing a Christian symbol. This forced the organizers to allow the red crescent to be adopted in Muslim countries. During the Balkan wars, again, Indian

Muslims organized in defense of the Ottomans in order to reflect the strength of a specifically Indian nationalism in its defiance of the imperial power.[23] More recently, the state of Israel has tried to insist on the use of the red Star of David in its own sphere.

Its Christian organizers intended the World Parliament of Religions of 1893 to celebrate humanity's global quest for religious experience. They hoped to mitigate hostilities between different religious traditions. The context was the rise of anti-Semitism, increased Protestant-Catholic hostility, and the Western fear of pan-Islamism. From the beginning, however, the organization of the meeting was dogged with controversy over the status of national religious bodies. In the tense political situation of the period, it was found possible in many cases only to allow the representatives of national churches to represent religions.

Though uninvited, the great Bengali seer Swami Vivekananda turned up at the meeting and by force of character became the "Indian" representative.[24] He achieved three things by his passionate speeches to the Parliament. First, he managed to consolidate the American sense that Hinduism was a powerful international force. He did this by eliding sects and pointing to the ancient Hindu civilizations of Southeast Asia and the diaspora Hindus of South Africa and the Caribbean. Second, he managed to project the idea of Hindu difference from other religions and its superiority to them. He recorded his horror at the daily massacre of the sacred cow, which he saw in the Chicago stockyards. This stirred not only Hindu sentiment, but also the conscience of vegetarians around the world. Most significantly, Vivekananda firmly welded the notion of Hinduism to the claims of Indian nationalism. His moral dominance of the parliament was celebrated in India as the precise moment when Indian nationhood was recognized universally as a force in its own right, separate and superior to British imperialism.

On his return, Indians hailed Vivekananda as the embodiment of India's specifically national spirituality. A few years earlier, he had wandered the subcontinent as a pilgrim in search of traces of God, like the archaic sacred globalizes. Now, his devotees subordinated caste, culture, and sacred geography to the nation. Indian princes personally dragged the chariot of this lower-caste renounce, bodily inverting the old hierarchy. Vivekananda was meanwhile serenaded with the triumphal march from Handel's "Judas Maccabeus." This music had been itself composed as a celebration of the fusion of religion with the once-and-future nation. A Calcutta daily newspaper wrote, "India celebrated its conquering champion. All sections of Hinduism came together to thank the American people."[25]

This chapter has suggested how we might understand the shift over the last two centuries from global networks to what increasingly became international networks. It has suggested that the shift took place in the register of ideology, of actual human diaspora, and, critically, of bodily practice and consumption. This last register encompassed the linkage between the ideological and the material through the consumption and transformation of commodities. The strategic collection by people of the exotic and health-giving made way increasingly for the consumption of uniform commodities that were markers of status in international arenas. Many people now talk of the decline of the nation-state and the power of the new globalization. My impression is that contemporary globalization still begins from assumptions about the nation-state and its aims. We are probably still immobilized in an age of internationalism. We are not yet citizens of Cosmopolis.

NOTES

1. I have tried to develop the concept archaic globalization more fully in A. G. Hopkins, ed., *Globalization in Historical Perspective* (London: Pimlico, 2002); much of this material can also be found in my *The Birth of the Modern World: Global Connections and Comparisons, 1780–1914* (Oxford: Blackwell, 2004), where it is conceptualized in a more general discussion of world history over this period.

2. James L. Hevia, *Cherishing Men from Afar: Qing Guest Ritual and the Macartney Embassy of 1795* (Chapel Hill: University of North Carolina Press, 1995).

3. Evelyn Rawski, *The Last Emperors: A Social History of Qing Institutions* (Berkeley: University of California Press, 1998), pp. 46–47, passim.

4. See, for example, Firdausi, "Shahnamah," written for the Emperor Akbar, circa 1595 (Add. Mss. 12208, ff. 280 b, British Library), where Iskander (Alexander) meets the Brahmins in a Persianate landscape, recalling his earlier meeting with the Greek sages.

5. For example, Moorcroft Papers. Mss Eur D 25 1, ff. 300–39, Oriental and India Office Collections, British Library, London.

6. See, for example, "Akhlaq-1-Jalali," trans. W. F. Thompson, *The Practical Philosophy of the Muhammadan People* (London: Orient Translation Fund, 1836), esp. introduction.

7. Napoleon famously stated that in Egypt he was a Muhammadan and that he would return the Jews to the Temple; for Tone, see *The Autobiography of Theobald Wolfe Tone*, ed. R. Barry O'Brien (London: n.p., 1893), pp. ii, 303.

8. This, of course, is not to say that much local and even some interregional trade in archaic Eurasia was not generated by the more pragmatic exchange of basic food and other commodities, but merely that long-distance transactions were particularly influenced by the exchange of charismatic items of this sort.

9. Arjun Appadurai, *Modernity at Large: Cultural Dimensions of Globalization* (Minneapolis: University of Minnesota Press, 1996).

10. P. J. Marshall and G. Williams, *The Great Map of Mankind: British Perceptions of the World in the Age of Enlightenment* (London: Dent, 1982).

11. N. Leask, "Francis Wilford and the Colonial Construction of Hindu Geography," in Amanda Gilroy, ed., *Romantic Geographies: Discourses of Travel, 1775–1844* (Manchester: Manchester University Press, 2000), pp. 204–223; C. A. Bayly, "Orientalists, Informants and Critics in Benares, 1790–1860," in Jarnal Malik, ed., *Perceptions of Mutual Encounters in South Asian History, 1760–1860* (Leiden: Brill, 2000).

12. Compare M. C. G. Saiz, *Las Castas Mexicanas: Un Genero Pictorico Americano* (Mexico City: Olivetti, 1989).

13. F. Dikotter, *The Discourse of Race in Modern China* (London: Hurst, 1992).

14. Compare, for example Helen Ward, "Worth Its Weight in Gold: Women and Value in Northwest India." Ph.D. dissertation, Cambridge University, 1999.

15. Avner Offer, *The First World War: An Agrarian Interpretation* (Oxford: Clarendon Press, 1991).

16. Christopher Clark, *Kaiser Wilhelm II* (London: Longman, 2000).

17. Elizabeth Collingham, *Imperial Bodies: The Physical Experience of the Raj, c. 1800–1947* (London: Polity Press, 2001); the indigenous dimension has been traced by Charu Gupta, *Sexuality, Obscenity, Community: Women, Muslims and the Hindu Public Sphere in Colonial India* (New York: Palgrave, 2002).

18. John Torpey, *The Invention of the Passport: Surveillance, Citizenship and the State* (Cambridge: Cambridge University Press, 2000).

19. For example, "The Magistrate of Trichinpoly Asks the Madras Government What Action Should Be Taken in the Case of a Greek Named Jacob Lucas and a Persian Himes Ebba Usuf Who Had Been Arrested for Traveling without Passport," Board's Collections, vol. 1685/64431, Oriental and India Office Collections, British Library, London.

20. The parallel process of using the fingerprint as a method of internal surveillance has been recently tackled by Radhika Singha, "Settle, Mobilize, Verify: Identification Practices in Colonial India," *Studies in History* 16:2 (2000): 151–198.

21. Stanley Fisher, *Ottoman Land Law* (Oxford: Clarendon Press, 1919).

22. This is mostly based on Caroline Moorhead, *Dunant's Dream: War, Switzerland and the History of the Red Cross* (London: HarperCollins, 1998).

23. Mushirul Hasan, *A Nationalist Conscience: M. A. Ansari, the Congress and the Raj* (New Delhi: Manohar, 1987), chaps. 6–8.

24. *The Life of Swami Vivekananda by his Eastern and Western Disciples*, 2 vols. (Calcutta: Advaita Ashrama, 1981); Vivekananda, *Chicago Addresses*, 16th impression (Calcutta: n.p., 1971).

25. Romain Rolland, *Ramakrishna the Man God and the Universal Gospel of Vivekananda* (Calcutta: Advaita Ashrama, 1960), p. 103.

THREE

Sufi Brotherhoods
Transcultural / Transstate Networks
in the Muslim World

John O. Voll

Religion is one of the major arenas for significant cross-cultural interactions. Although religions play a vital role in defining the distinctive characteristics of cultures and societies, they also have been major vehicles for transcending the boundaries and limits of regionally identified civilizations. The faith traditions of the major world religions, when viewed within the framework of global history, are multicultural and multicivilizational. The world of premodern Buddhism brought together Indian and Chinese civilizations as well as nonurban societies in central and Southeast Asia, while premodern Christendom included African and Middle Eastern as well as European societies. The world of Islam by the sixteenth century brought together peoples from the four major traditions of civilization in the Eastern Hemisphere (Middle Eastern, European, Indian, and Chinese) as well as numerous societies of Africa and central and Southeast Asia. The expansions of these major faith traditions and then their development as cohesive worlds of faith represent some of the most important interregional and cross-cultural interactions in world history.

Transcultural and transstate religious organizations and networks of believers involve processes and issues that are of crucial importance for understanding cross-cultural and global interactions. "World religions" have long provided important examples of groups and institutions that interact successfully across political, cultural, and civilizational boundaries. Examination of the actual historical development and experiences of such networks can provide a basis for a better understanding of transcultural and transstate interactions in both the premodern and contemporary worlds.

In the world of Islam, the large Sufi (mystic) devotional traditions and the organizations that represent them provide important examples of multicultural, interregional, and multicivilizational networks of interaction. These Sufi organizations have played and continue to play an important role in the expansion of the world of Islam as well as providing important vehicles for interaction among the diverse peoples within that world. This chapter examines the development of the Sufi organizational format and then follows the history of one of the major Sufi brotherhoods, the Naqshbandiyyah, showing how it provided and provides a major vehicle for interactions across cultural boundaries in premodern and contemporary history.

The history of the Naqshbandiyyah provides more than an account of an important and long-lasting religious organization. The experiences of the Naqshbandiyyah highlight some of the major themes in the study of global processes and cross-cultural interactions, and this chapter will draw attention to those broader themes. The activities of individual teachers and preachers as they traveled widely spreading the ideals and devotional practices of the brotherhood emphasize the importance of individual agency, even when operating in the context of broader societal structures and organizations. Similarly, throughout its history the Naqshbandiyyah interacted with rulers and states in many different ways. The Sufi order was not identified with any particular state and operated as a significant transstate actor. Sometimes a state and the order were mutually supportive, as was the case in some of the states in central Asia. At other times, as in the era of European imperial expansion in the nineteenth century, the brotherhood was a major vehicle for revolutionary opposition to the imperial state. Similarly, the Naqshbandiyyah tradition was an important arena within which broader, more global modes of religious thought and experience interacted with local traditions, often creating distinctive syntheses of global and local elements. As a reflection of the Islamic traditions of religious renewal and reform, however, the Naqshbandiyyah frequently was an important force for emphasizing the more "global" dimensions of Muslim global-local syntheses.

The communities created by the believers in the world religions are themselves representative of an important framework for intercultural relations. A study of the history of the Naqshbandiyyah and its place in the world of Islam and global interactions can provide a vehicle for understanding how these interactions operate. The case study of the Naqshbandiyyah needs to be placed in the context of the broader dynamics of Islamic history and the development of Sufism and then can be seen as an important case study in the dynamics of transcultural and transstate relationships in world history.

ISLAMIC EXPANSION AND SUFI ORDERS

The community of Muslims rapidly grew from the small group of believers around the Prophet Muhammad in the early seventh century C.E. in western Arabia into a major world of faith stretching from central Asia to the Atlantic Ocean by the middle of the eighth century C.E. In its first centuries, the Muslim world was primarily a Middle East regional world having some sense of identification with a broadly conceived political system centered on the rule of the "successors" (*khalifahs*, or "caliphs") to the Prophet as leaders of the community, which had also become a major world empire. Within this world, conversion of the peoples to Islam was relatively gradual, with Muslim majorities emerging in the major societies such as Egypt and Persia no earlier than the tenth century C.E.[1]

Distinctively Islamic social institutions and structures developed gradually within this context of an increasingly Islamized society. The formal construction of the mystic brotherhoods came relatively late in this process. From the early days of the Islamic community, ascetic and mystical devotional styles were reflected in the religious life of popular and well-known teachers and exemplars, but the systematization of this Sufi tradition into schools of thought and piety and then into broader formal associations did not take place until the eleventh and twelfth centuries C.E.[2] These associations developed around the distinctive devotional practices and teachings of individuals famous for being "friends of God," or *walis*.[3] The term *tariqah*, or "path," is used for both the devotional path of the *wali* and the broader social organization of the people who practice that path. Usually people identify the first formal *tariqah* or brotherhood as being that based on the memory of the devotional path of Abd al-Qadir al-Jilani (died 1166) and called the Qadiriyyyah Tariqah.

*Tariqah*s represent a mode of religious life rather than a particular doctrinal or theological position. They vary more in terms of how they are organized and in the sets of prayers and litanies that are used than in the theological content of the teachings. The core of the *tariqah* is a regular meeting of those associated with the order for recitation of the litanies, usually in a rhythmic manner associated with physical motion. In some orders, the ceremonies result in trances or some form of higher order of awareness on the part of the participants. Although the Sufi masters are highly skilled specialists, participation in the brotherhoods and their activities has been open even to those with little knowledge of Islam. *Tariqah*s rapidly became an important vehicle for incorporating new people into the Islamic community as individual Sufi teachers began to travel widely within the Muslim world, bringing their particular sense of spirituality to the processes of the expansion of the Muslim community. It has been suggested that the physical activity of the devotions themselves opened the way for a "muscular unison" that worked to create a stronger sense of community among Muslims.[4]

In the period from the eleventh to the eighteenth centuries, the world of Islam virtually doubled in size. Islam ceased to be the religion of a civilizational region identified with one large world empire, as it had been in the days of the Umayyad and early Abbasid caliphates. Instead, the world of Islam came to include significant populations in many different civilizations and nonurban societies. This expansion was not identified with one culture or one state or set of states and represents a major example of transcultural and transstate interactions in that era. One of the key elements in this interaction was the Sufi *tariqah*, which provided vehicles for bridging cultural boundaries and integrating a wide variety of peoples into a sense of belonging in the *Dar al-Islam*, "the House of Islam." The experiences of a particular *tariqah*, the Naqshbandiyyah, can provide some insight into the actual processes involved in these interactions.

NAQSHBANDIYYAH ON THE FRONTIER OF ISLAM

The devotional tradition that is called the Naqshbandiyyah Tariqah originated in central Asia. The cultural frontiers between the Middle East and central Asia had long been porous, with merchants, soldiers, and teachers moving back and forth between the more nomadic peoples and oasis settlements of central Asia and the more urban-based societies of the Middle East. By the twelfth century, central Asians, especially Turkic peoples, had become an important part of Middle Eastern Islamic society as a result of migrations and conquests. Many of the settled and nomadic peoples in the region beyond the Oxus River had come into contact with traveling Muslim merchants and teachers and Trans-Oxus became increasingly Islamized. It was the Sufi teachers who provided the most effective links between the indigenous spiritual traditions and Islam, incorporating and Islamizing local practices into the fabric of the emerging central Asian Muslim societies. In these societies smaller states developed out of the organizations of earlier ethnic-tribal traditions. The Sufi teachers within these societies provided a vehicle for the creation of an identity that transcended the smaller tribal and clan traditions, and they assisted in the creation of broader identities for state and society.

In the areas around Bukhara, a series of teachers in the thirteenth and fourteenth centuries developed a tradition of a number of similar devotional paths that were widely recognized by both rulers and common people. This broad movement of a number of different lines of transmission was consolidated and brought together with the development of the Naqshbandiyyah Tariqah. Later Naqshbandi historians identify this synthesis of traditions of the earlier teachers with the work of Baha'uddin Naqshband (died 1390), hence the identification of the path as the "Naqshbandi" path. Because this teacher "did not commit to writing either his doctrine or any systematization of his mystical practice," however, the definition of the Naqshbandi path is the result of the writings of his students and subsequent generations of Naqshbandi teachers.[5] By the end of the fifteenth century, the *tariqah* had a clear organization centered around a single leader in the third generation from Baha'uddin, Khwaja Ubayd Allah Ahrar (1404–1490).

Ahrar transformed the Naqshbandiyyah in a number of ways. Although the *khwajas* (teachers) before him had had some influence on military and political leaders in the region, Ahrar expanded this role. Several times he "intervened decisively in the political sphere . . . and through his numerous disciples made the Nakshbandiyya supreme in most regions of Transoxiana."[6] Ahrar also, and possibly more importantly, laid the foundations for the effective expansion of the order on an interregional basis. It seems clear that Ahrar made an active and "deliberate attempt to spread the *tariqa* outside of its Transoxianian homeland."[7] He gave special training to some of his students so they could act as transmitters of the order and then sent them out to a number of different areas. In this way, his disciples established the order in major cities in Iran and in Istanbul in the years following the conquest of that city by the Ottomans. Similar missions laid the foundations for the Naqshbandiyyah in eastern Turkistan and India.[8]

Thus, in its early years the Naqshbandiyyah shows the interesting intercultural character of the Muslim world of the fourteenth and fifteenth centuries. Students came from a variety of areas to study with Ahrar and his successors and returned to their homelands or were sent elsewhere with the task of spreading the Naqshbandi devotional path. Dina Le Gall makes important observations about the cultural diversity and unity that is involved in this expansion. She suggests that the region of this Naqshbandi activity was a world of four major languages—Arabic, Persian, Cagatay, and western Turkish—but because of the intermixture of the languages that had developed within the context of the expansion of the world of Islam, for "the missionaries active in the early diffusion of the *tariqa* westward, the geographical area stretching from Transoxiana to Anatolia must thus have been one linguistic world. In this sense, the Naqshbandiyya may be thought of as a unifying force in later Islamic history, but just equally it was the beneficiary of a measure of cultural unity that had existed in the Islamic world from much earlier times."[9]

In the days of Khwaja Ahrar, the Muslim world was no longer a single political unit, even in imaginative theological political theory. Already in the tenth century, the Abbasid caliphs had ceased to be effective rulers of the broader Muslim world. The Mongol conquests, culminating with the capture of Baghdad in 1258, brought an end to most general recognition of the existence of the caliphate, and military authorities ("sultans") replaced the caliphs as the recognized legitimate protectors and rulers of Muslim societies. Throughout the Muslim world, relatively small sultanates provided the basic organization for political authority. Teachers and students moved freely across the political boundaries of the sultanates within the framework of the organizations like the Naqshbandiyyah. The teachers sent by Ahrar had no difficulty in moving among the sultanates of central Asia, India, and the Middle East, making the *tariqah* an effective transstate organization. The only obstacle to this came in the sixteenth century, with the development of the Safavid state in Iran as an officially Shi'ite state that suppressed groups that were explicitly identified with Sunni Islam.

By the beginning of the sixteenth century, the Naqshbandiyyah developed a distinctive mode within the broader framework of Sufi devotional traditions. Some *tariqahs* represent more ecstatic devotional practices or may be more flexible in including non-Islamic elements in their repertoire of rituals and litanies. The distinctive Naqshbandi style was "sober" rather than ecstatic, emphasizing the importance of "fidelity to the Shari'a [Islamic law] in the political and social spheres as well as in devotional life."[10] As the order expanded, it did not develop or maintain a centralized organized structure. Instead, "it consisted of circles of *murids* [followers] that revolved around individual shaykhs and *zawiyas* [centers], sharing little more than common subscription to Naqshbandi beliefs and practices and a common descent from the Naqshbandi *silsila* [chain of transmission of the beliefs and practices]."[11] This flexible organization and distinctive mode provided an effective means of interaction for people and ideas in a broad area that stretched from the western borders of China to India, the Middle East, and the emerging Ottoman territories in the Balkans.

The Naqshbandiyyah and Networks of Renewal

In the generations following Khwaja Ahrar, this "sober" style continued to be affirmed, although, as the order expanded, special traditions identified with particular transmitters of the Naqshbandi path came to be recognized. The order did not maintain a centralized organization but rapidly became an interregional identity, passing on a distinctive devotional path and, frequently, an advocacy of reformist renewal. Despite the absence of a formal centralized structure, members of the order moved from region to region in the Muslim world and beyond, finding identity and like-minded people using the same devotional path in many different places.

As a movement reflecting a spirit of reformist renewal, the Naqshbandiyyah often played an important role in the evolution of Islamic identity in different societies. Because of the order's more "sober" mode, it sometimes opposed the syncretistic styles of Sufi teachers who adapted local devotional practices as a part of the beginnings of Islamization in new areas. Naqshbandis often were in the next stage of Islamization, correcting "syncretistic excesses" and advocating a more strict and explicit adherence to the rules and norms set in the Quran and the sunnah (traditions and precedents of the Prophet Muhammad and the early community of believers). As the Naqshbandiyyah became established in societies in the Middle East that had long been part of, or even the core of, the Muslim world, the order became an important voice there as well for reformist renewal and a cosmopolitan awareness of the broader horizons of the world of Islam. The Naqshbandiyyah emerged as a part of the longstanding traditions of renewal in the Muslim world.[12] In this way, different modes of Sufism developed throughout the Muslim world and often interacted in the contexts of political change and societal development.

One of the best known of the special traditions within the Naqshbandi path has its origins in India. Sufi orders had long been an active part of the processes of spreading Islam in South Asia, and many of the traditions developed in a context of more active synthesis with local and broader Indian civilizational traditions. The order became firmly established in India during the sixteenth century, as South Asia became politically unified by the conquests of new Muslim rulers, the Mughals. As a Muslim empire ruling a predominantly non-Muslim society, the Mughals faced the problems of ruling a highly pluralist realm. Mughal adjustments reached a climax with the policies of Akbar (reigned 1564–1605), who attempted to create an administrative and ideological synthesis of Hindu and Muslim elements

within Mughal society. Some of the older Sufi brotherhoods were supportive of this process. For some Muslims, however, these efforts represented an
unacceptable syncretism, and these views found a voice in a scholar named
Ahmad Sirhindi (1564–1624). Early in his career, Sirhindi was associated
with the Mughal court, but, after he was initiated into the Naqshbandiyyah, he "set out to redefine its doctrine along more radical and militant lines"
and "vigorously opposed Akbar's attempt to work out a synthesis of Hindu
and Muslim religious attitudes."[13]

There has been considerable scholarly debate about the nature of Sirhindi's message, but he became, by the nineteenth century, the symbol of
efforts of activist Islamic renewal. Regardless of whether he was as reformist, as subsequent generations claimed, even during his lifetime he was
clearly recognizable as a dynamic force in affirming a distinctively Islamic
identity. One of his major messages was that 1,000 years after the beginning
of the Prophet Muhammad's career, a new era was beginning. The keystone
in the emergence of this new era was the leadership to be provided by the
"Renewer of the Second Millennium" *(mujaddid-i alf-i thani),* and Sirhindi
claimed that he was that Mujaddid or "Renewer."[14] The line of Naqshbandi
transmission through Sirhindi is identified as Mujaddidi and is one of the
most important parts of the Naqshbandi tradition.

The Mujaddidi line spread into many different areas, and its expansion is an important illustration of transstate and transcultural interactions
in the Muslim world. A more detailed examination of how the Naqshbandiyyah spread within the Ottoman Empire in the Middle East and, in particular, how it became established as an important presence in Damascus
provides a useful case study. By the seventeenth century, affiliation with a
Sufi order had become an important part of social, economic, and religious
life in Ottoman society. Major orders were associated with professional
guilds, associations of artisans, and important sections of the military. Most
of the religious scholars were members of more "sober" *tariqahs*; however,
although various lines of transmission of the Naqshbandiyyah were already
present in Ottoman territories relatively early, the tariqah "was unable to
take root anywhere in the Arab lands except for Arabia" before the coming
of the Mujaddidi line in the late seventeenth century.[15]

The key figure in bringing the Mujaddidi line to the Middle East was
Murad b. Ali al-Bukhari (1640–1720), the founder of the "Muradi" family
in Damascus. He was born into a notable family of Samarkand and traveled to India, where he received the Mujaddidi transmission from Muhammad Ma'sum, the son of Ahmad Sirhindi. According to his great grandson,
Murad was commissioned by Muhammad Ma'sum for instruction in guid-

ing the masses.[16] Through extensive travels, Murad became a key figure in the spread of the Naqshbandiyyah within the Ottoman Empire, especially among the political and economic elite. He received substantial awards of properties from the sultan and settled finally in Damascus, where his family became politically and intellectually influential. His son, Muhammad Murad (1683–1755), continued to spread the order and received substantial patronage from the sultan. Scions of some of the major Damascene families, like Ahmad al-Manini and Abd al-Hayy al-Ghazzi, received the *tariqah* from Murad, and the major families continued to have close relationships through instruction and marriage.[17]

The experience of the Naqshbandis in Damascus represents a microcosm of the operation of the informal interregional networks created by *tariqah* affiliations. The network around the Muradi family was remarkably cosmopolitan. Murad's companion in travel for almost forty years, and then his successor in his place of instruction was identified as "al-Rumi," implying an origin in the central Ottoman lands.[18] An itinerant scholar from Lahore who was identified as being Naqshbandi, he traveled widely and then settled in Damascus, where he received support from a special fund established by a grandson of Murad.[19] A third person benefiting from Muradi patronage was a popular poet who was born in Hama, Syria, and then traveled as far as India. Eventually he settled in Damascus and became popular as a storyteller in coffeehouses. He received the *tariqah* from Muhammad Murad, and the historian Muhammad Khalil al-Muradi provided assistance and support to him in times of illness and poverty.[20] It would appear that this type of support for wandering Naqshbandis was common among wealthier members throughout the Muslim world and provided one of the means whereby teachers could move relatively freely from region to region, crossing political and cultural boundaries.

Life in eighteenth-century Damascus gives additional examples of the transregional nature of Naqshbandi life. In addition to the Mujaddidi, other lines of transmission were also propagated in Syria. One important line originated in the central Asian city of Balkh and was older than the Mujaddidi line, in both its origins and in its arrival in the Arab world. One of the major figures in the intellectual life of Mecca in the late seventeenth century, Ahmad al-Nakhli, received the Naqshbandiyyah from Mir Kalal al-Balhki.[21] And the doyen of scholars in Damascus, Abd al-Ghani al-Nabulusi (1640–1731), received it from Abu Sa'id al-Balkhi.[22] Scholars from Balkh, like Muhammad al-Balkhi and Rafi' al-Uzbaki, settled in Damascus, and Ghayath al-Din al-Balkhi, a member of a lineage of famous Naqshbandi shaykhs in Balkh, fled persecution by the Shi'ite Safavids and, after extensive travels in India, Egypt, and Arabia, settled in Aleppo, where he became an important teacher.[23] These details reflect the cosmopolitan nature of the Naqshbandis in Syria. Scholars came and went between central Asia, India, Arabia, and the central lands of the Ottoman Empire with relative ease. Affiliations such as adherence to a Naqshbandi tradition facilitated this movement.

The Naqshbandiyyah in eighteenth-century Syria illustrates the cosmopolitan nature of its activities, while the careers of Chinese Naqshbandi teachers at the time show the informal interregional network in operation. The Naqshbandiyyah had long been well established in the Gansu and Xinjiang regions of China, with roots possibly back to the time of Khoja Ahrar. Although these regions were under the control of the Chinese emperors, they had close ties with central Asian societies, and central Asia Sufi brotherhoods were an important part of religious life among these minority peoples within Qing domains. During the eighteenth century, Naqshbandi *khojas* led a series of rebellions against the Qing dynasty, even succeeding briefly in establishing an independent Islamic state in the Tarim Basin in the 1760s.[24] Also by the middle of the century, new and activist "missionary" lines had come to China. Ma Laichi was the son of a Chinese imperial office holder who became a transmitter of the central Asian line of Khoja Afaq in 1690. After teaching for a number of years, he went on pilgrimage to Mecca and followed an extensive study tour. Although the biographical sources differ in describing where he went and how long he stayed, the sources agree that he engaged in enhancing his Naqshbandi expertise and that "he remained at some center of Muslim learning, probably more than one, for many years and returned to China bearing a deep desire to reform Islam in his homeland. . . . His charisma and his message won many Muslims, both Chinese- and Turkic-speaking, to his version of Sufi ritual practice."[25]

Ma Laichi is reported to have met in Bukhara, during his return trip from his extended pilgrimage, with Ma Mingxin (1719?–1781), a younger Chinese scholar who was setting out on his own travels. Ma Mingxin engaged in extensive study, settling for an extended period of time in Zabid in Yemen. There were links between the Naqshbandis of Bukhara and Yemen, and Ma Mingxin may have been following up on contacts already established by Ma Laichi.[26] In Yemen, Ma Mingxin became closely associated with a broader network of renewal-oriented scholars in which the Naqshbandiyyah played an important role.[27] "Trained with budding revivalists from all over the Muslim world, Ma Mingxin returned to China in 1761 intending to purify Islam, establishing Koranic orthopraxy, and purge the faith of accretions from the surrounding culture. Like all mainstream Naqshabandis, he held the observance of Islamic law, *shari'a,* to be central to Muslim orthopraxy."[28]

The major centers of Naqshbandi life were connected in a network of relationships that bridged the boundaries of states, cultures, and regions.[29] Scholars moved freely from China to northwest Africa, finding support and instruction throughout the region. In return, they were also active in working to affirm the Islamic nature of societal life, in both the places they visited and their homelands. The structure of the relationships, however, was not centralized. "One remarkable fact about the politically active *tariqa* to which Baha al-Din Naqshband gave his name is that, like all Sufi brotherhoods, it had no overall organization. The only lines of authority were between shaykh and disciple. There were always, at any given time, many leading shaykhs, so that although Naqshbandi activities in various parts of the Islamic world may appear to have been interconnected, they were in fact never part of any common plan or coordinated effort. But neither were they mere coincidence."[30] From the early days, there was a common mode in which "Naqshbandi shaykhs preached a combination of religious reformation and political activism."[31] It was as a complex network of relationships within the framework of a shared devotional tradition that the Naqshbandiyyah functioned as a transstate and transcultural feature of the Muslim world.

The mode of transstate and transcultural interactions seen in the Naqshbandiyyah multiregional networks illustrates some important aspects of what Chris Bayly calls "archaic globalization."[32] Religion represented an important dimension of this globalization and Bayly observes that "Sufi orders" were "archaic globalizers *par excellence.*"[33] The idea of cosmic religion in the major world faith traditions provided the conceptual foundation for global perspectives and the incentives for commitment to the expansion of the faith community. The organizational structures of the Sufi orders could provide the material framework for travel, and the shared devotional practices helped to create a sense of communal identity that crossed political, cultural, and geographical boundaries. The Naqshbandiyyah shows how the religious dimensions of archaic globalization actually worked.

NAQSHBANDI NETWORKS IN THE MODERN ERA

The Naqshbandiyyah continues to be an important and dynamic part of life in the modern Muslim world. In many ways the challenges of the modern era have been well suited to the style of religious organization that the order represents. The changing conditions of modern history, however, are reflected in the different responses made by the Naqshbandiyyah to the issues faced by Muslims in the past two centuries. Two different experiences illustrate the continuities and changes in the Naqshbandiyyah as a transstate and transcultural set of networks in modern times: responses to European imperialism and the utilization of the opportunities and resources of contemporary globalization.

One of the remarkable features of the responses of Muslims to European imperial expansion in the nineteenth century was the surprising effectiveness of Sufi brotherhoods in organizing resistance. The Qadiriyyah Tariqah provided the organization basis for resistance to European expansion in many areas, providing the framework for opposition to the French in Algeria under the leadership of the Amir Abd al-Qadir from 1830 to 1847 and to Russian expansion in the Caucusus (along with the Naqshbandiyyah), especially in the major revolt of 1877, and in an uprising against the Dutch in Java in 1888.[34] Similar records can be seen for a variety of other brotherhoods throughout the Muslim world.

The Naqshbandiyyah, true to its traditions, was frequently at the heart of movements of renewal that had the potential for becoming movements of resistance. Early in the nineteenth century, the Mujaddidi line was rearticulated and given new dynamism by Shaykh Khalid al-Baghdadi (died 1827). Khalid was born in Kurdistan and traveled widely, becoming initiated into the Mujaddidi line while in India and ultimately settling in Damascus.[35] He has been described as "the last—and most important link—between Sirhindi and modern *Naksibendi* [Naqshbandi] activism."[36] Followers of Shaykh Khalid brought an active spirit of renewal to a variety of areas, with the most dramatic results in the Caucasus region. Russian imperial expansion had made significant advances already in the eighteenth century. A shaykh thought by some scholars to be Naqshbandi had already raised the banner of opposition in a jihad in 1785–1791, but it had little impact. It was not until the Mujaddidi-Khalidi line came to the Caucasus that effective opposition to Russian expansion was organized.

Local society in the Caucasus was a divided mosaic of clans and small, distinctive ethnic groups. These groups fiercely defended their own special identities and were often at war with each other. By the beginning of the nineteenth century, however, local Sufi teachers were beginning to create some sense of identity with a group that transcended specific clan loyalties. When the Russians invaded, local leaders of clans and small cities were quickly defeated and accepted Russian rule, despite its harshness. The "people felt that they were abandoned by their leaders just when they needed them most—when their physical and spiritual world was crumbling. It was at this precise moment that the Naqshbandiyya-Khalidiyya arrived on the scene with what seemed to be the right answers."[37]

The Naqshbandi movement of resistance reached its most effective form under the leadership of Imam Shamil (1796–1871). Although his movement was defeated in 1859, after more than three decades of fighting, Shamil became a major symbol of opposition to foreign and infidel rule. The *tariqah* provided the necessary vision that could unite the normally divided and feuding peoples of the mountains and valleys of the Caucasus. In this case, the order's ability to provide bridges across difficult cultural boundaries operated on a small scale, once the broader vision had been brought to the region by disciples of Shaykh Khalid.

The Sufi responses in general and the Naqshbandi responses in particular to European imperial expansion in the nineteenth century reflect the continuing interactions among the peoples within the Muslim world. None of the Sufi jihads occurred in isolation. Leaders were part of informal and decentralized networks that extended beyond the boundaries of the areas where they were struggling to maintain control. The Naqshbandiyyah-Khalidiyyah was not a long-established local order in the Causcasus. It came to that region as a part of the normal mode for the expansion of the order but arrived at the right time to provide the basis for a unified opposition to Russian expansion. This was typical of the interregional interactions within the Muslim world of the time.

The continuing viability and adaptability of the Naqshbandiyyah in this era of protoglobalization and imperialist globalization is remarkable. It suggests the strength of the traditions and structures developed through the long history of the order. The ability to blend local and global elements into effective anti-imperialist movements, for example, shows that modern globalization was not as capable of destroying premodern modes of society and life as has been thought.

Naqshbandiyyah history in the nineteenth century suggests that some of the discussions of archaic and modern globalization might be modified. The emerging world order of capitalist and imperialist globalization was powerful and at many levels succeeded in imposing a new ordering of social identity and institutions. In particular, Bayly argues, the new globalization was a pattern of "internationalism" in which the "nation-state increasingly dominated global networks. . . . Archaic patterns of global interactions persisted. But they were increasingly represented in terms of national essences."[38] When looking at the larger Sufi organizations, however, it might be possible to exaggerate the "nationalization" of Sufism.

Bayly argues that the "great Sufi orders, bearers of a global message of culture and humanity, were penned in to national boundaries both by government officials and by the agency of normalizing religious 'reformers.'"[39] Although the general trend was powerful, organizations like the Naqshbandiyyah maintained transnational/transstate identities and modes of operation. Resistance to Russian expansion in the Caucasus represented a synthesis of global and local rather than the "nationalization" of the Naqshbandiyyah. Even though that was early in the era of modern globalization, the Naqshbandiyyah later played a similar role of resistance to Soviet rule and in that context, one major element was the attempt of the Soviet rulers to impose "national" (and constructed ethnic) identities on the Muslim peoples.[40] Islam survived as a vital part of a transstate identity that has reemerged following the collapse of the Soviet Union.

The Naqshbandiyyah continued to be an important nonstate organization in an increasingly "international" world shaped by interstate relations. Its members moved with the great modern diasporas, and, although they as individuals became increasingly identified by their passports and citizenship, the *tariqah* continued not to be identified with a state or national construct.

The Naqshbandiyyah at the beginning of the twenty-first century is operating in very new and different conditions and continues to flourish. Some of its specific ways of doing things have changed, but its general tradition of decentralized organization built on a number of distinctive lines of transmission but sharing a common commitment to a sober affirmation of Islam and of the need to renew the life of Muslim societies continues. The structure of communications in the new electronic age is well suited to the multiple lines of direct communication among spiritual guides and disciples across political, cultural, and civilizational boundaries. The active expansion of the order in the United States in the second half of the twentieth century reflects the development of new lines of transmission that are both independent and in dynamic interaction with other lines in other regions. The leading Naqshbandi shaykh in Syria, who also serves as the grand mufti of Syria, has said that his "most recent top priority is on developing American moral leadership to make the twenty-first century an era of universal justice."[41]

Major Naqshbandi shaykhs are important cosmopolitan international figures, although the news media tend to pay less attention to them than to more overtly political figures. Shaykh Muhammad Nazim Adil al-Haqqani, often called al-Qubrusi because he was born in Cyprus (al-Qubrus) in 1922, is a good example.[42] He studied under a number of teachers in the Mujaddidi tradition and then settled in Damascus while regularly traveling first in the Middle East and then farther. Beginning in 1974 he went annually to Europe, and in 1986 he made a major tour to South and Southeast Asia. In 1991 he made his first trip to the United States, and in 1993 he made a trip to the homelands of the *tariqah* in central Asia. Modern technology has effectively globalized the scope of the activities of major Naqshbandi shaykhs, but the tradition of renewal remains, as is reflected in a summary description of Shaykh al-Haqqani by a disciple: "As Shah Naqshband was the reviver in Bukhara and central Asia, as Ahmad Sirhindi al-Mujaddidi was the reviver of the 2nd millennium, as Khalid al-Baghdadi was the reviver of Islam, the Divine Law and the Way in the Middle East, now Shaykh Muhammad Nazim Adil al-Haqqani is the reviver, the renewer and the caller to God in this age, the age of technology and material progress."[43]

CONCLUSION

At the beginning of the twenty-first century, the major Sufi orders like the Naqshbandiyyah represent important vehicles for bridging the gaps between cultures. The Naqshbandiyyah remains, in some ways, what it has been for centuries: a network of people tied together by a common devotional path. This network is not a centralized organization with a single head leading a bureaucratic structure; rather, it is a loosely connected collectivity of peoples in many different societies whose loyalties transcend the boundaries of states, societies, and even civilizations.

This style of organization developed during the era of archaic globalization and was well suited to the distinctive conditions of that era, from the fourteenth through the eighteenth centuries. It also proved, however, to be effective in the eras of capitalist-imperialist globalization and now in the era of postcolonial/postmodern globalization as well. This confirms Bayly's conclusion that "agents of archaic globalization could become active forces in the expansion of the Euro-American dominated world economy and even survive and transcend it."[44]

Examination of the history and development of the Naqshbandiyyah provides two contradictory messages at the beginning of the twenty-first century. First, in terms of structures of social movements, the order represents a distinctive decentralized but effective framework for Islamic activism. A careful recognition of this type of structure as being part of the available organizational repertoire for contemporary Islamic movements should be required for those analysts and policy makers who seek to understand the elusive organization of terrorists such as Usama Ben Ladin. His organization has many similarities to the longstanding mode of decentralized but dedicated activism that is visible in the history of the Naqshbandiyyah.

Second, in many ways, the effective expansion of the Naqshbandiyyah in the contemporary era represents one of the most dramatic refutations possible of the "clash of civilizations" posited by Samuel Huntington. The desire for a renewal of human society based on moral values is not limited to one civilization or one religion. The transstate, transcultural, and trans-civilizational operations of the Naqshbandiyyah in the West, as well as in China, India, and the Middle East, show that significant forms of dialogue among peoples and civilizations are not just theoretically possible but currently taking place in many forms. Just as the major world religions already transcended the boundaries of regionally defined "civilizations" in the pre-modern eras, in the present world they represent a major element in the dynamics of contemporary globalization.

NOTES

1. See, for example, the analysis in Richard W. Bulliet, *Conversion to Islam in the Medieval Period* (Cambridge, Mass.: Harvard University Press, 1979).

2. A useful summary of these developments can be found in Alexander Knysh, *Islamic Mysticism: A Short History* (Leiden: Brill, 2000).

3. The usual translation of *wali* as "saint" can be misleading in the context of comparative historical analysis, so this paper will use the terms *wali* and "friends of God" for purposes of precision in terminology.

4. William H. McNeill, *Keeping Together in Time: Dance and Drill in Human History* (Cambridge, Mass.: Harvard University Press, 1995), pp. 92–94.

5. Jurgen Paul, *Doctrine and Organization: The Khwajagan/ Naqshbandiya in the First Generation after Baha'uddin* (ANOR 1; Berlin: Das Arabische Buch, 1998), p. 5.

6. Hamid Algar, "Nakshbandiyya," *The Encyclopaedia of Islam*, new ed. (Leiden: E. J. Brill, 1992), 7:935.

7. Dina Le Gall, "The Ottoman Naqshbandiyya in the Pre-Mujaddidi Phase: A Study in Islamic Religious Culture and Its Transmission," Ph.D. dissertation, Princeton University, 1992, p. 16.

8. Ibid., pp. 15–20.

9. Ibid., pp. 42–43.

10. Knysh, *Islamic Mysticism*, p. 221. For the emphasis on sobriety, see also Annemarie Schimmel, *Mystical Dimensions of Islam* (Chapel Hill: University of North Carolina Press, 1975), pp. 365–366.

11. Le Gall, "The Ottoman Naqshbandiyya," p. 119.

12. For a discussion of this tradition and its development, see. John O. Voll, "Reform and Renewal in Islamic History: *Tajdid and Islah*," in John L. Esposito, ed., *Voices of Resurgent Islam* (New York: Oxford University Press, 1983), pp. 32–47.

13. Knysh, *Islamic Mysticism*, p. 230.

14. For an introduction to his millennialist ideas, see Julian Baldick, *Mystical Islam: An Introduction to Sufism* (New York: New York University Press, 1989), pp. 120–121.

15. Le Gall, "The Ottoman Naqshbandiyya," p. 227.

16. Muhammad Khalil al-Muradi, *Silk al-durar fi 'a'yan al-qarn al-thani ashar*, reprint ed. (Baghdad: Maktabah al-Muthani, n.d.), 4:129.

17. Muradi, *Silk*, 1:133–145, 2:243–244.

18. Ali b. Husayn al-Rumi. Muradi, *Silk*, 3:213.

19. 'Alim Allah al-Hindi. Muradi, *Silk*, 3: 260–262.

20. Ahmad Shakir al-Jakawati. Muradi, *Silk*, 1:155–162. See also Carl Brockelmann, *Geschichte der arabischen Litteratur*, reprint ed. (Leiden: E. J. Brill, 1996), 2:283.

21. Muradi, *Silk*, 1:171–172.

22. Muradi, *Silk*, 3:30–38. An extensive analysis of al-Nabulusi's Naqshbandi affiliation can be found in Barbara Rosenow von Schlegell, "Sufism in the Ottoman Arab World: Shaykh Abd al-Ghani al-Nabulusi (D. 1143/1731)." Ph.D. dissertation, University of California, Berkeley, 1997, esp. pp. 142–144.

23. Muradi, *Silk*, 2:116, 3:274–275.

24. Joseph Fletcher, *Studies on Chinese and Islamic Inner Asia*, ed. Beatrice Forbes Manz (Aldershot: Variorum, 1995), 4:88–89.

25. Jonathan N. Lipman, *Familiar Strangers: A History of Muslims in Northwest China* (Seattle: University of Washington Press, 1997), pp. 66–67. See also Fletcher, *Studies on Chinese and Islamic Inner Asia*, 11:15–17.

26. Fletcher, *Studies on Chinese and Islamic Inner Asia*, 11:28.

27. For the broader context into which Ma Mingxin came, see John O. Voll, "Linking Groups in the Networks of Eighteenth Century Revivalist Scholars: The Mizjaji Family in Yemen," in N. Levtzion and J. O. Voll, eds., *Eighteenth Century Renewal and Reform in Islam* (Syracuse, N.Y.: Syracuse University Press, 1987).

28. Lipman, *Familiar Strangers*, p. 88.

29. A very important collection of essays that examines the utility of the concept of "network" in analyzing the nature of interactions within the Muslim world is Roman Loimeier, ed., *Die islamische Welt als Netzwerk: Moglichkeiten und Grenzen des Netzweransatzes im islamische Kontext* (Wurzburg: Ergon Verlag, 2000).

30. Fletcher, *Studies on Chinese and Islamic Inner Asia*, 4:90.

31. Ibid.

32. See C. A. Bayly, "'Archaic' and 'Modern' Globalization in the Eurasian and African Arena, c. 1750–850," in A. G. Hopkins, ed., *Globalization in World History* (London: Pimlico, 2002), pp. 47–73, and his keynote address in the Interactions conference on March 2, 2001, "Regional Histories, Global Processes, Cross-Cultural Interactions," as well as his chapter in the present volume.

33. Bayly, "'Archaic' and 'Modern' Globalization," p. 52.

34. Discussions of these movements in the broader context of Islamic renewal can be found in Voll, "Foundations for Renewal and Reform: Islamic Movements in the Eighteenth and Nineteenth Centuries," in John L. Esposito, ed., *The Oxford History of Islam* (New York: Oxford University Press, 1999), esp. pp. 537–545.

35. I acknowledge the research of Sean Foley, a graduate student in the Department of History at Georgetown University, and the insight that his work has given me into the career of Shaykh Khalid.

36. Serif Mardin, *Religion and Social Change in Modern Turkey* (Albany: State University of New York Press, 1989), p. 57.

37. Moshe Gammer, *Muslim Resistance to the Tsar: Shamil and the Conquest of Chechnia and Daghistan* (London: Frank Cass, 1994), p. 42.

38. This quotes the text of the keynote address by C. A. Bayly in the Interactions conference on March 2, 2001, which was distributed to participants.

39. Bayly, "'Archaic' and 'Modern' Globalization," p. 67.

40. An important study of the role of the Sufi orders in the Soviet Union is Alexendre Bennigsen and S. Enders Wimbush, *Mystics and Commissars: Sufism in the Soviet Union* (Berkeley: University of California Press, 1985).

41. Reported on his web site, www.kuftaro.org; accessed December 1, 2000.

42. The material in this section is drawn from his biography in Shaykh Muhammad Hisham Kabbani, *The Naqshbandi Sufi Way: History and Guidebook of the Saints of the Golden Chain* (Chicago: Kazi Publications, 1995), pp. 375–408.

43. Kabbani, *The Naqshbandi Sufi Way,* p. 396.

44. Bayly, "'Archaic' and 'Modern' Globalization," p. 48.

FOUR

Cotton
A Global History

Sven Beckert

I n 1835, John Masterson Burke, a young businessman from New York City, set sail for southern Mexico. His destination was the small colonial town of Valladolid. There, Don Pedro Baranda, a Spaniard who had emigrated to Mexico a few decades earlier, and John L. MacGregor, a Scot, had opened Mexico's first cotton manufacturing enterprise, a factory that Burke was to direct.[1] Although the entrepreneurs cited the "spontaneous growth of cotton around Valladolid" as the incentive for this venture, spreading stories of the wealth of cotton entrepreneurs from Lancashire to Lowell, from the Nile Delta to the mountain villages of Switzerland, must have encouraged Baranda and MacGregor as well.[2]

Building a cotton factory in Valladolid, far away from shipping facilities, major markets, or technical expertise was no small undertaking. Although a New Yorker who passed through the city in 1842 found the factory "remarkable for its neat, compact, and business-like appearance," setting up production in the Yucatan had been a struggle. To get the operation started, Burke had brought with him from New York not only the machinery, but also four engineers, two of whom died shortly afterward of malaria. With no architect to plan the buildings, moreover, the budding textile entrepreneurs ventured to design the factory themselves and in consequence "[t]wice the arches gave way, and the whole building came down."[3] Despite these and other tribulations, Baranda, MacGregor, and Burke got the factory up and running. With the help of fifty-three workers drawn from the local population, sixty-four Indian families who supplied the wood to fire the engines, and another 117 Indian families who planted cotton along their maize fields, they churned out 95,000 yards of cloth and about 1,700 pounds of yarn in the years before 1844.[4] Though modest by the standards of Lancashire, considering the factory's location, this was a spectacular success.

A number of factors helped them to accomplish this feat. Most important was their easy access to raw cotton, which the Maya had grown for centuries in the area surrounding Valladolid. Moreover, they faced little resistance from local spinners and weavers, because British textile imports that had come to the markets of Yucatan via British-Honduras a few decades earlier had already largely destroyed the indigenous spinning and weaving industry. This was quite different from other Mexican cities, such as Puebla and Veracruz, where workers had violently and, at first, successfully resisted the introduction of modern textile machinery. Furthermore, despite their isolation, they were able to draw on not only modern machines, but also Burke's body of knowledge about up-to-date production processes.

That a cotton manufacturing enterprise arose in the middle of the tropical wilderness of the Yucatan Peninsula, remote from sources of capital, access to modern machinery, and transportation infrastructure, testifies to the powerful attraction that cotton had for entrepreneurs all around the globe throughout the long nineteenth century. The promises of cotton, there and elsewhere, captured the imagination of merchants, manufacturers, planters, and consumers. As a result, cotton growing, cotton manufacturing, and cotton consumption expanded rapidly, turning cotton textiles from a luxury good accessible only to a few in the West into the first true mass-market commodity. Merchants, budding manufacturers, technically skilled workers, empire-building government bureaucrats, slaves, spinners, and weavers from all around the world linked in new ways plantations and factories, slavery and free labor, Asia, Europe, and the Americas, building the dynamic and at times explosive empire of cotton and with it the world of nineteenth-century capitalism. More than any other actors, they recast how people lived, produced, and consumed in places as diverse as Mississippi and Lancashire, the Nile Delta and the plains of Gujarat, Valladolid, and New York City.

Cotton, indeed, was the most important commodity of the nineteenth century. No other industry employed as many people. No other manufactured good inspired so many technical innovations, organizational improvements, or social changes or as many concomitant domestic and international conflicts. By inventing the factory as the most efficient way of producing textiles, cotton manufacturers recast the way humans worked. By searching for ever more hands to staff their factories, English, American, Brazilian, and Japanese cotton manufacturers, among others, encouraged a global and unprecedented move of people from the countryside into cities. By demanding ever more cotton to feed their hungry factories in Lancashire and elsewhere, manufacturers encouraged planters to expand cotton lands vastly, and the need for cheap labor to work all that land led to the forced migration of millions of slaves, as well as the colonialization of new territories. By producing ever more cotton textiles ever more efficiently, and selling them to markets throughout the world, cotton traders destroyed less-efficient indigenous ways of producing textiles and in the process decisively moved the center of the industry from Asia to Western Europe and the United States, for example by turning India from a region of cotton exporters to a colony that consumed vast quantities of British yarn and cloth. And in their search for labor, capital, and land, these capitalists wove together different regions of the globe.

Cotton's importance surpassed that of other fibers such as wool or flax, because it provided the impetus for the emergence of factory production and captured markets of an unprecedented elasticity. Cotton's unique dependence on both the plantation and the factory set it apart from other commodities, such as sugar or salt, that would never require the degree of manufacturing input to ignite an industrial revolution. In contrast to other commodities, moreover, cotton combined in explosive ways free and slave labor, an incendiary mix at the core of nineteenth-century capitalism. From the perspective of the century as a whole, cotton's importance can be compared only to oil's centrality a hundred years later. Cotton, in short, was so central to the nineteenth century that most of its history could be told from the vantage point of this agricultural commodity.[5]

It was the powerful draw of cotton that brought Burke, Baranda, and MacGregor to Valladolid in 1835. Their story, just like that of cotton more generally, tells us something important about the nineteenth century: Its history does not easily fit into the "container" of national historiography that is so familiar to all of us. Even the history of such a minor part of the empire of cotton as the "Aurora Yucateca" is about the porous nature of international boundaries and about the connections forged by merchants, manufacturers, state bureaucrats, workers, and slaves between vastly different regions of the world, different cultures, and different nations. In 1835, cotton had brought together a Spaniard, a Scot, and an American in the Mexican tropics, where they engaged with British technology, Mayan agricultural practices, the weakness of the Mexican state (which could not enforce its own custom laws), competition from Lancashire, and a cosmopolitan belief in progress equally at home in Mérida, Liverpool, Hamburg, or New York. The venture of Burke, Baranda, and MacGregor is a small part of the crucial epic of the global connections forged around cotton and the geographic and social spread of capitalism in the nineteenth century.

As the account of the "Aurora Yucateca" demonstrates, each element of the history of nineteenth-century cotton can be understood only in its global context. People in Valladolid and Lancashire, Pernambuco and Bombay, Alexandria and New York, New Orleans and the textile towns of Saxony, along with many other places, interacted in ways that created the particular shape of the world's cotton industry and with it of nineteenth-century capitalism. Despite this clearly global scope of the industry, the libraries of books that have been written on aspects of the history of cotton—on the cotton mills of Lancashire, on the development of cotton textile technology, on the history of the growing of cotton in the United States, on cotton in Egypt, the fate of the Indian cotton textile industry, the mills of Saxony and France, and the ventures of the Boston Associate, among others—have limited their view largely to specific countries, regions, cities, and towns. This is surprising, because it was both the global reach and the tight linkage of agriculture, trade, and manufacturing that made the industry so central to the Industrial Revolution. The empire of cotton depended on the plantation and the factory, the "core" and the "periphery," railroads and steamships, in short, a global network of supply, transport, manufacture, and sale. It was only the combination of these different and even contradictory elements that led to the explosive growth of cotton in the nineteenth century. The Liverpool Cotton Exchange had an enormous impact on Mississippi cotton planters; the Alsatian spinning mills were tightly linked to those of Lancashire; and the future of handloom weavers in New Hampshire or Calcutta was related to such diverse factors as the construction of a railroad between Manchester and Liverpool, investment decisions of Boston merchants, and the tariff policies of the United States and Great Britain. Although nation-states were important in channeling the trajectory of cotton, the commodity itself created networks, identities, institutions, and processes that transcended any particular nation. Nineteenth-century authorities who wrote on this commodity, indeed, understood this global context of cotton quite well.[6] Once professional historians got their hands on the subject, however, they tried to fit it into the container of their various national specializations. Because the emergence of professional history writing and the solidification of the nation-state went hand in hand, this is probably less surprising than it seems at first.[7] It did, however, unnecessarily limit our view of cotton and capitalism.

To come to terms with the history of cotton in the nineteenth century, we need to look at it in global terms. A global perspective puts many problems in context—labor relations on Mississippi plantations then can be seen in context of the way the growing of cotton in India was organized; the political efforts of Southern plantation owners or Manchester mill owners become more meaningful in the global context of the industry. Moreover, a global perspective on cotton brings together the agricultural, trade, and manufacturing aspects of the story that heretofore have been artificially separated, a flaw that ignores the relations of power between different actors and places in the industry. Last but not least, such a perspective puts into sharp relief that shifting capital across the globe, capturing new markets, spreading new production technologies and international migrations were as much developments of the nineteenth century as they are of today.

This chapter will first present a short version of the history of cotton in the nineteenth century, before ending with some more general observations about cotton and capitalism. The complex history the essay sketches, however incomplete, does suggest in powerful ways how a commodity-centered view of past economic life opens new and exciting vistas on the history of capitalism and its globalization. In the process of telling this story, I will make two main arguments. First, I claim that cotton forged unprecedented economic, social, and political links throughout the world and that its history—and with it the history of capitalism—can be understood only by putting these global networks, identities, institutions, and processes at the center of the story. Second, I emphasize the importance of politics to the forging of the empire of cotton in particular and capitalism in general. Public and private forms of coercion structured the global market system in decisive ways. States in particular structured labor, commodity, and product markets through military power, industrial policies, laws, tariffs, and the sanctioning of private forms of violence, especially slavery. Ironically, opening our view to global connections sharpens our appreciation for the importance of states.

Before expanding on these general points, let us review the explosive history of cotton in the nineteenth century.

Cotton is indigenous to Asia, Africa, and Central America, and people for thousands of years have harvested cotton and produced cotton fabrics, most of them for household or local consumption. When Cortez invaded the Aztec Empire in 1519, for example, he found the cotton fabrics he encountered of such superb quality that he sent some to his king.[8] In preindustrial settings, cotton has been used not only for making cloth, but also as a medium for tribute payments and even as a form of currency. Despite such small-scale production, however, some raw cotton and cotton fabrics also entered long-distance trade before the modern period, and indeed by the end of the fifteenth century an elaborate system of trade in cotton goods had unfolded, centering principally on the Indian subcontinent. This system of trade brought a limited amount of cotton cloth to Europe, though high transportation costs meant that only the very richest could afford to purchase these exotic fabrics. Most Europeans continued to dress in linens and woolens well into the nineteenth century.

With the expansion of European power into Asia in the early seventeenth century, however, Western merchants inserted themselves ever more powerfully into the networks of cotton trade in Asia, bringing an increasing number of cotton goods to Europe. From this involvement grew a deeper penetration of the manufacturing process, first in India and, by the eighteenth century, in Europe, especially in Great Britain. By then, merchants organized people in the countryside to spin cotton thread on hand-operated wheels and weave fabrics on handlooms. Operating largely out of their own homes, these outworkers produced a growing amount of cotton goods, and, by late century, British merchants alongside budding manufacturers invested capital into a dramatic reorganization of the production process. They were encouraged in doing so by the rapid expansion of markets for cotton goods, as people in Great Britain and on the continent discovered the advantages of cotton clothing and indigenous textile industries in all parts of the world were destroyed by cheap British imports. The heady combination of manufacturers' access to labor, capital, and markets allowed them to organize the most radical change in the ways humans worked, bringing with them machine-driven spinning wheels, looms, and the factory system. A tiny region centered on Liverpool and Manchester came to be the heart of the Industrial Revolution.

This explosion in cotton manufacturing had immediate repercussions throughout the world. First, the demand for raw cotton increased so rapidly that cotton plantations sprang up in large numbers. The lords of the loom had an insatiable appetite for cotton, most of it produced by slave labor. At first, cotton arrived in Great Britain from the West Indies and the Ottoman Empire, but, by 1781, Brazilian raw cotton was unloaded on the docks of Liverpool; two years later Surat cotton followed, and in the next year the first bales of American cottons were landed. It took almost no time for the United States cotton to dominate the world market. In 1800, 25 percent of cotton landed in Liverpool originated from the United States; twenty years later that number had increased to 59 percent, and in 1850 a full 72 percent of cotton consumed in Britain originated in North America. Indeed, cotton single-handedly established the importance of the United States in the world economy and set it on the path of indigenous capital accumulation.[9] The Southern states of the United States were perfectly suited for such an expansion because cotton plantations did not encounter resistance from powerful and entrenched interests in the countryside, and slaves provided plentiful labor for plantations.

Why did the United States turn into the world's most important supplier of raw cotton? The core competitive advantage of the United States was the availability of land suitable to the growing of cotton and the availability of cheap labor. In the areas where cotton was to be grown, no powerful and entrenched social structure needed to be dislodged. Instead, indigenous inhabitants were forcefully removed and workers forcefully moved in. Planters could then recast nature and the organization of work as they wished. This was distinctly different from places such as Egypt and India, where the expansion of cotton production was constrained by powerful social forces. In Brazil and the West Indies, moreover, sugar competed with cotton for labor, something that was largely absent from the United States, where the old labor-intensive export crop of tobacco had gone into a long period of decline.

These locational advantages allowed the United States to become the world's most significant source of cotton. As a result, cotton single-handedly established the importance of the United States in the world economy and set it on the path of indigenous capital accumulation.[10] As cotton became the country's most important export article in the early nineteenth century, it enabled the United States to pay for the import of manufactured wares, provided markets for the products of its free labor farmers, allowed for the accumulation of capital that could be invested in manufacturing enterprises, and, last but not least, invigorated slavery and with it domestic political tensions.[11]

The second impact of the rapid expansion of cotton manufacturing in Lancashire was that rulers and businessmen throughout the world saw the potential wealth and power that this revolutionary way of manufacturing brought to those who embraced it. Naturally, they tried to copy it. Spinning, as well as weaving, mills were built all over the European and North American countryside—in the mountain villages of Switzerland, the hills of Alsace and Saxony, the plains of Yucatan, along the rivers of Massachusetts, and next to the Nile in Egypt. These mills not only brought new production techniques to many corners of the world, but also helped deepen and spread capitalist social relations to regions previously untouched by them.

Moreover, the export of cotton goods from these burgeoning textile mills that now sprang up mainly in Western Europe and North America helped alter global textile markets as they destroyed hand spinning and put severe limits on handloom weaving throughout the world. This affected especially the once-dominant Indian export industry. The once-proud Dacca cotton spinners and weavers, for example, whose products had dominated global markets, were increasingly reduced to unemployment, as demand for Dacca fabrics fell globally as a result of the advances of British manufacturing. John Taylor, who wrote a detailed history of the clothing industry of Dacca in 1800, reported that the value of cloth exports from Dacca declined by 50 percent between 1747 and 1797 (from 2,850,000 to 1,401,545 rupees).[12] Spinners especially were hurt by British imports, and as a result, reported Taylor, a great number "died of famine."[13]

The sum of all these changes was that, by the second quarter of the nineteenth century, a global cotton system had evolved, one that largely focused on Great Britain and the United States, especially on Liverpool, Manchester, and the American South, but with new avenues of investment and trade that reached from Britain to the Americas, Africa, the Middle East, and Asia.

With the American Civil War (1861–1865) this system came into crisis. The war initiated a fundamental and long-lasting realignment in the world of cotton. It was an event of such magnitude in the empire of cotton that, tellingly, Egyptian economic historians consider it one of the most important events in Egypt's nineteenth-century history.[14] Most dramatically, the war encouraged Indian, Egyptian, and Brazilian planters and peasants to grow more cotton, leading to the first integration of large areas of the world into the emerging capitalist world economy.

Not only did the war decimate the supply of raw cotton to European cotton manufacturers, but it also effectively undermined the essentially colonial relationship that had emerged between the American South and Great Britain. By destroying the political power of Southern slaveholders and their acceptance of a subordinated economic development of the United States, the United States could emerge as a major player on the world economic scene. And indeed, after the Civil War, no other place in the world saw such a rapid program of import-substitution industrialization in textiles as the United States, expanding its number of spindles from 1.2 million in 1832 to 16.1 million in 1895—a growth rate more than twice as fast as that of Great Britain.[15] Other countries followed suit, Germany and Russia in particular seeing the emergence of significant domestic cotton industries, further undermining British dominance.

The Civil War also resulted in the destruction of slavery in North America, to the great concern of cotton manufacturers and merchants everywhere, who feared that the disruption of the "deep relationship between slavery and cotton production in the West" will "destroy one of the essential conditions of the mass production" of cotton.[16] Even the *Economist,* in general a strong opponent of slavery, was deeply concerned about the possible abolition of slavery in the American South. Its editors feared that, if slavery would come to an end in the South, "the catastrophe would be so terrible, its accompaniments so shocking, and its results everywhere and in every way so deplorable, that we most earnestly pray it may be averted."[17] Yet such fears proved unfounded as new forms of the organization of labor emerged in the American South and elsewhere that effectively forced sharecroppers, tenant farmers, and others to produce ever more raw cotton. And even though personal dependence declined drastically in this new regime of cotton production, coercion was hardly absent from this new world of labor. As late as 1909, the U.S. Department of Commerce and Labor reported to Congress that laborers on Mexican cotton plantations "are forced to work by the police," as "steady work can not be secured from this class of help in any other way."[18]

But perhaps the most important impact of the American Civil War was the realization of cotton manufacturers everywhere of the dangers of depending on a single supplier of cotton. In consequence, manufacturers appealed to their respective national governments to open new and more reliable sources of cotton supply, most prominently among them the Manchester Cotton Supply Association, the British Cotton Growing Association, the Association Cotonnière Coloniale, the Kolonialwirtschaftliches Komitee, and the Central Asian Trading Association.[19] Reliability, by implication, usually meant the political control of the territory in which cotton could be grown, and it was in these last decades of the century that cotton manufacturers and imperial states favored colonial cotton production—the French in Mali, the Russians in central Asia, the Germans in Togo, and the British in Egypt, Sudan, and India.[20]

Britain most forcefully pursued such a policy, but other governments followed suit. Germany, for example, diversified its suppliers after the war, with India and Egypt enjoying a significant share of what had become the continent's most important cotton market. When in 1901 the nation's cotton spinners, along with the imperial government, sent a "cotton expedition" to the German colony of Togo, they issued a "Mahnruf zum Baumwollbau auf eigener Scholle" because more than a million people in Germany, they argued, had come to depend on a regular supply of cotton. Relying on countries such as the United States, India, and Egypt was dangerous, they believed, not least because these nations used ever more of their own cotton in their own factories. The solution to these problems was to be the growing of cotton in German colonial possessions. Eventually, these cotton manufacturers also helped to hire a number of African American cotton farmers from Alabama to settle in Togo, all of them recent graduates of Tuskegee Normal and Industrial Institute.[21] These farmers, chosen personally by none other than Booker T. Washington, did turn Togo into a cotton-exporting colony.[22]

In Russia, efforts to grow cotton on native soil had begun during the Civil War but were vastly expanded after the solidification of Russian rule over Turkestan in the 1870s. During that decade, a group of cotton mill owners got together in Moscow, creating the Central Asian Trading Association to find ways to expand cotton production in central Asia, with the strong support of the imperial government. Over the ensuing years, large-scale infrastructure projects were undertaken, especially the building of railroads and irrigation projects. While at first cotton was transported on the backs of camels—which took three to four months to cover the 600 miles to the nearest railroad depot—the building of railroads cut transportation time to a few days. By 1890 so much cotton was grown in Turkestan (nearly one-quarter of the total amount of cotton used in Russian factories) that one historian has argued that the province had in effect become "the cotton colony of Russian capitalism."[23] By the end of the 1890s, thanks to these efforts, Russia had turned into one of the most important cotton-growing countries in the world, ranking fifth behind the United States, India, China, and Egypt.[24]

In a major shift, the world cotton industry now came to be structured more by imperial states and their colonies and ever less by the workings of the markets organized by capitalists themselves. States intervened further by raising tariff barriers to the import of manufactured cotton goods. As a result, export markets in countries controlled by the imperial powers themselves increased dramatically in importance. Most significantly, whereas Great Britain had exported 73 percent of its cotton textiles in 1820 to Western Europe and the United States, by 1896 only 24 percent went to those areas and 76 percent was shipped to Asia, Latin America, and Africa.

By the beginning of the twentieth century, cotton manufacturing had begun to slip out of the core areas of the developed world, most dramatically out of the pioneer region of the Industrial Revolution, Lancashire. It was a slow process, and its end was motivated as its beginning had been, by the cost of labor. Despite a century of technological modernization, cotton manufacturing remained labor intensive. With cheap labor as the periphery's most important asset, cotton mills increasingly left the areas in which they had thrived and moved to areas with lower labor costs—into the American South and Eastern Europe, but also to India, Latin America, and, especially, Japan. At the same time, cotton planting was increasingly mechanized, fundamentally altering the dynamics of the plantation world. And with the rise of heavy industries during the "second industrial revolution" at the end of the nineteenth century, cotton became much less important to the core economies of the West. With the migration of cotton manufacturing, the mechanization of cotton planting, and the emergence of new industries, the nineteenth-century cotton nexus came to a close.

It was this dynamic and interconnected world that had brought Burke, Baranda, and MacGregor together in the 1830s and introduced new technologies and social relationships to the Yucatan. This story, part of a much larger history of the empire of cotton, suggests a number of more general observations about how a global perspective on cotton changes our view of this commodity and with it of nineteenth-century capitalism.

First, and most important, starting from the global context changes how we view each of the cotton empire's constituent parts and raises new questions about them. Developments in India, Great Britain, the United States, Egypt, and even Valladolid suddenly become closely interconnected. Just one example illustrates this point: the American Civil War, viewed in the context of the world's cotton industry, becomes a decisive break of the United States from British tutelage, allowing for a fundamentally new and different integration of the United States into the world economy, because it did break apart the "Atlantic" coalition between the South and Lancashire forged by cotton. Also, the importance of a particular kind of gender relations to explaining the Industrial Revolution in the United States can be truly appreciated only if we understand that a different set of gender dynamics in China kept Chinese women much longer in their parents' household and therefore made them less available to join a factory proletariat of the Manchester and Lowell kind.[25]

Moreover, a global perspective suggests new questions about the relationships between different places. Also, it raises new questions about particular places, such as why it was the United States, of all countries, that turned into the world's premier supplier of raw cotton, and not, for example, India. It raises comparative questions as well, for example, about labor relations on cotton plantations and in factories. The story that emerges from such a perspective in effect allows us to see the connections between events and developments in distant areas of the world—that is, the global reach of capital and its power to integrate far-flung places unequally into a world system. What seems at first like a world of numerous particularities and conflicting developments becomes more comprehensible as we uncover the unity of the diverse, that is, how very different and geographically distant developments are linked (such as slavery and free labor) and how the logic of capitalism, by confronting entrenched local traditions and distributions of power, led to different outcomes—colonial control in India, slave labor in the United States, and debt peonage in Egypt, for example. Viewed through the lens of the history of cotton, the global, national, and local constituted a unity that conditioned one another, and not distinct spheres.

Second, a global perspective provides a fresh understanding of the history of capitalism. It demonstrates through one powerful example that the global reach of capital is not marginal to the history of capitalism, but is its essence. Capitalism, from the outset, was global in a way the earlier world had not been. With the emergence of capitalism, Europeans directly and indirectly recast the lives of people in distant places and reshaped the very look of the land. In addition, the history of a single commodity allows us to come to terms with how these global connections unfolded. It tells us that without slavery, without colonies, without the removal of Choctaws and Cherokees, and without the destruction of hand weaving and spinning in many areas of the world, the explosion in capital accumulation and technical knowledge that took place first in Britain and then in other regions of the world would not have occurred. The dynamics of capitalism, hence, cannot be explained solely by focusing on one region of the world; global connections were central to the unfolding of capitalist social relations in specific locales, as were the evolving hierarchies of developed versus underdeveloped economies.[26] A history of cotton, then, helps us understand the connections forged by nineteenth-century capitalism, most particularly its harnessing of contraries: slavery and free labor, markets and states, colonialism and free trade, industrialization and deindustrialization.

Third, global perspectives on cotton show in meaningful empirical ways that connections between different places were already well advanced in the nineteenth century. Two hundred years before the advent of "globalization," merchants sourced raw materials globally and manufacturers invested in far-flung places, while workers and peasants migrated over vast distances. The quality of global economic activity has decisively changed since the 1970s, to be sure, yet capitalists in 1800 already thought in global terms when it came to securing raw materials, accessing labor, and finding markets for their products. "Globalization" is not a child of the past three decades, yet the forms that particular moments of capitalist globalization took have changed decisively.

Fourth, a global history of cotton demonstrates that, although capital everywhere followed a similar logic, history weighed down on its particular articulations. The distribution of social power, cultural heritage, diverse natural endowments, and the relative power of a particular place in the larger global division of labor decisively shaped the particular ways in which a particular region was integrated into the larger capitalist economy. If we think about the question, for example, why it was the United States that emerged as the world's premier supplier of raw cotton, and not, for example, India, we need to consider the particular distributions of social power in areas in which cotton could potentially be grown. In similar ways, when we try to come to terms with the gender dynamics of the division of labor in the global cotton industry, the structure of preindustrial households as well as diverse traditions of a gendered divisions of labor need to be considered.

Fifth, because the distribution of social power in particular locales mattered a great deal in structuring local, national, and global markets, we need to understand also how people without access to capital or state power shaped the empire of cotton. They did so in manifold ways. Individually, for example, many African peasants refused to sell their cotton into world markets, making the expansion of colonial cotton production in Africa maddeningly difficult for Western powers.[27] Collectively, cotton workers throughout Western Europe and the United States organized into trade unions, improving their wages and working conditions, encouraging the move of cotton textile manufacturing into areas with lower wage costs. Freed people in the United States after 1865, collectively and individually, resisted the imposition of gang labor on Southern plantations, resulting in the emergence of a system of sharecropping that, among many other things, immobilized the Southern labor force and led to an ever greater reliance on cotton.[28]

Sixth, a history of cotton, while focusing squarely on capitalists and markets, also tells us about the importance of states to the development of nineteenth-century capitalism. It allows us to see the global market system as a construction created by public and private forces, rather than a given. Although historians have recently tended to emphasize the cultural, climatic, and religious factors in explaining the balance of economic power in the world, the story of cotton strongly suggests the importance of slavery, war, imperialism, tariffs, and violence.[29] Indeed, labor, commodity, and product markets all were structured by states and state-sanctioned coercion —slavery, indentured servitude, and forced labor by the poor structured labor markets. Imperial expansion, colonialism, and state-sponsored agricultural experiments influenced commodity markets. Last, but not least, tariffs and restrictive trade agreements, backed by the projection of military power abroad, shaped product markets. "Free" markets, hence, were to an important degree constructed by coercion. Yet, importantly, during the course of the nineteenth century the locus of coercion increasingly shifted away from private actors and toward states that consolidated their power and asserted ever more their monopoly of violence. As a result, the global cotton industry came to be structured by increasingly networks of states, and not, as before, by networks of capital.[30] States constituted and structured the "global," especially as the nineteenth century went on.

Just as states were central in structuring the emerging global world of capitalism, the story of cotton tells us that the blossoming of "free" markets is tightly linked to the exertion of private and public power. Access to military power and capital allowed particular actors to structure markets to their advantage, in effect allocating certain economic functions to particular regions of the world.

These are big arguments for a brief essay. What I want to suggest with this short excursion into the fascinating world of cotton, however, is that, in the wake of the Industrial Revolution, the character of global connections changed dramatically. No commodity played a comparably important role in forging these connections than cotton. It was this new quality of interchange that brought Burke, Baranda, and MacGregor to the small town of Valladolid in 1835 and encouraged them to do what many people throughout the world with access to capital, labor, and raw cotton tried to do at this very moment, manufacture yarn and cotton cloth. By the mid-1840s, however, despite their earlier successes, their venture failed. It failed not least because the weak Mexican state could neither patrol its borders to keep out smuggled British textiles that arrived from neighboring British Honduras nor effectively subdue the protonationalist aspirations of segments of the Yucatecan elite, forcing the American state to close its markets for Yucatecan goods as a way to reasserting its control.[31] It was only once the Mexican state had consolidated control over its territory that a thriving textile industry emerged. In this age of markets and entrepreneurial energy, it was states, after all, that forcefully shaped the global empire of cotton.

NOTES

1. For biographical information on Burke see *National Cyclopedia of American Biography* (New York: J. T. White, 1892–1894), 20:79.
2. John L. Stevens, *Incidents of Travel in Yucatan* (1843; reprint New York: Harper & Brothers, 1848), 2:329.
3. Ibid., 2:330.

4. Howard F. Cline, "The 'Aurora Yucateca' and the Spirit of Enterprise in Yucatan, 1821–1847," *Hispanic America Historical Review* 27 (1947): 41.

5. This argument is also made by Eric Hobsbawm, in *Industry and Empire: The Birth of the Industrial Revolution* (1968; reprinted New York: New Press, 1999), p. 34.

6. See, for example, Edward Baines, *History of the Cotton Manufacture in Great Britain* (London: H. Fisher, 1835); Morris Chew, *History of the Kingdom of Cotton and Cotton Statistics of the World* (New Orleans: W. B. Stansbury, 1884); and Thomas Ellison, *A Handbook of the Cotton Trade; Or, a Glance at the Past History, Present Condition and Future Prospects of the Cotton Commerce of the World* (London: Longman, Brown, Green, Longmans, and Roberts, 1858).

7. Historians of the United States have talked for more than a decade about the need to "internationalize" their field. See especially Akira Iriye, "The Internationalizing of History," *American Historical Review* 94 (1989): 1–10; Ian Tyrell, "American Exceptionalism in an Age of International History," *American Historical Review* 96 (1991): 1031–1055; Michael McGerr, "The Price of the 'New Transnational History,'" *American Historical Review* 96 (1991): 1056–1067; and Thomas Bender, ed., *Rethinking American History in a Global Age* (Berkeley: University of California Press, 2002).

8. U.S. Department of Commerce and Labor, Bureau of Manufactures, *Cotton Goods in Latin America*, part 1 (Washington D.C.: Government Printing Office, 1909), p. 19.

9. See Douglas North, *The Economic Growth of the United States, 1790–1860* (Englewood Cliffs, N.J.: Prentice-Hall, 1961), passim.

10. Ibid., passim.

11. North, among others, has argued for the prominent role of cotton in American economic development. See ibid.

12. John Taylor, "Account of the District of Dacca by the Commercial Resident Mr. John Taylor in a Letter to the Board of Trade at Calcutta dated 30th November 1800 with P.S. 2 November 1801 and Inclosures, In Reply to a Letter from the Board dates 6th February 1798 transmitting Copy of the 115th Paragraph of the General Letter from the Court of Directors dated 9th May 1797 Inviting the Collection of Materials for the use of the Company's Historiographer," British Library, London, Oriental and Indian Office Collection, Home Miscellaneous Series 456, Box F, pp. 111–112.

13. Ibid., p. 202. The story of Indian spinning and weaving is quite complicated and is mainly a story of how a once-global industry found itself losing its once-burgeoning export markets. Hand spinning, and, especially, hand weaving remained important throughout the nineteenth century. Dacca weavers and spinners, however, had produced mostly for export.

14. Roger Owen, *Cotton and the Egyptian Economy, 1820–1914: A Study in Trade and Development* (Oxford: Clarendon Press, 1969), p. 89.

15. D. A. Farnie, *The English Cotton Industry and the World Market, 1815–1896* (Oxford: Clarendon Press, 1979), p. 180.

16. *Bremer Handelsblatt,* October 11, 1862, p. 335.

17. *Economist,* January 19, 1861, p. 58.

18. U.S. Department of Commerce and Labor, Bureau of Manufactures, *Cotton Goods in Latin America*, part 1, p. 31.

19. Arthur Redford, *Manchester Merchants and Foreign Trade, 1794–1858* (Manchester: Manchester University Press, 1934), pp. 217, 227; Kolonial-Wirtschaftliches Komitee, *Baumwoll-Expedition nach Togo, Bericht* (Berlin: Kolonial-Wirtschaftliches Komitee, 1901).

20. See, for example, Allen Isaacman and Richard Roberts, *Cotton, Colonialism, and Social History in Sub-Saharan Africa* (Portsmouth, N.H.: Heinemann, 1995). See also the records of the Togo Baumwollgesellschaft mbh, Record Group 7,2016, Box 1, Staatsarchiv Bremen.

21. See Kolonial Wirtschaftiches Komitee, *Baumwoll Expedition nach Togo,* pp. 1, 6, 10.

22. For this story see also Sven Beckert, "From Tuskegee to Togo: Freedom and Imperialism in the Empire of Cotton," unpublished manuscript, 2004.

23. Quoted in M. Gately, *The Development of the Russian Cotton Textile Industry in the Pre-Revolutionary Years, 1861–1913* (Ann Arbor, Mich.: UMI, 1968), p. 126.

24. See ibid., p. 169.

25. For a discussion of this point see Kenneth Pomeranz, *The Great Divergence: China, Europe, and the Making of the Modern World Economy* (Princeton, N.J.: Princeton University Press, 2000), pp. 103–104.

26. There exists a vast literature on this topic, including Dale W. Tomich, *Slavery in the Circuit of Sugar: Martinique and the World Economy, 1830–1848* (Baltimore: Johns Hopkins University Press, 1990); Andre Gunder Frank, *ReORIENT: Global Economy in the Asian Age* (Berkeley: University of California Press, 1998).

27. See, for example, the records of the Togo Baumwollgesellschaft mbh, Record Group 7,2016, Box 1, Staatsarchiv Bremen, Bremen, Germany.

28. Gavin Wright, *Old South, New South: Revolutions in the Southern Economy since the Civil War* (New York: Basic Books, 1986).

29. David S. Landes, *The Wealth and Poverty of Nations: Why Some Are So Rich and Some So Poor* (New York: Norton, 1998); Jared Diamond, *Guns, Germs, and Steel: The Fates of Human Societies* (New York: Norton, 1997).

30. See also Sidney Pollard, *Peaceful Conquest: The Industrialization of Europe, 1760–1970* (Oxford: Oxford University Press, 1970), esp. pp. 252–277.

31. Cline, "The 'Aurora Yucateca,'" p. 44.

FIVE

From Red Crosses to Golden Arches
China, the Red Cross, and The Hague
Peace Conference, 1899–1900

Caroline Reeves

Today we take for granted the near-universal existence of national Red Cross Societies and their local branches. Most of the world unquestioningly accepts the basic tenets of the Red Cross, that medical personnel and war wounded be treated as neutral noncombatants in wartime. These principles have "acquired a taken-for-granted quality and are no longer a matter of broad public debate," that is, they have become an international norm.[1] Similarly, the institution is so much a part of our daily landscape that we no longer consciously notice it per se. This passive acceptance of the Red Cross's pervasive presence is significantly different from the social and intellectual controversy generated by the more recent spread of another world-renowned symbol, the Golden Arches. As recent attacks on McDonald's reveal, a broad range of people interpret McDonald's as a world-shaping force (although what that shape *is* remains ambiguous), a herald of the new age of globalization, a cultural hegemon of the worst ilk.[2] The globalization that the proliferation of these arches is seen to represent, although originally conceptualized as an economic phenomenon, is now recognized as a broader force, encompassing cultural, social, moral, *and* economic spheres.

Yet as the Red Cross story reveals, the processes creating culturally biased global systems were at work long before the Golden Arches dotted the globe. Almost a century ago, the recognition already commanded by the symbol of the Red Cross—like the Golden Arches today—marked the fact that many non-Western societies had been prepared for an analogous (albeit quite different) cultural invasion under the guise of diplomatic humanitarianism. The symbol of the Red Cross, like that of the Golden Arches, is recognized by millions and millions, and the International Committee of the Red Cross (ICRC) is casually accepted as a global actor. But many observers of "globalization" have never considered the impact the ICRC has had (and continues to have) in creating a superficially homogenous global moral system. This moral system is both explicit and specific and forms an important part of the larger phenomenon of globalization as we are beginning to understand it today.[3] The emergence of a national Red Cross Society in any given country and a state's inclusion in the treaties and conventions required for recognition by the ICRC mark critical steps in the expansion of global networks, institutions, and ideas, as well as in a country's national and international development. These steps and the creation of a ubiquitous Red Cross network, with members in more than 169 countries, have received remarkably little public or scholarly attention.[4]

How did this global moral system come into existence? Investigating specific instances of Red Cross history uncovers important intersections of local and international diplomacy, revealing how such a phenomenon can take root in even the most unlikely places. For example, China's first attempt to create a national Red Cross Society in 1899–1900 opens a window on the meanings and motivations prompting countries to join international organizations, as well as on a fundamental change in China's approach to international relations at a pivotal point in world history. These steps toward internationalization—that is, the formation of linkages among state actors—ultimately led to the creation of a new nonstate actor in China, the Chinese Red Cross Society, thereby linking China with a global organization and engaging it in an emerging global moral system.

This chapter has a twofold aim: first, to situate China historically in a larger international context by documenting its role in extending the reach of one of the interlocking global systems that form the larger phenomenon of "globalization" and, second, to discuss the particular case of China and how the domestic environment affected the Qing Empire's international interactions. The details of China's attempts to enter the international community of nations reveal much about the intersection of the local and the global. This information will allow us a more nuanced understanding of the contradiction between the tightly bound world in which we live and the large ideological rifts that constantly threaten that weave.

SITUATING CHINA

Unlike most national Red Cross movements, whose origins derive from localized catastrophic relief actions or war situations, the first impetus in China to form a national Red Cross Society was a primarily diplomatic maneuver, part of China's involvement in the First Peace Conference at The

Hague in 1899. Extensive documentary evidence shows that officials of the Qing dynasty (1644–1911) involved with the decision to become signatory to the first Geneva Convention of 1864, and thereby to create a national Chinese Red Cross Society, were highly cognizant of what they were doing and why. Much like the Qing actors in Adam McKeown's study of Chinese labor migration and governmental responses, these men "had a growing . . . desire to develop and participate in the institutions that encouraged recognition of China as a member of the 'family of nations.'"[5] Intent on state building, the diplomats were stepping determinedly into international society. In a dramatic move pushing China from a centuries-old tradition of bilateral foreign relations to a new policy of multilateral engagement, influential Qing statesmen now saw involvement in multilateralism and internationalism as an important direction for China's state-building efforts. This policy shift, although short lived, foreshadowed initiatives implemented after the Boxer Uprising (an antiforeign, anti-Christian peasant rebellion in 1900) conventionally seen as motivated by the Allied Expedition's defeat of the Boxers.[6] My research shows that it was not the Sino-Manchu defeat in 1900 that served as the impetus for a new, more open foreign policy stance in the Qing court. Instead, the incident represented a brief hiatus in a diplomatic trend already in place before the uprising overwhelmed it.

Examining the decision-making processes behind these specific changes, we can uncover answers to larger, non-area-specific questions such as, Why do states join international treaties and organizations? How do domestic politics influence those decisions? How did noncolonized, semi-sovereign states respond to the "civilizing mission" of the colonizing powers? What did ostensible support for the Red Cross's humanitarian mission mean to the state actors adhering to the so-called Red Cross Treaty (the Geneva Convention)? In answering these questions, we can understand more fully the historical local processes that have coalesced into the more recent worldwide phenomenon known as "globalization," "the world-wide linkage and integration of previously local, national, and regional phenomena into organizational arrangements on a global scale."[7]

This work builds on a growing multidisciplinary literature on globalization, international norm formation, and international society.[8] It links these three areas to show how each phenomenon must be understood in conjunction with the others, and further adds an important, but largely missing, dimension—a historic contextualization of the individual incidents that make up the process of globalization.[9] Rather than creating a periodization of globalization or abstracting sweeping generalizations about norm formation, this chapter highlights a particular event and the actual debates of state actors as they made the decision to engage in international society and to create a nongovernmental organization.[10] Adding historical depth to the work of two schools of international relations, the English School and the neoinstitutionalists, my research supports their assertion that international society wields a normative force that powerfully motivates states' behavior.[11] It also independently confirms the norm life cycle that political science scholars of international relations, sociologists, and legal theorists have posited.[12]

Unlike many of these scholars, however, I do not agree that the world "constituted a single polity" or that the international social system was "unitary" in the late nineteenth century.[13] Nor do I believe that universalism was actually necessary to create the normative force of international society. The articulation of a cleavage between the powerful "haves" (those possessing "civilization," the salient term of the time) and the "have-nots" (those states deemed to be lacking civilization) created the impetus for the marginalized to seek admission into a society founded and shaped without them.[14] Thus, the Chinese case uncovers an important stage in the process of the creation of normative change and the global spread of a specific moral order—an instrumental acceptance of a nonstate institution to facilitate future international influence, without a corresponding acceptance of the mentalité behind the institution.

By applying these theoretical literatures to the field of Chinese history, we can begin to situate late-Qing China in the increasingly important context of "world history" or, as Akira Iriye challenges scholars of all areas, "to develop a scheme in which local forces integrate themselves into a global situation."[15] This reexamination of China's historical relations with the international community of the late nineteenth and early twentieth century is long overdue.[16] Understanding China's entrance into international society will help us better understand both China's position there today and the way in which international society had to adapt to include noncolonized, semisovereign states such as China.

THE HAGUE CONFERENCE OF 1899:
CIVILIZATION AND THE POLITICS OF PEACE

"Civilization" was a critical term in the international society of the late nineteenth century.[17] With it came many of the dominant European states' assumptions of cultural, racial, religious, and moral superiority. "Being civilized" was the sine qua non of entry into the so-called family of nations. (Contemporary international society still offers similar assessments, sometimes using the same language of civilization and labeling those states outside the family as "pariah" or "rogue" states.[18]) The criteria of civilization were neither static nor impervious to outside influence and evolved substantially over time. Solidarity based on Christianity and the commitment to Christianize, paramount in the eighteenth century, became less imperative with the secularization of Europe in the wake of industrialization, and other values took Christianity's place as benchmarks of civilization.[19] While still rooted in Christianity, secular Enlightenment values such as the rule of law and the supremacy of progress (including material prosperity) began supplanting earlier criteria in the nineteenth century.[20]

In 1899, what did it mean to be civilized? The First International Peace Conference at The Hague, convened by Russian tsar Nicholas II to discuss peace, provides an answer repeated at all successive peace conferences and still appropriate today. To be civilized, a state must have the capacity to wage war, but choose instead to pursue peace.[21] Despite its failure to achieve many of its stated goals, the Hague conference was an important and enduring success in establishing the terms and structure of the discourse on warfare in the civilized world. The Hague conference helped establish the way state actors thought and talked about international arms reduction and peacekeeping efforts, and about war and its legality.[22] This discourse is as pervasive and relevant today as it was at the turn of the twentieth century.

The tsar's diplomatic circular of August 24, 1898, announcing the conference emphasized the link between peace and civilization. It read, "In the course of the last twenty years, the longings for a general state of peace have become especially pronounced in the consciences of civilized nations. . . . All these efforts nevertheless have not yet led to the beneficent results of the desired pacification."[23] The main obstacle to peace, according to the circular, was "above all, the . . . progressive development of existing armaments."[24] This buildup of arms was particularly harmful economically, because "the ever-increasing financial charges strike and paralyze public prosperity at its source, the intellectual and physical strength of the nations, their labor and capital."[25] Ultimately, the circular predicted, the economic hardship caused by arms expenditures would bring on "the very cataclysm it is desired to avert, and the impending horrors of which are fearful to every human thought."[26] The tsar proposed the peace conference to consider "this grave problem."[27] The conference thus had a tripartite agenda—"the reduction of armaments on land and on sea, through a pacific understanding; . . . the organization and extension of arbitration; and, in the case that war could not be avoided, a lessening of its horrors by the adoption of rules intended to reduce them to a minimum."[28]

Although the agenda of the conference was to be "peace," much of what was to be discussed actually concerned the tsar's third imperative: how war should be fought in the civilized world. On January 11, 1899, a second circular presented the program for the conference.[29] Three categories of articles were to be covered. The first concerned the limitation of armaments, including the prohibition of certain weapons. The second covered the adaptation of the Geneva Convention of 1864 to maritime warfare and the review and ratification of the conventions of the 1874 Conference of Brussels on the law and customs of land war. The third category was the most specifically concerned with promoting peace and suggested the drafting of an international arbitration treaty "with the purpose of preventing armed conflicts between nations."[30]

The extension of the first Geneva Convention of 1864 was a critical piece of the conference. The Geneva Convention, also known as the "International Red Cross Treaty," was the international judicial instrument that provided the legal framework for the Red Cross organization. This organization, begun in 1863 in Switzerland, had found an enthusiastic audience in Europe and beyond and had already grown to considerable international stature.[31] States signatory to the Geneva Convention were obligated to set up Red Cross medical relief services during war time, and to respect the neutrality of other states' Red Cross workers. The 1864 convention itself was a rather uncomplicated document. It stipulated that the sick and wounded of war were to be cared for humanely, regardless of nationality. Wounded soldiers were not to be treated as enemies, but simply as human beings in need of care. The convention also specified that all personnel and materiel working on behalf of the wounded were to be treated as neutral by the belligerents and protected as such. Their neutrality was to be signaled by distinctive flags and armbands marked with the Red Cross. The convention, although limited in scope, made important breakthroughs in promoting humanity in warfare, an idea that was increasingly taking hold in the civilized world.[32] The Hague conference was the first attempt to extend the reach of the 1864 document to cover more than land war.

The equation between the existence of a national Red Cross organization and the presence of civilization was popular in the late nineteenth century. States that did not participate in the organization were suspect, and their status as civilized compromised, regardless of racial or religious credentials. For example, America's attitude as a relative latecomer to the Red

Cross movement puzzled many Europeans, as well as some Americans.[33] Refusing to sign the Geneva Convention for many years, and even more hesitant about creating a national Red Cross organization, the United States was something of a renegade when it came to this international humanitarian movement.[34] When Louis Appia, one of the Swiss founders of the Red Cross, asked Clara Barton, well known for her relief work in the American Civil War, why the United States would not support the new Red Cross movement or sign the Geneva Convention, Barton reflected, "Not a civilized people in the world but ourselves missing, and saw Greece, Spain, and Turkey there. I began to fear that in the eyes of 'the rest of mankind' we could not be far from barbarians. This reflection did not furnish a stimulating food for national pride. I grew more and more ashamed."[35] Barton was not alone in this view of the importance of the Geneva Convention in delineating the civilized world. The line between civilization and barbarism was a clearly marked one, and the existence of a national Red Cross Society helped put a state on the right side of the divide.

Yet, despite the apparent weight given to these humanitarian measures of civilization, there was also a less delicate side to civilization, as the Hague conference agenda reveals. As Iriye argues, by the late nineteenth century, despite lofty rhetoric stressing humanitarianism and legal regulation, the "prerequisites for membership" in the society of nations—and thus presumably the ultimate determinant of civilization—were actually "armaments, successful military campaigns, and colonies."[36] This paradoxical situation is evident in the case of Japan. Pursuing inclusion in the so-called comity of nations, the Japanese realized the importance to this project of both the capacity to make war and the simultaneous advocacy of humanitarianism. As disaffected Western observer and journalist Arthur Diosy recounted in 1898, "[By the 1890s, the Japanese] had seen through the sham of Occidental international ethics. For thirty years the West has been urging the Japanese onward in their adaptation of Occidental civilisation, ever replying to their claim to be treated as equals: 'Not yet! Go on building railways, erect more schools, establish new hospitals. Study, work, trade, become learned, peaceful, rich—in one word, a civilised nation—and we will admit you willingly into our midst on an equal footing.' The Japanese took the advice to heart."[37]

According to Diosy, the Japanese indeed built more railways, created a national educational system, and opened hospitals "that aroused the admiration of foreign medical men," but all to no avail. The Western Powers continued to treat Japan "like an interesting, clever child." But when Japan's military became successful (in 1894–1895, during the first Sino-Japanese War), when "Japan went to war, she conquered by land and sea... hey, presto!—the scene changed. The great, civilised Christian Powers stood in a line, bowing courteously to the victor and exclaiming in unison: 'Here is a nation that has cruisers and guns, and torpedoes and long-range rifles, and that knows how to use them so as to kill a great number of people with small loss to herself. Truly this is a great nation and one worthy of our respect!'"[38] Clearly, both nonmartial *and* martial attributes played a role in building international status. Having the capacity to wage war, yet choosing to negotiate peace—both according to Western standards, of course—brought a country into the ranks of the civilized.

REACTIONS

In 1899, despite the tsar's grand rhetoric about peace and its importance to the project of being civilized, the reality of civilization's darker side made the Hague initiative a controversial one. The international community viewed the Russian proposal with deep skepticism. At this stage, the main point of contention was the idea of limiting armaments. Many considered the whole idea simply infeasible, contrary to political and human nature. In China, one foreign resident wrote to the *North China Herald*, "The idea is magnificent ... but more practical minds, taking into account the inevitable imperfections of human institutions and human nature, may see in the Peace Conference nothing but a solemn farce which it is well to play in order to prove that men know the good though they cannot ensue [*sic*] it."[39] Diplomats scheduled to attend the conference also felt this way.

Why the world's largest army would propose limiting armaments also puzzled many. Indeed, scholars of international relations still hotly debate this question today. Contemporary observers saw the Russian involvement as suspect, fraught with hidden agendas. Some suggested what would now be considered neo-Realist, geopolitical explanations for the Russian initiative—that the treaty was proposed to preserve the status quo of international power relationships. Along these lines, contemporary American observers believed that the recent American victory over Spain and the American takeover of the Philippines had forced Russia's hand.[40] The Russians, they felt, feared the emergence of a new power in the Far East, a power made all the more threatening because of Russian anxiety about an alliance between Britain and the United States.[41] Other observers thought that Russia was attempting a diversionary tactic to draw attention away from its voracious expansion in China.[42] The Chinese themselves believed that Russia had fixed on a topic that was "good for discussion" but that was actually an exercise in self-delusion and a cover-up for other issues. "Everyone knows that Russia is 'covering her ears to steal the bell,'" commented the Chinese minister to Saint Petersburg, "but all the nations promote disarmament as a good topic."[43]

Another set of observers, however, particularly the adherents of the growing international peace movement, found the conference to be truly "visionary," genuinely expressing all that was good in human society.[44] In Japan (where he had fled after the Hundred Days Reforms of 1898, when he had challenged the status quo of the Qing government), prominent Chinese philosopher and reformer Kang Youwei enthusiastically welcomed the tsar's peace initiative, which he felt dovetailed with his own utopian ideas.[45] Although his view was quite different from the Western conception of the term, Kang also saw a triumph for civilization close on the horizon.

In fact, the whole issue of what might anachronistically be called arms control had long been a subject of lively debate in China. Zhang Zhidong's famous essay *Quanxue pian* (An exhortation to learning), written in 1898, devotes an entire chapter to this topic and to the related topic of international law.[46] Both a reaction to Kang Youwei's and Liang Qichao's ideas and an impassioned plea for a heartfelt point of view, the chapter begins by saying, "Troops are to the country what breath is to the body . . . yet there are many influential Chinese today who think that China should connect herself with the Western Disarmament Society, arguing that . . . such a move would guarantee a lasting peace to the Orient. Our contention is that a procedure of this kind, instead of promoting peace, would serve as an occasion of further insult to China by other Powers."[47]

Zhang goes on to exhort his readers how "important it is now to be on our guard when all the powerful countries of the world are talking of disarmament! Are they fooled or blinded?"[48] Instead, he proposes, "By all means get the army first and then consider the question of disarmament; for if we talk of disarmament to the other countries without the force to back up our words, we will become the laughing-stock of the world."[49] Zhang also dismisses the idea that international law will make disarmament work, insisting that until China is on equal footing with the West "it is useless to prate about international law."[50] In fact, he concludes, "China is really not in the comity of nations [at all]. . . . Disarmament is an international joke and international law is a deception. There is nothing for it but to seek help in ourselves."[51]

Despite the wide range of reactions to the conference's agenda careening from skepticism to enthusiasm, *all* participants were determined to put the best face possible on the event, to represent their countries as "the most enthusiastic advocates of international peace," as American conference delegate G. William Frederick Holls wrote to President McKinley in March 1899.[52] This public display of enthusiasm was an imperative for all invited states. Failure to seem engaged would be domestically and internationally disadvantageous. Even at this early stage in the development of international society—pre–League of Nations, pre–World War, pre–Nobel Peace Prize, and pre-CNN—states sent their representatives to the conference to be seen doing the right thing. The *official* reactions to the conference, despite unofficial misgivings, show the normative force of international society, demanding that states at least give lip service to the promotion of a more peaceful, civilized world.[53]

The Importance of Being Invited: China Joins the Ranks of the Civilized

The conference was considered important not only in defining civilized behavior for states, but also as a critical arbiter in determining which states were to be considered civilized. Contemporary American observer Joseph Choate remarked that any country participating in the Hague conference had "been recognized as an equal power vested with complete and perfect nationality and equal sovereignty, and entitled *to be treated as a civilized nation,* and not to be classed with African aborigines as a fair prey for the spoiler."[54] The guest list for the conference thus became cause for much international interest.

When finally released, invitations were sent to all countries with regular diplomatic representation at St. Petersburg, plus three more (Luxemburg, Montenegro, and Siam).[55] Non-European governments invited were the Americans—the United States, Mexico, and Brazil (the only invited state to decline)—and the Asians—Turkey, Japan, China, Persia, and Siam. But there were many states that were not included. Notable among those *not* invited were the South and Central American republics, Korea, the South African republics, and the Vatican.[56] Although much popular sentiment in the international community still echoed Emerson's nineteenth-century summation of China's international position ("China, reverend dullness! hoary ideot!, all she can say at the convocation of nations must be—I made the tea"), China had made it onto the guest list. Tsar Nicholas II had invited China to the conference as a full player.[57]

For China, the conference offered a much-coveted opportunity to join with the Great Powers to sculpt the legal framework of international society—or at least to been seen as so doing. China, like many non-European states, interpreted the invitation as a marker of inclusion in civilized society.[58] For the Qing state, or at least a small but significant coterie within the Qing court, the invitation represented important international recognition and gave China considerable "face."[59] This event allowed China to appear on the world stage as participating in Great Power diplomacy—this time, not as a victim or as a defeated enemy, as in many previous treaty negotiations, but as an equal. Although welcome, the recognition the invitation seemed to convey can also be seen as deeply ironic, in light of the international scramble for territorial concessions simultaneously taking place within Qing boundaries.

But the recognition for China was critical. In 1899, Qing dynasty China had already faced the Great Powers in a less than equal capacity on more than one disastrous occasion. From the Opium Wars to the most recent ignominious defeat by the Japanese in 1895, Qing China had not fared well at the hands of international forces in the latter half of the nineteenth century. Unequal treaties, extraterritoriality, treaty ports, and concessions brought home the dominant force of the West—and Japan—over China. China, unlike Japan, lacked a Red Cross organization and much more and, to this point, had been seen as far from achieving the necessary levels of civilization to be considered part of the international community. The Sino-Japanese War of 1894–1895, fought on many fronts—both military and humanitarian—had served to highlight China's weaknesses. Catapulting Japan's progress toward attaining civilization into the international spotlight, China's defeat had shown observers how far "behind" China was, especially compared to her island neighbor. The subsequent "scramble for concessions" resulted after this realization of China's vulnerability. The invitation to the conference, therefore, was all the more attractive to China. It seemed to offer an intimation of diplomatic parity and the chance to join the civilized, particularly because it came at a moment when China was facing the specter of being "carved up like a melon."

Despite China's marginal status in the international community and the irony of being recognized at the same time the Qing were struggling to maintain territorial integrity, China *did* receive an invitation to the Hague conference, where certain other countries did *not*. On March 26, 1899, an imperial edict was issued to Yang Ru, China's minister to Russia, Austria, and Holland, then in residence at the St. Petersburg court, ordering Yang to proceed to the Netherlands to serve as China's chief delegate to the peace conference at The Hague.[60]

CHINA GOES TO THE HAGUE

China took its first major steps toward participation in international society through participation in the Hague conference. Attendance at the conference marked an important shift in China's approach to international relations, from a bilateral approach based on short-term political contingencies to a multilateral approach based on the importance of belonging to the new international order. Although this period of China's foreign relations is often characterized as increasingly xenophobic, in reality Qing diplomacy was breaking out in new directions.[61]

China's diplomats reveled in their inclusion in the conference, revealing their new orientation toward engagement in the world arena. In a reply to the Qing court's order to proceed to The Hague for the conference, Chinese minister Yang wrote,

> China has negotiated [with foreign nations] for several decades, yet we have never before been included in an important conference on either the American or the European continent. . . . [When] Russia invited us to participate in this conference, the foreign minister approached me in person to tell me "[You are invited] because the tsar considers our two countries to have good relations, and hopes that China will thus enter the ranks of the Great Powers." The minister's words were meant to flatter us, of course, but still, if we are compared to Korea, Brazil, or Argentina, whose ministers were in Russia and yet were still not invited to join the conference, we are being treated in a totally different manner. . . . This is a great turning point in China's recent foreign relations.[62]

For China, the invitation itself was an important international achievement and marked a "great turning point" in China's foreign relations.[63] Inclusion meant more than good bilateral relations with Russia; it meant that China had a new *world* status compared to the China of the past, and a different status than Korea, Argentina, or Brazil. Unspoken was the comparison with even more downtrodden countries, particularly colonized countries in places such as Africa. China was *not* to be viewed as "fair prey for the spoiler."[64]

The acceptance of the invitation was even more important than the invitation itself. China's decision to attend the Hague conference reflected not only China's desire for international recognition, but also a new approach to foreign relations. Attendance at the conference announced a decision to participate in international society proactively, by dealing multilaterally with the states that made up that powerful cabal. China's long tradition of dealing with foreign powers on a strictly bilateral basis, engaging in tribute relations, treaty port diplomacy, and barbarian management, meant approaching states one at a time, except when playing one off against another. Now Qing officials were taking a major step into the new world of international agreements and multilateral diplomacy.

In the years immediately preceding the Hague conference, there had been controversy over the choice between Russia and Japan as a key geopolitical ally for the Qing state.[65] Disagreement over which neighbor was more territorially predatory and whose designs on China more threatening rocked the court, involving prominent regional leaders Li Hongzhang, Liu Kunyi, and Zhang Zhidong (who all supported a pro-Russian, anti-Japanese policy during this period). After a brief reign by a pro-Japan faction (spearheaded by Kang Youwei and Liang Qichao) cut short by the dramatic end of the Hundred Days Reform in late 1898 (when the empress dowager imprisoned her nephew emperor who had tried to institute sweeping social, political, and economic reforms), the empress dowager reasserted control over foreign policy and reinstituted a pro-Russian stance in the Qing court. In view of this background, participation in the Hague conference moved beyond the opportunity to reaffirm the Russian-Chinese friendship; it also included Japan.

Qing involvement in the Hague deliberations revealed a critical shift in the locus of foreign policy decision making after 1898 and, with that shift, a move toward heightened awareness of the need to expand China's position in international politics. But domestic politics and foreign policy were in disjuncture; control of the two areas of policy making was split.[66] Despite the accepted interpretation of court politics during this period as broadly xenophobic, the actual picture is more complicated. A clique of antiforeign Manchus, loyal to the empress dowager, is usually said to have been in control of both domestic affairs *and* foreign policy.[67] But, in fact, *foreign* policy was in a different set of hands, controlled by a group of men in the Zongli Yamen (China's recently established foreign affairs bureau) with an internationalist, not an isolationist, bent, led by Prince Qing (Yikuang) (1836–1916), and including a newly developed cadre of capable, trained diplomatic personnel, such as Yang.[68] These men, in direct contrast to the Manchu princes running domestic affairs, saw China's future lying in a broad involvement in the international community.[69] To them, strengthening China meant demonstrating that the country could succeed as a player in world society. Yang's order to proceed to The Hague reveals the power of this internationalist group in controlling foreign policy—while at the same time, domestic policy was swirling toward its isolationist nadir in the hands of pro-Boxer officials.

The First Hague Peace Conference opened on May 18, 1899. Clearly enthusiastic for the proceedings, Yang was the second delegate to enter the conference hall in the Netherlands.[70] During the conference, which lasted through July 29, Yang actively joined the meeting's discussions.[71] George William Frederick Holls, the American secretary, noted, "It should be remarked that the distinguished Chinese delegate and his associates followed the discussions most carefully."[72]

Yang had been posted in St. Petersburg since 1897. Previously, the bannerman had served for five years as minister in the Washington legation, where he had arrived in 1892. Yang's appointment as minister to the United States, Spain, and Peru (one post), with a concurrent promotion to the rank of expectant grand secretary, added an international dimension to a previously domestic official career.[73] Yang had served as *daotai* (circuit intendant) in Jiangsu in 1888; Wenzhou (Zhejiang) in 1891; and Wuhu (Anhui) in 1892.[74] Yang's presence as China's chief representative to the Hague conference and that of his subordinates (Lu Zhengxiang [*zi* Zixin], Hu Weide, and He Yancheng, secretary to the delegation) elicited intense interest from Western delegates at The Hague.[75] The "Chinamen" in their "outlandish costume[s]" were considered exotic and a curiosity to many, despite their credentials.[76] In contrast, the Japanese delegation—already civilized in their Western dress—aroused no such response.

QING DELIBERATIONS

China came to The Hague as a delighted participant and left a cautious, yet enthusiastic, advocate of portions of the Hague treaty, particularly the second section on the extension of the Geneva Convention. Qing officials' interest in the actual treaty—rather than simply attendance at the conference—derived from many factors. First, they felt that this treaty offered an opportunity for the Qing state to show its new interest in participating in the world community and particularly that it could work with other countries: in their own words "following the majority" *(cong zhong)*.[77] Second, many parts of the treaty itself, such as arms reduction, now watered down by the major state players, presented no important challenges to the Qing government, because those articles were not being signed by any of the attendees. Third, involvement with the treaty would set a precedent for Qing involvement in future international affairs. Conversely, *not* participating would isolate China. And finally, signing certain parts of the treaty would mark China as a civilized nation, in step and on a par with other world powers.

For all his involvement, China's chief delegate, Yang, like many other national representatives, did not actually sign any of the conventions or declarations at the treaty's official signing on July 29, 1899, citing his responsibility to wait for his government's instructions before proceeding.[78] Reporting to China after the close of the conference, Yang corresponded with the Qing court about which treaty articles would be most advantageous for China. This correspondence reveals the Qing statesmen's concerns about China's place in international society and her inclusion in international treaties.

The international benefits to China far outweighed Qing concerns about other aspects of the treaty. They carried more weight than the material obligations outlined in the treaty (such as the provision of biomedical relief services in wartime), which Qing officials immediately recognized as impossible, in light of China's current economic and scientific condition. They even overcame reservations about the symbol of the cross, which the Red Cross organization imposed on signatories of the Geneva Convention (although it was not until 1904 that the Chinese would actually display a Red Cross flag). Furthermore, any disparities in belief systems were overcome by reinterpreting the obligations of the treaty in terms of China's own cultural context. Becoming a recognized member of the civilized international community was a critical component of China's state-building mission; it was *primus inter pares*.

In his memorials to the throne about the conference, Yang explained the articles of the Hague treaty in general terms, evaluating the benefits and obstacles China would encounter from each. Yang offered sophisticated appraisals of the views held by other countries' delegates as well as detailed reports of who signed what. Yang's recommendations frequently suggested "following the majority," a stance revealing a primary concern with demonstrating China's willingness to cooperate with the world powers.[79]

Yang discussed the treaty "based on [his] own understanding" of the difficulty he felt the items would present to Qing foreign-policy makers. His memorials singled out the extension of the 1864 Geneva Convention and the Red Cross Society for special attention. The conference had produced three major conventions. The first, the Convention for the Peaceful Settlement of International Disputes, covered voluntary mediation and arbitration for international disputes. This convention was considered the most important and far-reaching success of the conference, establishing a world court.

Yang immediately dismissed this convention and the three declarations prohibiting certain lethal weapons. These, he felt, "did not pose obstacles" for China. He described the arbitration issue as straightforward (something with which China was already acquainted, presumably in her many military defeats) and explained the unproblematic nature of the arms declarations by saying that, "since China's armament factories are not yet refined," signing a ban on weapons not yet developed in China would not present any difficulties. The second and third sections, dealing with land war and the Geneva Convention, however, deserved more attention.

Yang believed the second item on the agenda, the Land War Convention, would be troublesome for China. This section codified regulations concerning qualifications of belligerents, treatment of prisoners of war, treatment of the sick and wounded, and issues regarding spies, flags of truce, and terms of surrender, as well as other technical issues. This convention was based on the Laws and Customs of Warfare document adopted by the Brussels Conference of 1874, which had found much of its original inspiration in Francis Lieber's American Civil War code, *Instructions for the Government of Armies in the Field* (commissioned by the U.S. government in 1863).[80] Yang pointed out how unaccustomed China's army was to the basic precepts embodied in the new code. "In Western countries," he explained, "armies train and drill together. The [European-based] laws of war are familiar concepts to them." Although China was pursuing military refinement and had already partially switched to Western drill techniques, China's army was "not yet totally acquainted with Western laws [of war]. If China were to approve this convention, and China became embroiled in a war with foreign powers, China's army would be forced to fight according to the treaty." Officials would be unable to enforce compliance among China's troops, and the penalties imposed by foreigners for noncompliance would undoubtedly be severe.

The Convention for the Adaptation to Maritime Warfare of the Principles of the Geneva Convention of 1864 was similarly problematic. After some amendments, this convention had met with unanimous approval at The Hague. Yet to China, these ideas, too, were new. Yang pointed out that the Qing bureaucracy did not have the personnel or the resources to set up Western-style hospitals in Chinese port cities (where foreigners congregated) or to build and man the hospital ships called for in the convention. This convention also led to the same predicament as the previous one: if war broke out with a Western power, or if Westerners were to wage war on Chinese soil, the Chinese would be bound to treat all sick and wounded soldiers according to the treaty, which China would probably be unable to do. "So," Yang concluded, "it seems that these two sections of the treaty are both troublesome for us."

In Yang's estimation, however, there was one significant difference between the two conventions—their relative importance in the Western public eye. Comparing the two, Yang argued that the Geneva Convention could not be easily avoided; the popularity of this convention in the world community made it of special concern to China. Although signing this item would certainly cause difficulties, that obstacle could—and would have to—be overcome. Yang insisted that adherence to the Geneva Convention and the formation of a national Chinese Red Cross Society were critical moves for China's world status.

The key point was that adhesion to the Geneva Convention and the establishment of a national Chinese Red Cross Society would make a favorable impression on the international community. Yang explained,

> All other countries regard the Red Cross Society as a humane endeavor, a product of Civilization *(wenhua)*.[81] Japan has already established such a group, sponsored by the government and supported by the people. This group has had much success. If we do not join [the ICRC], it will seem as if we are the only country not performing these good deeds. It will be hard to justify ourselves. If we follow the Japanese model and create such a Society, however, it will be a swift and easy way to show that China can conform with others. . . . If we do not sign, the foreigners will suspect China of segregation, and later, when there is another treaty beneficial to China, the foreigners will not be willing to negotiate with us as cordial friends.[82]

Yang's concern with the treaty was as much one of setting precedent in the world community as it was of interest in the content of the agreement. Assessing the Geneva Convention pragmatically, Yang did not address debates of Eastern versus Western humanitarian philosophy. His focus was squarely on China's international status. Yang wanted to make sure China was not left behind or left out, "the only country not performing these good deeds."

In a later memorial, he elaborated, "If we join [this treaty], in the future when international conventions deciding postal issues, commercial matters, or international law [are being held], we can cite China's involvement in this conference as a precedent, and thus we will no longer be excluded. The advantages here are numerous and significant. This is a great turning point in China's recent foreign relations."[83] Yang was articulating the new foreign policy position of the diplomatic wing of the Qing court, an increasingly active involvement in a multilateral international policy, which would bestow "numerous and significant" advantages on China. China no longer wanted to be "excluded."

Yang was speaking in concert with the Zongli Yamen. There, other important Qing figures shared his view that China must set a precedent of involvement. Prince Qing (Yikuang) supported Yang's recommendations. "[Yang Ru's] discussion of each article is quite careful," the prince wrote in a memorial to the throne; "we ministers have reinvestigated them." Speaking out strongly in favor of Yang's position, Prince Qing concluded, "China is coming to the Hague Conference as a neophyte *(yishi)*. We should not overly segregate ourselves, which would cause the foreigners to discriminate against us."[84]

Here we see the split in opinion within the Qing bureaucracy between internationalists and isolationists over the correct way to handle foreigners. On November 24, 1899, the throne sent an edict to respond to the Zongli Yamen's memorial of the same date. The first item of the Hague treaty, the Arbitration Convention, might not be as harmless as Yang had painted it, the edict declared. The Westerners might band together and use mediation as a way to deprive a victor (China) of her spoils, were there a war.[85] The throne thus disagreed with Yang on the advisability of signing the Arbitration Convention, fearing that this item was "in appearance, mediation; in reality, a way to obstruct China."[86]

Prince Qing dealt carefully and diplomatically with the throne's concerns. His arguments explained the items of the Arbitration Convention in detail, stressing the nonbinding and voluntary aspects of the document. Prince Qing directly addressed the issue of China going to war, by December 1899 a real threat because of the increased domestic unrest of the Boxer movement. "Domestically, we will seriously prepare for war, while externally, we will appear weak. . . . It will not do for China to appear to segregate herself [internationally]. As for this Arbitration Treaty, we ministers have investigated again and again, and there is no obstacle to our signing it. We request that an edict be issued to Yang to sign this item along with the rest of the group." The clash between domestic policy and foreign policy emerges explicitly here. Despite domestic antiforeignism, however, the Zongli Yamen recommended pressing ahead for international inclusion. The throne, deciding to leave foreign policy in Zongli Yamen hands, finally complied.[87]

Prince Qing next addressed the Extension of the Geneva Convention to Maritime War, which, in the Chinese discussion, had become increasingly focused on the creation of a Red Cross Society in China. The prince explained that, although the Red Cross was "something China's army and navy have never had before, the trend is that China must not become isolated. It does no harm to show that China can follow along and demonstrate that China, too, performs moral and virtuous deeds."[88] Agreeing with Yang, Prince Qing also expressed the opinion that in this case, particularly, China needed to demonstrate its ability to function according to Western precepts of civilized behavior and to join the Western nations on their terms.

Apparently intrigued, the court ordered more information about "the so-called Red Cross activities."[89] In response, Prince Qing delivered another memorial, introducing a brief history of the Red Cross Society. Here the conflation of the Red Cross Society and the Geneva Convention was complete. For this audience's intents and purposes, the Geneva Convention was primarily a call for the creation of a national Red Cross Society.

Situating the Red Cross organization in a Chinese context, the prince suggested that establishing a Red Cross Society was a political custom of Western governments, one that was actually based on a concept resembling the ancient Chinese philosopher Mozi's idea of *jian ai*, universal love.[90] Echoing Yang, the prince explicitly stressed the fact that nations around the globe considered the Red Cross mission a most desirable, compassionate undertaking. The peer pressure of international society was clearly at work here. This approach also played to imperial concerns about the traditional Confucian responsibility of the emperor to perform as benevolent patron of the people. The prince, on behalf of the Zongli Yamen, also recommended that China join the treaty.[91]

On December 6, 1899, the throne approved the signing of the 1864 Geneva Convention and all articles of the Hague treaty except the Land War Convention.[92] Yang's final report, dated January 28, 1900, summarized Yang's experiences at The Hague and confirmed his authorization to sign the approved parts of the treaty.[93] Yang, aware of the triumph, actually petitioned for the signature of the land war article, which the court had already decided not to sign. The bulk of his memorial, however, was dedicated to the Red Cross Society. Yang's enthusiasm for the formation of a Red Cross Society in China and his desire to take part in that project bubbles through the formal language of the official memorial.

This final memorial focused for a large part on the creation of a national Chinese Red Cross Society. Again, the public face of the endeavor was the crucial one. China should quickly establish a Red Cross group to show China's good intent to the world, he wrote. The Japanese Society's rules and regulations could serve as a model for China's organization (Japan's Red Cross had been functioning since 1873).[94] Funds would initially come from the imperial treasury, which would "lead the country" in supporting the organization. Later, solicitations would be made, presumably among the elite *(shenshi)* and "from small sums, a great sum would be collected," according to Yang's vision.[95] Yang's plans for the Society's immediate future also included "building hospitals, purchasing [hospital] ships, storing medicines, training personnel, and setting up establishments in treaty ports." Yang even went so far as to suggest himself as head of the Chinese Red Cross Society. "My term ends next spring," he noted. "If I receive your favor and may return to China, I would be more than happy to take charge of this endeavor, as well as to donate 5,000 taels of silver from my salary as a meager contribution, so that we can quickly set up a model."

Yang had only one reservation about the organization as it stood. Following the examples of Persia, the Ottoman Empire, and Siam (all of which voiced similar objections at the conference), Yang proposed a modification of the Red Cross symbol for use within China, a proposal he had already raised with the Dutch foreign ministry.[96] "Because China's culture and religion *(wenjiao)* are unlike [those of the Europeans], it would be inappropriate for China to adopt the sign of the cross," he noted. This departure from the policy of "following the majority" may have been a concession to China's domestic isolationists, signaling recognition of the anti-Christian feeling already beginning to crest in China as part of the Boxer movement. As an alternative, "in order to show China's difference," Yang suggested adding two strokes to make the cross a *zhong,* as in *Zhonghua* (China) or adding four strokes to the cross to make it into the character *wan* (the Buddhist swastika). Here Yang was not afraid to differentiate China and China's culture from the assembled Western nations and depart from "following the majority." Although sensitive to the will of the majority at the conference, Yang saw this issue as an opportunity to align China with other non-Western states. Siam, Persia, and Turkey were countries whose outspoken resistance to the Christian chauvinism of the Western majority (although ostensibly unintentional in the case of the Red Cross symbol) was inspiring to China's representative.[97]

Yang, representing China's government, had come to The Hague to advocate China's accession to a treaty whose particulars were all but impossible for China's domestic situation but whose general thrust was almost irresistible: inclusion in the world polity. In signing on, the Sino-Manchu government committed itself to a process that would become increasingly prevalent in the new century, willing submission to a constitutive process of global social and political construction, leading to a superficial isomorphism among states.[98] Yet even Yang, enthusiastic as he was for these proceedings, ultimately felt he needed to "show China's difference" in some small way, "because China's culture and religion are different." Although China—like Persia, like the Ottomans, like Siam—was indeed there at The Hague, with all that its representatives' presence entailed and hoped to entail, China's representatives were as aware as members of the civilized states that the world was *not* a single polity, nor would it so become, even after they "joined" the international community. Even if China were to be recognized as a Great Power, those differences would remain.

DOMESTIC CRISIS: THE END OF THE INITIATIVE

Here Yang's discussions with the court come to an abrupt halt. Ironically, just as China was taking specific diplomatic steps to improve her status in the international community, the Boxer Uprising erupted in China. The Boxer movement, supported by the empress dowager herself, marked the last great triumph of isolationism within the Qing court. The internationalists were temporarily eclipsed, as peasants wielding magic incantations closed on Beijing to rid China of the foreign scourge and return the Qing to its former glory.[99] The treaty of The Hague was quickly put aside by officials overwhelmed by the domestic crisis, and the documents for ratification lost. The same "international community" China was trying so hard to join banded together to crush the uprising and impose yet another staggering indemnity on China. The only Red Cross activity during the uprising was that organized by the Japanese, whose Red Cross hospital ships waited offshore to care for the wounded of the "civilized" nations crushing China's revolt.[100] Yang's energies were turned to negotiating an exit from this crisis.[101] The Hague treaty would not be ratified by China, nor would the Red Cross initiative be rekindled until 1904, when the pendulum swung back to a more open foreign policy and the Russo-Japanese War once more brought national and international humanitarian relief into the domestic Chinese spotlight. The initiative *would* be picked up again, and China would continue to move toward inclusion in civilized society, signing the Geneva Convention in 1906 and finally becoming recognized by the ICRC in 1912. But as contemporaries noted after the Boxer events in late 1900, China had "reached a stage of national degradation so low that she . . . retained few of the attributes of a sovereign and independent state," and the events of The Hague seemed long ago and far away.[102]

To Yang, a diplomat with extensive overseas experience, and to Prince Qing, chief member of the Zongli Yamen, the signing of the Hague treaty and participation in the International Red Cross Society offered China an opportunity to "join in great power diplomacy on equal footing." [103] China's diplomatic statesmen were well aware of the clout wielded by Western-dominated civilized society and were determined to have China take her place in that powerful company. Perhaps these prescient statesmen even saw their actions as a possible prelude to later renegotiations of the unequal treaties. The general philanthropic thrust promoted by the international Red Cross organization could be contextualized in a Chinese tradition and thus rendered familiar to the Chinese bureaucracy when need be. But for the most part, the importance of joining the international community overcame any other considerations.

Rather than springing out of an actual relief action or war situation (the usual genesis of national Red Cross Societies), in 1899 the formation of a Red Cross Society was seen by the Qing imperial court as a diplomatic tool, a badge of civilization worn to enter a certain club, a mark of belonging, and a sign of incipient sovereignty. Very much a diplomatic initiative, inclusion in the Geneva Convention and the formation of a national Red Cross Society were seen as methods to enhance China's position in the world community. Although the move posed various domestic difficulties, the immediate international prestige such a move would bring seemed invaluable. In a period of growing domestic antiforeignism, despite the recent rejection of the reforms of the Hundred Days, the imperial government nonetheless decided to act on Yang's and Prince Qing's suggestions to sign the Hague treaty and form a national Red Cross Society. The decision was based on neither important reevaluations of China's moral standards nor a radical reinterpretation of the meaning of civilization in China's own cultural and historical context, but instead on the importance of being included. The normative force of international society, although a very fledgling society compared to that of today, was already working powerfully.

CONCLUSIONS

The Chinese example reveals that some states join international organizations not necessarily because of a confluence of values between the interested state and the organization, nor simply for the material assets membership confers, but instead to exploit the symbolic importance of belonging. Although membership in the International Red Cross movement certainly confers many material benefits on countries seeking international humanitarian aid or direction in setting up a national disaster relief organization (including mutual assistance among member states; the sharing of medical and relief information, supplies, and personnel; participation in an international network of actors; and access to financial resources), less tangible benefits are equally important to countries seeking affiliation with the Red Cross organization.

At the turn of the twentieth century, sponsorship of a national Red Cross Society conveyed a state's seriousness on the world stage as an actor —one that could live up to the material and moral standards set by the emerging world powers. These standards were no less normative for their newness in the international arena. The ICRC's recognition of a national Red Cross Society was seen as "a standard early sign of statehood," and was highly coveted by marginalized states.[104] The withholding of that recognition (as in the modern cases of Taiwan's Red Cross Society or Israel's Red Shield of David)—or the lack of a national Society—suggested a certain precariousness about a state's international status or sovereignty.[105] Like membership in the United Nations (although long predating that organization), membership in the Red Cross family was broadly assumed of any legitimate state. It was this symbolic meaning that the Qing hoped to exploit by signing the Geneva Convention and the Hague treaty articles, signaling legitimation and strength to both international and domestic audiences.

By examining the Chinese case, we can see how international society grew to include a more "global," "universal" representation of states at the turn of the twentieth century, thereby laying the groundwork for increasingly global (rather than simply international) processes as the twentieth century progressed. The more states included in international society, officially adopting the standards it espoused (like the Red Cross credo or the need for state-controlled travel documentation), the more influential that normative force became, ostensibly championing the beliefs and standards of a growing segment of the global polity. Yet at the same time, we can also begin to see the dilemma caused by the inclusion of states and state actors whose values and priorities were unlike those of its founding members. In officially signing onto the treaties and documents codifying the existence of international society, latecomer states such as China paradoxically reinforced claims of universalism that they did not (and still do not) necessarily accept. The myth of a single world polity was recognized as such even by the actors of the times. The "norm" was clearly not universal in a deeply significant sense.

In addition, these state actors were often also at variance with the domestic constituents they were assumed to represent. The disjuncture between the new members' reasons for joining and the impression "joining" projected created a gap which has allowed hopeful, yet misguided, ideas of "universalism" and global homogeneity to flourish. Like the Golden Arches, the Red Cross does not mean the same thing to all peoples around the globe. Despite this disjuncture, the power of humanitarian norms has become increasingly recognized, and their educational influence has expanded.[106] In light of this influence, the global moral system promoted by the international Red Cross movement may some day indeed become truly universal.

NOTES

1. Martha Finnemore and Kathryn Sikkink, "International Norm Dynamics and Political Change," *International Organization* 52:4 (autumn 1998): 895.

2. On globalization, see James L. Watson, ed., *Golden Arches East: McDonald's in East Asia* (Stanford, Calif.: Stanford University Press, 1997). On cultural hegemony, compare the *New York Times*, July 1, 2000, p. A1, and October 12, 1999, p. A1, for recent French assaults on McDonald's

3. The multiplicity of meanings now comprising the term "globalization" is immediately evident in many public fora on globalization. For example, see a recent edition of *Foreign Affairs* 80 (January/February 2001), which hosts a series of articles collectively titled "Bridging the Globalization Gap." Some of the articles address globalization as an explicitly economic phenomenon (Scott, Wolf), whereas others refer to a larger, more inclusive conception of globalization (Franck).

4. Caroline Moorehead, *Dunant's Dream: War, Switzerland and the History of the Red Cross* (New York: Carroll & Graf, 1998), p. 714.

5 Adam McKeown, "Diaspora and Bureaucracy in the World Order: Chinese Migrants Meet the American Empire, 1880–1936." Paper presented at the conference "Interactions: Regional Studies, Global Processes, and Historical Analysis," Washington, D.C., February 28–March 3, 2001.

6. Even recent articles take this position. For example, an essay on Zhang Zhidong's *Quanxue pian* (An Exhortation to Study) broadly concludes that after 1898, "the opportunity for peaceful and orderly reform based on a critical reevaluation of Chinese traditional institutions and substantial borrowings from the West seems to have been lost" (Tze-ki Hon, "Zhang Zhidong's Proposal for Reform: A New Reading of the *Quanxue pian*," in Rebecca Karl and Peter Zarrow, eds., *Rethinking the 1898 Reform Period: Political and Cultural Change in Late Qing China* [Cambridge, Mass.: Harvard University Press, 2002], p. 98). I would argue that, although this might be true in the domestic sphere, officials dictating China's foreign relations were still able to expand the scope of reforms in the diplomatic sphere.

7. Jeffrey Sobal, "Food System Globalization, Eating Transformations, and Nutrition

Transitions" in Raymond Grew, ed., *Food in Global History* (Boulder, Colo.: Westview Press, 1999), p. 171.

8. See Jan Nederveen Pieterse, "Globalization as Hybridization" in Mike Featherstone, Scott Lash, and Roland Robertson, eds., *Global Modernities* (London: Sage, 1997), p. 45, for an overview of disciplinary approaches to this topic; see Finnemore and Sikkink, "International Norm Dynamics and Political Change," for a review of scholarship on international norms.

9. Compare political scientist Martha Finnemore's discussion of the history of the International Red Cross, *National Interests in International Society* (Ithaca, N.Y.: Cornell University Press, 1996), with that of historian John F. Hutchinson, *Champions of Charity: War and the Rise of the Red Cross* (Boulder, Colo.: Westview Press, 1996), for differing approaches to the "data" of history.

10. Anthony Giddens, *The Consequences of Modernity* (Stanford, Calif.: Stanford University Press, 1990), and Piertese, "Globalization as Hybridization," pp. 46–48.

11. On the English School, see Gerritt W. Gong, *The Standard of "Civilization" in International Society* (Oxford: Clarendon Press, 1984), and Hedley Bull and Adam Watson, eds. *The Expansion of International Society* (Oxford: Clarendon Press, 1989). On neoinstitutionalism, see George M. Thomas, John W. Meyer, Franciso O. Ramirez, and John Boli, *Institutional Structure: Constituting State, Society and the Individual* (Beverly Hills, Calif.: Sage, 1987); Finnemore, *National Interest in International Society;* and Yasemin Soysal, *The Limits of Citizenship: Migrants and Postnational Membership in Europe* (Chicago: University of Chicago Press, 1994).

12. See Finnemore and Sikkink, "International Norm Dynamics and Political Change," pp. 895–909; however, I take issue with their "stage I characterization" of the ICRC.

13. John Boli and George M. Thomas, *Constructing World Culture: International Nongovernmental Organizations since 1875* (Stanford, Calif.: Stanford University Press, 1999), pp. 14.

14. On the notion of "civilization," see Prasenjit Duara, "The Discourse of Civilization and Pan-Asianism," *Journal of World History* 12:1 (spring 2001): 99–130; Thongchai Winichakul, "The Quest for 'Siwilai': A Geographical Discourse of Civilizational Thinking in the Late 19th and Early 20th C. Siam," *Journal of Asian Studies* 59:3 (August 2000): 528–549; Gong, *The Standard of "Civilization";* and Thomas Risse, Stephen Rapp, and Kathryn Sikkink, eds., *The Power of Human Rights: International Norms and Domestic Change* (Cambridge: Cambridge University Press, 1988), p. 8. On the admission of previously marginalized states to the "civilized" community of nations, see Bull and Watson, *Expansion of International Society*, p. 124; and Yannis A. Stivachtis, *The Enlargement of International Society: Culture versus Anarchy and Greece's Entry into International Society* (New York: St. Martin's Press, 1998), pp. 72–93.

15. Akira Iriye, *Cultural Internationalism and World Order* (Baltimore: Johns Hopkins University Press, 1997), p. 179.

16. The field is still depending on venerable but increasingly outdated classics such as Immanuel C. Y. Hsu, *China's Entrance into the Family of Nations* (Cambridge, Mass.: Harvard University Press, 1960); Hosea Ballou Morse, *The International Relations of the Chinese Empire*, 3 vols. (London: Longmans, Green, 1910); and Mary Wright, ed., *China in Revolution: The First Phase, 1900–1913* (New Haven, Conn.: Yale University Press, 1968). Samuel

S. Kim deals with China's international involvement in the latter half of the twentieth century. Much of his work is particularly interesting when understood against the backdrop of the pre–World War II period in Chinese history. See, for example, Kim's "China and the United Nations," in Elizabeth Economy and Michel Oksenberg, eds., *China Joins the World: Progress and Prospects* (New York: Council on Foreign Relations Press, 1999).

17. Gong, *The Standard of "Civilization"*; Thongchai, "The Quest for 'Siwilai.'"

18. Noam Chomsky, *Rogue States: The Rule of Force in World Affairs* (Cambridge, Mass.: South End Press, 2000); Richard Price, "A Genealogy of the Chemical Weapons Taboo," *International Organization* 49:1 (winter 1995): 95–98; Robert S. Litwak, *Rogue States and U.S. Foreign Policy: Containment after the Cold War* (Baltimore: Woodrow Wilson Center Press, 2000), pp. 47–48. I disagree with Thomas Risse and Kathryn Sikkink, "The Socialization of International Human Rights Norms into Domestic Practices: Introduction," in Risse, Rapp, and Sikkink, eds., *The Power of Human Rights*, who state, "Today, the idea of 'civilized' nations has gone out of fashion" (p. 8). The idea is not only still used, but also remains powerful, especially after the events of September 11, 2001.

19. Stivachtis, *Enlargement of International Society*, pp. 73–76; Bull and Watson, *Expansion of International Society*, p. 125.

20. Thongchai, p. 530 and, particularly, note 5; Baron Alexander Von Siebold's *Japan's Accession to the Comity of Nations* (London: K. Paul, Trench, Trubner, 1901), pp. 47 and 66, gives a contemporary observer's comments on the Japanese case that is very revealing of these values.

21. This discussion was echoed in the post–September 11, 2001, descriptions of civilization versus barbarism, at least until the United States declared its intentions to invade Iraq.

22. Price, "Genealogy of the Chemical Weapons Taboo," particularly pp. 82–83 and 90–92, agrees.

23. James Brown Scott, ed., *The Hague Conventions and the Declarations of 1899 and 1907* (New York: Oxford University Press, 1915), p. xiv.

24. Ibid.

25. Ibid.

26. Ibid., p. xv.

27. Ibid.

28. James Brown Scott, dir., *The Proceedings of the Hague Peace Conferences: Translations of the Official Texts* (New York: Oxford University Press, 1921), p. 1.

29. The second circular is dated and frequently referred to by the date December 30 (1898), according to the Russian "old-style" calendar. See Scott, *Hague Conventions*, p. xvii.

30. Ibid., p. xvii.

31. Pierre Boissier, *Histoire du Comite International de la Croix-rouge de Solferino a Tsoushima* (Paris: Plon, 1963); Hutchinson, *Champions of Charity*.

32. Price, "Genealogy of the Chemical Weapons Taboo," pp. 95–103.

33. Moorehead, *Dunant's Dream*, p. 92.

34. For this chapter of the American Red Cross story, see Hutchinson, *Champions of Charity*, pp. 226–227.

35. Clara Barton, *The Red Cross: A History of this Remarkable International Movement in the Interest of Humanity* (Albany, N.Y.: J. B. Lyon, 1898), pp. 60–72; Ishbel Ross, *Angel of the Battlefield: The Life of Clara Barton* (New York: Harper, 1956), p. 106.

36. Akira Iriye, *China and Japan in the Global Setting* (Cambridge, Mass.: Harvard University Press, 1992), p. 18.

37. Arthur Diosy, *The New Far East* (London: Cassell and Company, 1898).

38. Ibid., p. 34.

39. *North China Herald,* May 29, 1899, p. 953.

40. Calvin D'Armond Davis, *The United States and the First Hague Peace Conference* (Ithaca, N.Y.: Cornell University Press, 1962), p. 38.

41. Ibid.

42. Ibid., p. 47.

43. Wang Yanwei and Wang Liang, comps., *Qingji waijiao shiliao (QWS)* (Taipei: Wenhai Chubanshe, 1964), vol. 5, p. 40.

44. Davis, *The United States and the First Hague Peace Conference,* pp. 54–63.

45. On the Hundred Days Reforms, see Luke Kwong, *A Mosaic of the Hundred Days* (Cambridge, Mass.: Harvard University Press, 1984); and, for a long overdue reappraisal of the significance of many aspects of the Hundred Days, see Karl and Zarrow, eds., *Rethinking the 1898 Reform Period.* On Kang Youwei, see Laurence Thompson, trans., *Ta T'ung Shu: The One-World Philosophy of K'ang Yu-wei* (London: Allen and Unwin, 1958), pp. 90–91, 104.

46. I use the Chinese version in *Xu xiu si ku quan shu;* for an English translation, see Chang Chih-tung, *China's Only Hope: An Appeal* (New York: Fleming H. Revell, 1900), pp. 139–143.

47. Ibid., p. 139.

48. Ibid., p. 140.

49. Ibid., p. 141.

50. Ibid., p. 143.

51. Ibid.

52. Cited in Davis, *The United States and the First Hague Peace Conference,* p. 70.

53. In "The Socialization of Human Rights Norms," Risse and Sikkink discuss a similar process occurring later in the next century as "norms socialization," pp. 1–38.

54. Joseph H. Choate, *The Two Hague Conferences* (Princeton, N.J.: Princeton University Press, 1913), p. 26; emphasis added.

55. Frederick Holls, *The Peace Conference at The Hague and Its Bearing on International Law and Policy* (New York: Macmillan, 1900), p. 34.

56. Davis, *The United States and the First Hague Peace Conference,* pp. 52–53; Holls, *The Peace Conference at The Hague,* pp. 35 and 87.

57. Cited in Paul Cohen, *Discovering History in China* (New York: Columbia University Press, 1984), p. 59.

58. *QWS* 5:40, Guangxu 25.12.28 memorial (January 28, 1900).

59. See "China Goes to The Hague," below, for this discussion.

60. *QWS* 4:552.

61. See, for example, Joseph Esherick, *The Origins of the Boxer Uprising* (Berkeley: University of California Press, 1987), p. 273.

62. GX25.12.28 memorial (January 28, 1900), in *QWS* 5:40.

63. Ibid.

64. Choate, *The Two Hague Conferences,* p. 26.

65. See, for example, Chung-fu Chang, *The Anglo-Japanese Alliance* (Baltimore: Johns

Hopkins Press, 1931), p. 83; Li Guoqi, *Zhang Zhidongde waijiao zhengce* (Taibei: Zhong-yang Yanjiuyuan Jindaishi Yanjiusuo, 1970), pp. 95–108; Dong Haojun, "Lun wan Qingde 'Yiyi zhi yi,'" *Yanan Daxue Xuebao* [Journal of Yanan University] 3:16 (1994): 42–47.

66. This split, resulting in a schizophrenic disparity between domestic behavior and foreign policy, has obtained numerous times in Chinese history—for example, during the Mao years just before the Sino-Soviet Split (1962) and again before Sino-American rap-prochement (1971–1972).

67. See, for example, Esherick, *Origins of the Boxer Uprising*, p. 273.

68. Although Paul Cohen examines Esherick's work on the domestic situation, he does not challenge Esherick's assessment of the foreign policy atmosphere of the time. See *History in Three Keys: The Boxers as Event, Experience, and Myth* (New York: Columbia University Press, 1997).

69. For a discussion of the development of this new breed of Chinese diplomat, experienced and trained in Western matters, see Richard Horowitz, "Central Power and State Making: The Zongli Yamen and Self-Strengthening in China, 1860–1880," Ph.D. dissertation, Harvard University, 1998, pp. 248–297.

70. *New York Times*, May 19, 1899; *The Times* (London), May 19, 1899, cited in Davis, *The United States and the First Hague Peace Conference*, p. 92.

71. Scott, *Proceedings*, passim.

72. Holls, *The Peace Conference at The Hague*, p. 325; note the condescending tone.

73. GX22.10.19 edict in QSL 396:3602, cited in Linda Pomerantz-Zhang, *Wu Ting-fang, 1842–1922: Reform and Modernization in Modern Chinese History* (Hong Kong: Hong Kong University Press, 1992), p. 100.

74. Kenneth W. Rea, ed., *Early Sino-American Relations, 1841–1912: The Collected Articles of Earl Swisher* (Boulder, Colo.: Westview Press, 1977), p. 193. Yang would later serve as principal negotiator between Russia and China after the Boxer Uprising and also during the recovery of telegraph and railway rights in Manchuria. See Chester Tan, *The Boxer Catastrophe* (New York: Columbia University Press, 1955), pp. 157–214.

75. Lu went on to a distinguished career as a diplomat and statesman, becoming minister to the Netherlands in 1905 and minister to Russia in 1911, serving briefly as prime minister during the Republican period, and being appointed multiple times as minister of foreign affairs throughout the 1910s. See *Who's Who in China, 1926* (Shanghai, 1926), pp. 563–564. On the response of Western delegates, see Scott, *The Hague Conventions*, p. 8.

76. Davis, *The United States and the First Hague Peace Conference*, p. 108.

77. GX25.10.22 in *QWS* 5:32.

78. Scott, *The Hague Conventions*, passim; Holls, *The Peace Conference at The Hague*, p. 325. "All powers represented signed the final act, but only seventeen of the powers signed all the conventions and declarations. Of the Great Powers, Russia and France had signed all documents. Delegates of Great Britain, Italy, Germany, and Austria-Hungary [of the Great Powers] chose to sign no conventions or declarations, preferring to leave to their governments all decision concerning these documents. The United States signed the first convention and the first declaration." Davis, *The United States and the First Hague Peace Conference*, p. 182.

79. The following material is taken from a memorial from Yang dated GX25.9.4 (October 4, 1899). Taibei, Waijiaobu Archives, 1-28-1 (3). For a revised version of this memorial, leaving out many of Yang's pithy comments, see *QWS* 5:26, document dated GX25.9.11 (October 11, 1899).

80. Choate, *The Two Hague Conferences*, pp. 12–13; Geoffrey Best, *Humanity in Warfare* (New York: Columbia University Press, 1980), pp. 155–156.

81. Although *wenhua* is now usually translated as "culture," I would suggest that a less anachronistic translation of the term would be closer to "civilization." See Norbert Elias, *The Civilizing Process: The History of Manners* (New York: Urizen, 1978), particularly chap. 1, "On the Sociogenesis of the Concepts 'Civilization' and 'Culture,'" pp. 1–50, for a discussion of the controversy in Europe between the concepts of "culture" and "civilization" over the previous two centuries.

82. GX25.9.11 memorial in *QWS* 5:26–27.

83. GX25.12.28 in *QWS* 5:40.

84. GX25.12.28 in *QWS* 5:40.

85. GX25.10.22 in *QWS* 5:32.

86. GX25.11.5 in *QWS* 5:34.

87. GX25.11.5 in *QWS* 5:34.

88. GX25.9.28 in *QWS* 5:27–28 (November 1, 1899). Neither Prince Qing nor Yang mentions the foreign missionary Red Cross activities of 1894–1895 in Manchuria during the Sino-Japanese War, nor is there any indication that these officials or the throne were aware of that enterprise. For details of that work, see Caroline Reeves, "The Power of Mercy: The Chinese Red Cross Society, 1900–1937," Ph.D. dissertation, Harvard University, chap. 1.

89. GX25.9.28 in QSL 57:957.

90. For an English translation of Mozi, see Burton Watson, trans., *Mo Tzu: Basic Writings* (New York: Columbia University Press, 1963), esp. pp. 39–49, "Universal Love."

91. *QWS* 5:31–32.

92. *QWS* 5:34.

93. *QWS* 5:39–41, memorial dated GX25.12.28 (January 28, 1900). The next section is based on this memorial.

94. See Eleanor Westney, *Imitation and Innovation: The Transfer of Western Organizational Patterns to Meiji Japan* (Cambridge, Mass.: Harvard University Press, 1987), for a comparative case study on the importance of organizational modeling in Japan.

95. This fundraising strategy was deeply rooted in the Chinese philanthropic tradition. For example, Joanna Handlin Smith notes the late-Ming landowner and philanthropist Chen Longzheng advocated a similar strategy ("Benevolent Societies: The Reshaping of Charity during the Late Ming and Early Ch'ing," *Journal of Asian Studies* 46:2 [May 1987]: 325).

96. Scott, *The Hague Conventions*, p. 181, notes Persia's and Turkey's official reservations, that Persia was permitted to use the Lion and Red Sun and Turkey to use the Red Crescent. Holls, *The Peace Conference at The Hague*, pp. 125–126, notes Persia's and Siam's reservation of the right to use distinctive flags. Siam "reserved the right to change the sign on the Geneva flag to a symbol sacred in the Buddhistic cult, and calculated to increase the saving authority of the flag." Also Choate, *The Two Hague Conferences*, p. 16.

97. Ultimately, both Siam and China would concede to the cross. China unofficially adopted the red cross symbol for the Chinese Red Cross Society in 1904 and officially recognized it in 1907 at the Second Hague Conference.

98. Boli and Thomas, *Constructing World Culture*, pp. 2–3.

99. Cohen, *History in Three Keys*; Esherick, *The Origins of the Boxer Uprising*, p. 1987.

100. Hutchinson, *Champions of Charity,* pp. 208, 211. The French sent nurses, but not Red Cross nurses; see Hutchinson, p. 257.

101. Tan, *The Boxer Catastrophe,* pp. 157–214, for details of Yang's post-Hague career.

102. Morse, *The International Relations of the Chinese Empire,* vol. 3, p. 359.

103. Mary Wright, ed., *China in Revolution: The First Phase, 1900–1913* (New Haven, Conn.: Yale University Press, 1968), p. 8.

104. Best, *Humanity in Warfare,* p. 345.

105. See *New York Times,* November 7, 1999, for recent developments on that front.

106. Paul Gordon Lauren, *The Evolution of International Human Rights: Visions Seen* (Philadelphia: University of Pennsylvania Press, 1998), pp. 296–298; David Halloran Lumsdaine, *Moral Vision in International Politics: The Foreign Aid Regime, 1949–1989* (Princeton, N.J.: Princeton University Press, 1993), pp. 283–284; Finnemore, *National Interests in International Society,* pp. 128–149.

SIX

Constructing Africa
African American Writers before Emancipation

Colin Palmer

The African diaspora in the Americas has become a very vibrant area of intellectual inquiry. Beginning in 1502, the peoples of African descent constituted ever-increasing parts of a coerced migratory stream to various societies of this hemisphere. By the time the commerce in African slaves finally ended in the nineteenth century, as many as twelve to thirteen million persons had disembarked in the Americas. Today, the peoples of African descent in this hemisphere comprise an estimated 150 million. They form the majority of the residents in several Caribbean islands such as Haiti, Jamaica, Barbados, and Antigua; constitute a significant minority, as in the United States of America; or are a relatively minor presence, as in Chile or Argentina.

The descendants of these African slaves historically have had an ambivalent relationship with the African continent. Although some embraced Africa and an African heritage with pride, many others distanced themselves from any identification with their ancestral continent. Africa and her peoples were the victims of a pernicious denigration by those Europeans who enslaved the Africans in the West and who colonized the Americas. This denigration was the product of a cultural prejudice that, in time, was supported by claims of white supremacy that rested on pseudoscientific data.[1]

No slave society in the Americas was immune to this contagion. The enslaved peoples, particularly those who were born in the Americas, were socialized from birth into the notion of being human property. Although it is fashionable for some contemporary scholars to celebrate the remarkable cultural production of the enslaved peoples, we know a good deal less about the psychological impact of slavery and the ideology that legitimized it on the slaves and on those who held them in thrall. Thomas Jefferson was one of the first persons to note the impact of slavery on the personality of the slave owners. He observed, "The whole commerce between master and slave is a perpetual exercise of the most boisterous passions, the most unremitting despotism on the one part, and degrading submissions on the other. Our children see this, and learn to imitate it. . . . The parent storms, the child looks on, catches the lineaments of wrath, puts on the same airs in the circle of smaller slaves, gives a loose to the worst of passions, and thus nursed, educated, and daily exercised in tyranny, cannot but be stamped by it with odious peculiarities."[2]

Slaves, to be sure, were not entirely powerless and did engage in a variety of forms of resistance with varying degrees of success. The forms of physical resistance have been widely studied, and the literature on runaways and revolts is quite extensive for most of the societies of the Americas. In societies where topography allowed, many slaves deserted and established free settlements, as in Jamaica, Mexico, and Brazil. Slaves in Haiti executed a successful revolution between 1791 and 1803, and others in Jamaica, Demarara, and elsewhere posed serious challenges to the institution.

It is a mistake, however, to view slave resistance solely in terms of escape or physical assaults on those who oppressed them or on their property. Nor does it seem plausible to characterize the cultural production of the enslaved population as constituting, in the main, forms of resistance. As human beings, the enslaved created the cultural forms and institutions that sustained them and affirmed their humanity. In other words, the enslaved peoples created vibrant cultures not because they were slaves reacting primarily to white society, but because they were human. Slavery affected the peoples of African descent in many pernicious ways, but it did not destroy their essential humanity.[3]

Enslaved peoples and those who were colonized fought largely similar battles to affirm their humanity and selfhood. Although the colonized were not defined as property, their human possibilities were circumscribed and they were relegated to second-class status in the land of their birth. The ideology that sanctioned their condition drew much from the one that nourished racial slavery. Colonial rule, as did slavery, produced forms of resistance, and the colonized were at times able to place limits on their oppression. The opposition to colonialism did not always take a violent form. The intellectual assaults on the imperial power could be sharp, pugnacious, and effective. Colonial critics challenged and undermined the basis of European claims to sovereignty over them.

I mention colonialism in the context of this discussion because slavery and colonialism have played critically important roles in the history of the peoples of African descent in the Americas. These two forms of societal oppression exacted a price from their victims and required them to contest their subjugation. During the late eighteenth and early nineteenth centuries, African American writers began a long struggle to cleanse the society in which they were born of the twin evils of slavery and racism. They laid the intellectual foundations of the assaults that the peoples of African descent would launch against the systems of oppression that would bedevil their lives in the Americas.

These early black writers were the children and grandchildren of American slaves. With the exception of Phillis Wheatley, all of them were born in the United States, although none could claim citizenship. They were outsiders, even though their presence in the society was longer than many of those who denied them their birthright. In fact, by the turn of the nineteenth century, most of the black people resident in the United States were native born. Beginning around the 1730s, the enslaved population in the American colonies had begun to experience an annual rate of natural increase, thereby creating the foundations of an African American Creole population. The official end of the slave trade in 1808 did not halt the human commerce to the new republic, but only an estimated 50,000 additional slaves trickled in before the signing of the Emancipation Proclamation, in 1863. It is quite safe to suggest that by 1820, about 90 percent of the black population was American born. In other words, America's slave population was homegrown during the nineteenth century.[4] The nation was enslaving its own, even if the society continued to maintain the fiction that blacks were not, and could not be, citizens.

Those blacks who were free while slavery existed occupied a peculiarly uncertain status. Not only were they strangers in the nation they inhabited, but most manifested an ambivalent attitude to their ancestral continent. The trade in slaves had severed the link between those who survived the Atlantic passage and those who remained in Africa. Few African Americans during the nineteenth century or later could claim a particular African ethnic heritage with any degree of certitude.

There were several free blacks, however, who urged the nurturing of a black identity that reflected a people's history and condition. The New York intellectual William Hamilton observed in 1809 that "it makes no difference whether a man is born in Africa, Asia, Europe, or America, so long as he is progenized from African parents."[5] In 1829, Robert Young published his *Ethiopian Manifesto,* in which he called for the "collecting together" of the peoples of African descent.[6] David Walker, the most widely known of the early black nationalists, also published his treatise, *David Walker's Appeal in Four Articles,* in 1829. Walker's *Appeal* admonished blacks to develop and cherish a common identity and to liberate themselves through collective action. As he put it, "I advanced it therefore to you, not as a *problematical*, but as an unshaken and for ever immovable *fact*, that your full glory and happiness, as well as all other coloured people under Heaven, shall never be *fully consummated, but with the entire emancipation of your enslaved brethren all over the world*. . . . Our greatest happiness shall consist in working for the salvation of our whole body."[7]

Such unity was easier said than done. These early writers had first to resolve the question of who they were. Were they Africans in a general sense, Americans, or a particular category of Americans? What ought to be their relationship with the peoples of their ancestral continent? What were their responsibilities, if any, to them? Such complex and difficult questions could not be easily resolved, and the conflicts they engendered reflected a people's anguished search for a usable and sustaining identity.

This quest for a usable identity was manifested in the prolonged controversy over an appropriate nomenclature for themselves. Were the peoples of African descent in the United States to be called Africans, Negroes, coloreds, Afro Saxons, Afro Americans, or other?

Samual Cornish, the editor of the *Colored American*, preferred the nomenclature, "Colored American." He maintained, "We are written about, preached to, and prayed for, as Negroes, Africans, and blacks, all of which have been stereotyped, as names of reproach, and on that account, if no other, are unacceptable. Let us and our friends unite, in baptizing the term 'Colored Americans,' and henceforth let us be written of, preached of, and prayed for as such. It is the true term, and one which is above reproach."[8] Frederick Douglass, the distinguished abolitionist, was not so certain. As he asserted, in 1853, "We are Americans, and as Americans we would speak to Americans. We address you not as aliens nor as exiles, humbly asking to be permitted to dwell among you in peace; but we address you as American citizens asserting their rights on their own native soil."[9]

The Reverend Henry Highland Garnet thought the struggle over nomenclature consumed energies that might otherwise be placed in the service of liberation. The clergyman and abolitionist complained, "How unprofitable it is for us to spend our golden moments in long and solemn debate upon the question whether we shall be called 'African,' 'Colored Americans,' or 'Africo Americans,' or 'Blacks.' The question should be, my friends, *shall we arise and act like men*, and cast off this terrible yoke?"[10]

The struggle over nomenclature has still not been completely settled; its emotional wellsprings are deep and enduring. Similarly, the early black writers—and later ones, too—have embraced competing images of Africa and her peoples. Unlike many of their counterparts of more recent times, the vast majority of the early writers had never visited Africa. Consequently, they had to construct images of their ancestral societies and imagine what life was like on the African continent and for their own ethnic group if they knew it. Alexander Crummell, the Episcopal priest and missionary, recalled, "From my earliest childhood, my mind was filled with facts and thoughts about Africa."[11] The young boy's imagination was shaped, in part, by his African-born father's "vivid remembrances of scenes and travels with his [own] father into the interior, and his wide acquaintance with divers tribes and customs."[12] But, as Crummell's later views would amply demonstrate, the image that he framed of Africa was also influenced by the culture into which he was socialized, by the prevailing negative and pejorative descriptions of Africa and her peoples that he had internalized, by the content of his formal education, and by the Christian principles that he embraced.

Crummell and the other African Americans who wrote about Africa before 1863 had much in common, but there were fundamental differences among them as well. They were all products of a society that denigrated blacks, and they all struggled to contest white definitions of themselves. But, as children of America, few were able to eschew the prevailing Western assumptions about Africa and her peoples. Indeed, many black intellectuals embraced these assumptions, even as they sought explanations for Africa's otherness and committed themselves to what they characterized as the "regeneration," "redemption," or "civilization" of her peoples.[13]

These black intellectuals were writing at a time when an emerging body of pseudoscientific literature served to bolster white claims to superiority. Science lent its tremendous authority to those who sought to justify the treatment of Africans on the grounds that they were biologically inferior to the peoples of European descent. Lacking the scientific data to contest these claims, black intellectuals employed other strategies. Invariably, they conceded that Africa was a benighted continent, but one that had had a history of considerable achievement prior to its "fall." The apparent "backwardness" of African peoples, they maintained, should be seen as a consequence of their punishment for having committed terrible offenses, particularly against the Christian God.

In contesting the assertions that Africans had made no contributions to humanity, these early black intellectuals consistently invoked the achievements of ancient Africa. In 1815, Hamilton observed that the continent had "a proud account to give of herself." He noted that Africa "can boast of her antiquity, of her philosophers, her artists, her statesmen, her generals, of her curiosities, her magnificent cities, her stupendous buildings, and of her once widespread commerce."[14] Hamilton spoke respectfully of Egypt, noting that some scholars believe that "China, that very ancient settlement, was originally a colony peopled from Egypt." He pointed out that those who "occupy the country [Africa] from the tropic of Cancer to the Cape of Good Hope were originally from Egypt."[15]

To Hamilton, Africa was a veritable Garden of Eden. With the exception of "her sandy deserts," he asserted, the continent "is very fertile, producing its fruit with very little labour of the husbandman, and as virtue carries with it no corroding thoughts, they must have been a very happy people." To him, Africa was the "first fair garden of God's planting"; it was the "spot of earth, where fair science first descended and the arts first began to bud and grow."[16]

Walker, the pamphleteer who wrote his *Appeal* in 1829, also praised African and Egyptian achievements. He saluted Egyptian strides in "the arts and sciences" and their "magnificent buildings." According to Walker, "learning" originated in Egypt and "was carried thence into Greece, where it was improved and refined." Such knowledge, he continued, "has been enlightening the dark and benighted minds of men from then, down to this day." Walker felt "cheered" by the "renown of that once mighty people, the children of our great progenitor."[17] A letter writer to *Freedom's Journal*, the first African-American newspaper, struck a similar note: "While Greece and Rome were yet barbarous, we find the light of learning and improvement emanating from this, by supposition, degraded and accursed continent of Africa, out of the midst of this very wooly haired, flat nosed, thick lipped, coal black race, which some persons are tempted to station at a pretty low intermediate point between men and monkeys. It is to Egypt, if to any nation, that we must look as the real *antigua mater* of the ancient and modern refinement of Europe."[18]

The Reverend Peter Williams gave an equally positive assessment of African life before the arrival of the Europeans. He claimed, "Before the enterprising spirit of European genius explored the western coast of Africa, the state of our forefathers was a state of simplicity, innocence, and contentment. Unskilled in the arts of dissimulation, their bosoms were the seats of confidence, and their lips were the organs of truth. Strangers to the refinements of civilized society, they followed with implicit obedience the (simple) dictates of nature. Peculiarly observant of hospitality, they offered a place of refreshment to the weary, and an asylum to the unfortunate."[19]

The fact that hardly any black American or black person in the Americas could claim an Egyptian heritage was not an issue for Walker and the others who extolled that civilization's accomplishments. Buffeted by the racially inspired assaults on themselves and their heritage, these intellectuals sought to celebrate their continent's achievements to counter the pejorative claims of their more numerous, usually more formally educated, and certainly more highly placed white counterparts. Whites scarcely noticed the countervailing claims of blacks, because it was they who defined the agenda and claimed a special legitimacy for their points of view. Black intellectuals, in keeping with the temper of the times, hardly questioned the assumptions upon which white definitions of human achievement rested. This was not an age of cultural relativism. European and European-derived cultures constituted what was normative. Thus, black intellectuals, like those of European descent, applied a yardstick, a measure to African cultures that reflected Western values and priorities. This led them, willy-nilly, to assess African achievements in European terms, highlighting those aspects of African life that closely approximated the European. The terrain upon which the nature of African life and accomplishments were contested was European in its texture and content.

This conceptualization created a dilemma for the early black intellectuals. If they applied a European measure to Africa, it was clear that their ancestral continent was not only different, but also inferior in its achievements. There was the stark reality that Africans had been enslaved by the Europeans and the imbalance of power was an uncomfortable fact of life. If the Africans were at one time superior to Europeans in terms of their achievements, their present status had to be explained. Did Africa's decline vis à vis Europe result from terrible crimes her peoples had committed? Why were her peoples enslaved? Could the continent regain its former greatness, and, if so, how could that be achieved?

The answers to such questions animated the thought of black intellectuals throughout the nineteenth century. With one or two exceptions, these writers were American born and had embraced Christianity with varying degrees of fervor. As children of the West, they had internalized the existing claims to cultural and religious superiority and saw it as their duty to "redeem" and "civilize" their benighted and "barbaric" African brethren. But they had to come to some understanding of the reasons for Africa's condition before they could prescribe a cure.

The depictions of Africa by these intellectuals had much in common with that of their white detractors. The Reverend Nathaniel Paul observed in 1833, "Africa is enveloped in darkness, infinitely deeper than the sable hue of its degraded sons." The Reverend Williams spoke of the "barbarous customs of Africa."[20] Hamilton thought that their condition had "descended to the ultimate point of degradation."[21]

Several writers blamed the Africans' degradation on the depredations of the Europeans. Hamilton was convinced that the European-induced slave trade had "crushed the peace and happiness of our country" and turned African "princes" into "tyrants and scourges."[22] Africa had suffered "horrible inhumanities" at the hands of the Europeans. "Thy shores, which were once the garden of the world, the seat of almost paradisiacal joys, have been transformed into regions of wo [sic]," he lamented.[23] In this rendering, the Africans were the victims of European avarice and power.

Whereas several writers blamed outsiders for Africa's perceived travails, others attributed responsibility to the Africans themselves. As Christians, such commentators bemoaned the absence of Christian beliefs among the majority of the African peoples. In 1808, the Reverend Absolom Jones hoped that a Joseph would "rise up" who "shall be the instrument of feeding the African nations with the bread of life, and of saving them, not from earthly bondage but from the more galling yoke of sin and Satan."[24] Crummell characterized Africa as "the benighted fatherland" that could be redeemed only by Christianity. The Westernized Episcopal clergyman blamed the idolatry of the Africans for their condition. As he put it, "If a people think that God is a Spirit, that ideas raises, or will raise them among the first of nations. If, on the other hand, they think that God is a stone, or a carved image or a reptile they will assuredly be low and rude. A nation that worships stocks, or ugly idols, can never while maintaining such a style of worship, become a great nation."[25]

Crummell was certain that Liberia, the country in which he served as a missionary, should adopt Christianity to "live on forever mindless of decay and fearless of ruin."[26] Crummell and Jones were not alone in seeing the absence of Christianity as constituting the basis of African redemption and regeneration. Nineteenth-century black Americans—as did some white Christians—embraced the view that Africa and Africans would play a fundamental role in the rejuvenation of the Christian religion, cleansing it of its past errors. They were strengthened in this view by the prophecy contained in Psalms 68:31, "Princes shall come out of Egypt, Ethiopia shall soon stretch out her hands unto God." In interpreting this prophecy, African American Christians saw it as their obligation to assist in its realization. The striking fact, of course, was that its fulfillment would mean the eradication of the traditional religions of the Africans and, to a large extent, the cultural reconstruction of the continent. The acceptance of Christian beliefs and their practice would produce deeper changes in the social and cultural arrangements and the ethos of the believers. African American Christians were not insensitive to some of these ramifications, but as children of the

West and as Christians, they welcomed them. In fact, they thought that the embrace of Christianity would lead inexorably to the moral improvement of the African converts.

In defining a role for the African American in the Christianization of Africans, a few persons even suggested that the enslavement of African peoples had been ordained by the Christian God for that very purpose. In 1808, Jones enquired, "Why has god permitted slavery?" "It has always been a mystery," Jones said, "why the impartial Father of the human race should have permitted the transportation of so many millions of our fellow creatures to this country, to endure all the miseries of slavery. . . . Perhaps his design was, that a knowledge of the gospel might be acquired by some of their descendants, in order that they might become qualified to be messengers of it, to the land of their fathers."[27]

Some years earlier, the poet Phillis Wheatley, who spent all of her adult years in America, was grateful for her enslavement, because it exposed her to Christian conversion. She wrote,

> 'TWAS mercy brought me from my *Pagan* land,
> Taught my benighted soul to understand
> That there's a God, that there's a *Saviour* too:
> Once I redemption neither sought nor knew.[28]

In this poem at least, Wheatley did not suggest, as had Jones, that the Christian God designed the enslavement of Africans so they might return to their ancestral land and become the instrument for the Christianization and redemption of her peoples. Her sentiments, however, were repeated in 1778 by the poet Jupiter Hammon when he wrote,

> O come you pious youth!
> Adore The Wisdom of thy God,
> In Bringing thee from distant shore
> To Learn His holy word.
> Thou mighst been left behind,
> Amidst a dark abode;
> God's tender mercy still combin'd,
> Thou hast the holy Word.[29]

These sentiments seemed to have been held by the lettered and the unlettered alike. Chloe Spear, a slave who worked in New England, reportedly observed, "[Whites] meant [the slave trade] for evil, but God meant it for good. To his name be the glory."[30] As late as the 1880s, the African American historian George Washington Williams maintained, "God often permits evil on the ground of man's free agency but he does not commit evil. The Negro of this country can turn to his Saxon brothers and say, as Joseph said to his brethren who wickedly sold him, 'As for you, ye meant it unto evil, but God meant it unto good; that we, after learning your arts and sciences, might return to Egypt and deliver the rest of our brethren who are yet in the house of bondage.'"[31]

Such views, at one level, manifested an anguished search for the meaning of the enslavement of African peoples. But, at another level, they showed how Christian dogma helped to shape negative images of Africa, allowing African Americans to absorb and express pernicious views about their heritage and about themselves. But blacks apparently did not all speak with one voice on the reasons for black enslavement, although there is no evidence in the written records of any dissent from views such as those expressed by Jones before slavery ended. Toward the end of the nineteenth century, however, the journalist T Thomas Fortune observed, "The talk about the black people being brought to this country to prepare themselves to evangelize Africa is so much religious nonsense boiled down to a sycophantic platitude. The Lord who is eminently just had no hand in their forcibly coming here, it was preeminently the work of the devil."[32]

Garnet, the missionary and emigrationist, did not accuse his God of ordaining the enslavement of Africans, but he thought that black and white Americans shared the obligation to Christianize the continent. He believed that black men were "bound by the laws of love and humanity, and the principles of the Gospel to do all they can for the land of our forefathers." He felt that whites were required to act similarly, "since they have robbed us of our lives, and become rich by our blood, and it is therefore for them to make sacrifices that Africa may be redeemed, and that they may bless it as they have so long cursed it."[33]

Many of those, like Garnet, who believed that Africa could and should be "redeemed" advocated emigration to that continent. They were driven by humanitarian impulses and were thoroughly convinced of their cultural superiority. Crummell, in appealing to free blacks to devote their energies to the uplift of the continent, spoke of "our ancestors" who were "unfortunate," "miserable," and benighted" and who had a history of "heathenism" and "benightedness."[34] He thought that "all men hold some relation to the land of their fathers," but each person should decide whether he would serve his fatherland and in what capacity.[35] In addition to those who possessed a missionary zeal, the continent, Crummell suggested, needed people with "that class of sentiments in the human heart which creates a thirst for wealth, position, honor, and power." The continent needed "skill, enterprise, energy, worldly talent, to raise her; and these applied here to her needs and circumstances, would prove the handmaid of religion, and will serve the great purposes of civilization and enlightenment through all her borders."[36]

The emigrationist Martin Delany also thought that Africa needed the expertise of black Americans to achieve its fullest potential. During his visit to West Africa in 1859–1860, Delany observed that "the missionary duty has reached its ultimatum." As he put it, "Religion has done its work, and now requires temporal and secular aid to give it another impulse. The improved arts of civilized life must now be brought to bear, and go hand in aid of the missionary efforts which are purely religious in character and teaching. . . . But it is very evident that the social must keep pace with the religious, and the political with the social relations of society, to carry out the great measures of higher civilization."[37]

Delany, it must be said, was driven less by Christian imperatives and more by the need to promote economic development on the continent. He looked askance at the presence of Europeans reaping economic benefits at the expense of Africans. He thought that the Africans could excel in the production of cotton, sugar, and palm oil, all of which could be exported. Black Americans were needed to instruct the Africans in the agricultural arts and they would be important as entrepreneurs and teachers as well. Thus, a mutual and mutually beneficial partnership could develop between the Africans and their brothers across the Atlantic. As Delany remarked, "My duty and destiny are in Africa, the great and glorious, even with its defects, land of your and my ancestors . . . we desire no promiscuous or general emigration to Africa (as the country needs no laborers, these everywhere abounding, industriously employed in various occupations). But [it needs] select and intelligent people to guide and direct the industry and promote civilization with the establishment of higher social organization, and the legitimate development of our inexhaustible commerce which promises not only certain wealth to us, but all the rest of the world."[38] African American participation in the cause of Africa's uplift, in Delany's eyes, would produce economic rewards. Africa's regeneration would carry a price tag.

Finally, there were those who interpreted Africa's fall from greatness not in terms of the absence of Christianity or as a product of God's will. Some saw it as part of the rise and fall of civilizations. Writing to *Freedom's Journal* in 1827, one observer noted,

Each great division of the species has had in its turn the advantage of civilization, that is in industry, wealth, and knowledge, and the power they confer; and during this period of conscious triumph, each had doubtless been inclined to regard itself as a favoured race, endowed by nature and Providence with an essential superiority over all the others. But on reviewing the course of history, we find this accidental difference uniformly disappearing after a while, and the sceptre of civilization passing from the hands of the supposed superior race into those of some other, before inferior, which claims in its turn, for a while, a similar distinction.[39]

The images of Africa that I have described came principally from the pens of clergymen, and this may help to explain their nature, the focus on heathenism, and the call for the Christian regeneration of the Africans. Accordingly, we must be cautious about making absolute statements about the representativeness of their observations. One clue that there were other constructions of Africa may reside in the names that African-Americans gave to many of the organizations they founded before 1863. These names suggest an embrace of an African heritage and a secure identification with the peoples of the continent. Hence, the two Christian denominations that African Americans founded before 1863 were named the African Methodist Episcopal and the African Methodist Episcopal Zion Church. Many secular organizations and publications also had Africa as a part of their names such as the African Union Society founded in 1780, the Free African Society (1785), the *Anglo-African* magazine (1859), and so on.

To the degree that competing images of Africa existed, this should be no surprise. African Americans then, as now, did not all speak with one voice, follow a common drummer, or embrace the same images of their ancestral lands. These images, seemingly ambivalent and contradictory, reflect an anguished search for a meaningful connection with a homeland that had been the subject of a harsh and sustained denigration by outsiders.

African Americans appear to have been the only peoples of African descent in the Americas who wrote extensively about Africa before the end of slavery in their respective societies. They were, to be sure, the most literate of those who enjoyed a free status while slavery lasted, a factor that helps to explain their intellectual productivity. Their ambivalent embrace of Africa was driven by a compelling need to claim an ancestral homeland, a development that was given some urgency by the harshness of the racism they confronted in the land of their birth. Some African Americans even abandoned the United States for Liberia, the site of their projected regeneration. If African Americans imagined and depicted Africa in largely pejorative terms, this demonstrated the inescapable fact that they were Americans, products of a society that devalued African peoples even as it became increasingly dependent on their labor for its well-being.

A century and a half after these persons wrote, the construction of Africa by black intellectuals has not changed fundamentally. Many black writers still invoke Egypt as the birthplace of Western civilization, and some speak of the continent's past in glowing terms, depicting it as having been a paradise with spectacular civilizations and powerful empires. Others still see it as a continent that needs the tutelage of the West, and some view it as a place to seek their fortunes. But there are differences in the construction of Africa as well. Most writers today would not refer to the continent as a "country," as did their nineteenth-century counterparts, and most would recognize the heterogeneity of the continent and her peoples and would be sensitive to the claims of cultural relativism.

The distressing thing, of course, is that far too many writers still view Africa and Africans through a Western and Christian lens and apply analytical paradigms born of the Western experience to societies that—in the main—still possess their own internal compasses. The measure that is applied is one that is constructed in the Western societies. It should be stressed that societies should be assessed on their own terms, because there has never been a set of common and universal priorities that have transcended time and place. The peoples of the world did not all follow a common trajectory and did not ascribe the same value to all forms of human endeavor. The images of Africa that have been framed over time frequently tell us more about the framers and their complex needs than they do about the objects of their imagination. African American and diaspora scholars cannot enter the new millennium without abandoning old constructs and representations of Africa. The times call for new conceptual frameworks, questions, debates, and comparative approaches.

NOTES

1. For a recent discussion of the nature and evolution of racism, see George Frederickson, *Racism: A Short History* (Princeton, N.J.: Princeton University Press, 2002).

2. James Oakes, *Slavery and Freedom: An Interpretation of the Old South* (New York: Knopf, 1990), p. 68.

3. For a discussion of these controversial questions, see Stanley Elkins, *Slavery: A Problem in American Institutional and Intellectual Life* (Chicago: University of Chicago Press,

1959); and Ann Lane, ed., *The Debate over Slavery: Stanley Elkins and His Critics* (Urbana: University of Illinois Press, 1971).

4. See Jack Eblen, "Growth of the Black Population in Antebellum America, 1820–1860," *Population Studies* 26 (1972): 273–289.

5. Sterling Stuckey, *Slave Culture: Nationalist Theory and the Foundations of Black America* (New York: Oxford University Press, 1987), p. 201.

6. See the reprint of Robert Young's *Ethiopian Manifesto*, in Sterling Stuckey ed., *The Ideological Origins of Black Nationalism* (Boston: Beacon, 1972).

7. David Walker, *David Walker's Appeal . . . to the Colored Citizens of the World . . .* (reprint; Baltimore: Black Classics Press, 1993). See esp. pp. 27, 34, 42–43, 50, and 85–90.

8. Stuckey, *Slave Culture*, p. 209.

9. Ibid., p. 224.

10. Ibid., p. 225.

11. Wilson Moses, *Alexander Crummell: A Study of Civilization and Discontent* (New York: Oxford University Press, 1989), p. 11.

12. Ibid., pp. 11–12.

13. For a discussion of these issues see Tunde Adeleke, *Unafrican Americans: Nineteenth-Century Black Nationalists and the Civilizing Mission* (Lexington: University of Kentucky Press, 1998).

14. Dorothy Porter, ed., *Early Negro Writing, 1760–1837* (Boston: Beacon, 1971), pp. 392–393.

15. Ibid., p. 394.

16. Ibid., p. 395.

17. Walker, *David Walker's Appeal*, p. 39.

18. Peter Hinks, *To Awaken My Afflicted Brethren: David Walker and the Problem of Antebellum Slave Resistance* (University Park: Pennsylvania State University Press, 1997), p. 186.

19. Porter, *Early Negro Writing*, p. 346.

20. Ibid., p. 297.

21. Ibid., p. 392.

22. Ibid., p. 347.

23. Ibid., p. 348.

24. Ibid., p. 340.

25. Moses, *Alexander Crummell*, p. 93.

26. Ibid., p. 94.

27. Albert Raboteau, *A Fire in the Bones: Reflections on African-American Religious History* (Boston: Beacon, 1995), p. 45.

28. For a collection of Wheatley's poems, see Julien D. Mason, Jr., ed., *The Poems of Phillis Wheatley* (Chapel Hill: University of North Carolina Press, 1966).

29. For the poems of Hammon, see Stanley Austin Ransom, Jr., ed., *America's First Negro Poet: The Complete Works of Jupiter Hammon of Long Island* (Port Washington, N.Y.: Kennikat, 1970).

30. William D. Piersen, *Black Yankees: The Development of an Afro-American Subculture in Eighteenth-Century New England* (Amherst: University of Massachusetts Press, 1988), p. 52.

31. Raboteau, *A Fire in the Bones*, p. 46.

32. Ibid., p. 50.

33. Stuckey, *Slave Culture*, pp. 181–182.

34. Alexander Crummell, "The Relation and Duties of Free Colored Men in America and Africa," in Okon Udet Uya, ed., *Black Brotherhood: Afro-Americans and Africa* (Lexington, Mass: Heath, 1971), p. 65.

35. Ibid.

36. Ibid.

37. Crummell, "Relation and Duties," p. 74; Stuckey, *Slave Culture*, pp. 226–231. See also Marin Delany, *The Condition, Elevation, and Destiny of the Colored People of the United States* (New York: Arno, 1969).

38. Ibid.

39. Hinks, *To Awaken My Afflicted Brethren*, p. 187.

SEVEN

Migration Control and the Globalization of Borders
China and the United States, 1898–1911

Adam McKeown

The international passport system offers an elegant and idealized vision of the relationship between individuals, political power, and global social order. A passport generally contains two forms of personal identification. The first is a unique number and description of personal characteristics that define a distinct individual in terms of a standardized matrix of identifiable qualities. The second form is the seals, insignia, and marks of the nation to which that individual belongs and that will take responsibility for that individual. These marks are ideally produced in a manner that is difficult to counterfeit. At the global level, this link between physical individual and nation is a fundamental social relationship. It is the foundation of a political order that rests on the interaction of discrete, autonomous nation-states understood to be a collectivity of individuals. Documentation of this relationship is, theoretically, all that is necessary for a person to claim the rights of recognition, protection, and movement around the world. Without such a document, a person is immobilized at international boundaries, assumed to be "illegal" or "stateless" until he can prove otherwise.

This elegant model of global order quickly breaks down when we remember that passports are often useless without visas. Passports imply formal equality between distinct individuals or nations. The granting of visas is a means by which nations assert their sovereignty and interact unequally within this international system. Regulations that specify visa categories and requirements for entry give form to those inequalities in terms of a spectrum of relationships that may include family, wealth, political alliance, or occupation. These categories and the methods of documenting them recognize a terrain of power and identity that is much more complex than the simple link between individual and nation. Visa-granting government bureaus strive to maintain the right of ultimately determining the relationship of individuals to these sources of identity, but the very fact that they must resort to such categories reveals the limitation of the tidy link between nation and individual.

As John Torpey argues in *The Invention of the Passport*, procedures of identification and migration regulation are inseparable from the definition of citizens and rights, which is inseparable from the growth of the modern state.[1] But the history of migration control and international identity documentation is also a fascinating example of how power, institutions, and identities are entwined at a global level. Much has been written on the role of institutions in the ordering and construction of social knowledge in particular societies.[2] The best of this work describes institutions as holistically embedded, inseparable from the economic, cultural, and political processes that make up our material lives and our very sense of self and identity. Holistic analyses, however, situate institutions squarely within the cultural logics and structures of particular, bounded societies. The influence of particular institutions depends on intense socialization from childhood, and many analysts emphasize the impossibility of translation between the institutions of different societies except through violent imposition and misrepresentation.[3]

An understanding of the rise of global passport and visa institutions can help show how institutions and identities also developed beyond particular states and societies and were structured at a global scale.[4] Threads of power extended from the use of diplomacy and police action to regulate international borders, down to the surveillance of individual bodies and our deepest feelings of social and personal identity as embodied in passports and citizenship. Unlike railroads, postal services, telegraphs, and other forms of international communication, no international convention established standards for the regulation of migration.[5] By the early twentieth century, most nations asserted their right to enforce migration policy unilaterally as an inviolable aspect of sovereignty. Globally standardized techniques, definitions, and forms of documentation emerged only through innumerable ad hoc decisions, encounters, and expedient compromises around the world. Most of the basic categories and procedures were already in place by 1910, developed especially in the context of regulating Asian migration to the Americas and British dominion.

The global standardization of passport and visa procedures was, in effect, the globalization of borders. Globalization is often conceived as the increasing interconnection of the world through flows of goods, peoples, and ideas that penetrate borders. As Caroline Reeves demonstrates in this volume, these flows can include the circulation of international norms about proper humanitarian actions and the proper activities that constitute a legitimate nation-state. The creation of an international system entailed the global replication of similar institutions and forms.[6] The ability to police territory, control borders in a manner that respects the rights of foreigners (especially those from powerful nations), and produce identity documents for citizens and subjects that will be recognized by other nations entailed institutional interactions at a global scale and the enforcement of global norms. The national units and borders that are now taken for granted as the basic units of a fragmented, unglobalized world were themselves a product of globalization. Perhaps the most astonishing aspect of this history is not that the nation-state form spread via the global replication of institutions and norms, but that we so consistently forget this global history and see nations as a fundamental unit in opposition to globalization. The history of the modern passport-visa regime is key to understanding the mutual globalization of flows and borders. The categories and procedures of international identity documentation determined which people had the right to move or not move, how such people could be identified, and who had the power to make these decisions.

The history of the modern passport-visa regime is still understood only in broad outline. This chapter will focus on a small portion of that history, the standardization from 1898 to 1911 of documentation procedures in China for Chinese traveling to U.S. territories. This moment in passport-visa history is significant for two reasons. The first is that the Chinese exclusion laws enforced by the United States were a pioneering attempt to regulate mobility by sifting through migrants one by one and assigning a particular status to each. The experience and administrative machinery that grew up around the exclusion laws shaped the nuts and bolts of subsequent immigration policy in the United States and across the world.[7] By the turn of the century, it had become clear that the exclusion laws could not be effectively enforced only within the borders of the United States. The reform of documentation procedures in China lay the foundation for later visa procedures that Aristide Zolberg has called "remote border control."[8]

This particular period is important because it encapsulates within a few concrete events many of the main transformations of the international standardization of migration control. These transformations included the usurpation of administrative responsibilities for determining the status of visa applicants by officials of the receiving country and the exclusion of a variety of lawyers, businessmen, commercial organizations, and other middlemen that had previously taken part in the process. The practical exclusion of Chinese officials was justified as necessary in the face of Chinese corruption and administrative incompetence, and it demonstrates how inequality was built in to the visa procedures. Procedural reforms also attacked the rights of nonofficial social networks to produce and verify identities. Many of the middlemen who were excluded from a voice in these procedures were embedded in economic and social networks that crossed cultures and nations. Reformed procedures not only confirmed the widespread assertion that China was incapable of responsible participation in the modern world, but also illegitimatized, and even criminalized, many of the businesses and social networks that facilitated migration. They established the ideal of an unmediated encounter between individual and state as the only legitimate means to channel movement and establish the identity of an individual.

Passport History

A brief account of the larger history of the modern passport regime provides context for an analysis of turn-of-the-century developments in China.[9] Before the 1850s, passports and travel documents were issued as means of controlling domestic movement or as letters of introduction and safe passage across domestic and international jurisdictions. As documents for domestic surveillance, they helped restrict the exit of subjects and monitor the activities of both natives and foreigners within a country. Russia and Turkey maintained rigid systems of internal passport control well into the twentieth century, and China required internal passports for foreigners until the fall of the Qing dynasty. As letters of safe passage, emphasis was placed less on the identification of the bearer than on the personage or power that issued the document and would take responsibility for the bearer. The manner, clothes, and social contacts of the bearer could confirm his identity as necessary. At times, such letters were even issued by powers other than those that claimed jurisdiction over the bearer.

The growth of a laissez-faire labor regime in Europe and the Americas after the 1850s contributed to reduced restrictions on international movement. Documentation was rarely necessary to cross borders, although lower class migrants often found it in their best interest to possess some kind of papers so as not to be mistaken for vagrants or Gypsies. An increasing number of bilateral treaties set up agreements whereby countries would accept the repatriation of any its citizens who had been deported from elsewhere, provided that documentary evidence of the deportee's country of citizenship could be produced. Vagrancy and enforcement of poor laws were the main causes of deportation (and imprisonment of foreigners), but lack of documents was not a cause for deportation in and of itself.

In the early twentieth century, international identity documentation gradually became linked with the international responsibilities of states. Italy was the first country in Western Europe to reinstitute passport requirements for all departing citizens, in 1901.[10] The Italian government wanted to promote emigration and avoid the humiliation of emigrants being turned back at the borders of the United States by health inspections and other restrictions. The passport law served to certify emigrants before departure. Migration and passport controls were instituted much more systematically across Europe during World War I, as military governments sought to control spies, monitor labor, and more closely determine citizenship for the sake of conscription. Looking at the coterminous growth of passport control in nonbelligerent countries, Leo Lucassen has argued that the rise of the welfare state was even more responsible than the war for the rising institutionalization of international migration controls.[11] Welfare states increasingly served the interests of native workers, the group most likely to oppose the free entry of foreign workers. The provision of welfare benefits also meant that states had a stronger interest in determining citizenship and keeping native workers employed. In more general terms, tightly monitored borders were an aspect of the growing managerial capacities of states.

The resulting passport regime, with which we are familiar today, is one in which the control of international migration by receiving states is accepted and even desirable. But this is the case only when migration control is enforced by receiving states (although restriction of movement out of and within states is frowned upon). This leads to difficult problems in documentation. When domestic surveillance is the main goal, a single government can standardize the means of identification. Responsibility for identification can be delegated to local communities, families, and officials familiar with the individuals and subject to punishment and control of identifications should they turn out to be false. At an international scale, a receiving country that wants to identify new immigrants has no way to ascertain the validity of documents produced in another country and no way to control local officials, institutions, and individuals that may produce fraudulent documents. Institutions charged with issuing visas and establishing identities of international migrants that conformed to visa categories had to produce their own sources of knowledge. These included specific interview procedures, extensive cross-referenced files, standardized forms of evidence, and procedures for interpreting that evidence.

ENFORCING EXCLUSION AND THE DIFFICULTIES OF SURVEILLANCE

The United States was a pioneer of migration regulation in the laissez-faire era. The Page Law against prostitutes and contract laborers in 1875, the Chinese exclusion laws of 1882, health inspections instituted at the turn of the century, and subsequent literacy tests and bans against other Asian immigrants impelled the construction of one of the most elaborate administrative machineries for migration control in the world. The most pioneering aspect of the exclusion laws was not the restriction of immigrants by race. Control of movement on the basis of broad categories such as race, culture, language, and nationality is nothing new in world history. The exclusion laws were much more pioneering in their goal of sifting through migrants one by one and applying a status to each that determined his or her right to enter. Race provided the broad framework of exclusion, but the laws specifically barred the entry of Chinese laborers only. A variety of "exempt classes"—a constantly shifting category centered on merchants, students, teachers, diplomats, and their families—were allowed "free" entry. The bulk of the regulations, administrative headaches, legal complications, and diplomatic crises arising from exclusion were related to efforts to determine who was "exempt." The process of identification increasingly required that people be isolated from existing social networks and subjected to government-orchestrated techniques of surveillance. In other words, the very process of dividing people into categories required that they first be constituted as isolated individuals subject to observation.

The administrative shortcomings of the original exclusion law of 1882 were apparent almost immediately.[12] It was far from obvious how to categorize many individuals, such as preachers, naval officers, wives of merchants, opera singers, bookkeepers, acrobats, cooks, landowners, and factory owners within the less-than-all-encompassing categories of laborer, merchant, teacher, student, or traveler. Fake and altered laborer return certificates were produced almost as soon as the originals were issued, and migration documents quickly became a valuable commodity on both sides of the Pacific. Decentralization of responsibilities further complicated enforcement, with duties divided between uncoordinated customs collectors at various ports, state and federal courts, Chinese officials required to issue certificates to the exempt classes ("section 6 certificates"), and shipping companies held legally responsible for transporting only admissible Chinese to American ports. Duties were further fragmented when consular visas were required for section 6 certificates, in 1884, and Internal Revenue agents were charged with the registration of resident Chinese laborers, in 1892. Nobody involved at any stage of exclusion escaped criticism and accusation from the press, diplomats, Chinese and American voluntary organizations, or each other.

Differences in interpretation between the Bureau of Customs and the courts quickly became the most intractable sources of tension. Immigrants could appeal to the courts against adverse Customs Service decisions. Immigration agents placed the burden of proof on Chinese to prove their admissibility, but the courts placed that burden on the government. Thus, in the courts, a Chinese was a U.S. citizen, merchant, previous resident, or whatever he claimed to be unless the Customs Service could produce incontrovertible evidence to the contrary. Such proof was generally impossible to obtain. Chinese detained at the ports quickly learned to take advantage of habeas corpus. From 1882 to 1891, 7,080 writs of habeas corpus were presented in California, with more than 80 percent gaining their liberty.[13] Over succeeding years, the Bureau of Immigration would win a series of Supreme Court cases that increasingly made administrative decisions final. These were landmark decisions that confirmed growing administrative power in the United States and the rights of a sovereign nation to define and exclude aliens above and beyond the claims of international treaties.[14] But they came too late to forestall entrenched schemes by Chinese migrants to circumvent exclusion.

Complications arising from the interactions with the Chinese government were dealt with more easily. Nothing in the law stipulated who had the right to issue laborer return certificates, but the San Francisco collector of customs, wanting to avoid "any appearance that this office is dominated by the Chinese consul-general," rapidly disabused Chinese of the "erroneous impression" that return laborer certificates could be issued by any Chinese institution in San Francisco.[15] When the Chinese government issued 1,141 section 6 certificates in China in 1883, loud complaints by the San Francisco collector and California press quickly highlighted difference of opinions on who qualified as a "merchant." A resolution of the question was deferred when the Chinese government, which had little interest in promoting emigration, issued no more certificates after November 14, 1883.[16]

To further complicate matters, the exclusion laws had a narrow conception of migration as taking place only between China and the United States and made no provisions for documentation of Chinese entering the United States from other nations. Land borders and complex waterways such as Puget Sound suddenly became formidable problems to customs collectors. Chinese gardeners in northern Mexico who routinely crossed the border to sell produce in the United States, trails in the Northwest that wound back and forth across the border with Canada, and Chinese who wintered on the Alaska coast between summer stints in Yukon gold mines all suddenly became problems.[17] Of course, smuggling of tariffed goods had always been a concern of customs officials but could be adequately controlled by stations on major transportation routes. The exclusion laws, however, demanded inspection of each and every entry and could not be sufficiently enforced with the existing infrastructure. Deportation was also a difficult international problem, as Canada would not accept the return of Chinese without payment of the head tax.

Chinese officials were also aware and critical of the inefficiency of the exclusion laws. In early 1886, former ambassador Zheng Zaoru wrote a long memorial to the emperor that described the inefficiencies and many forms of fraud perpetrated against the exclusion laws, "The laws of this country [the United States] are too loose. Local officials do not have the power to implement them among the common people, and the central government does not have the power to enforce it among the local officials. I sincerely believe these laws have shown their limitations, and one can only imagine what further calamities will ensue."[18] Zheng's description of U.S. administrative incompetence was part of a larger proposal that China assume responsibility for restricting migration. He reasoned that self-restriction was the only way to retain Chinese honor. It would remove the association with illegality engendered by American incompetence and corruption and avoid the embarrassment of having Chinese documents rejected by consuls and immigration officials. Zheng's analysis of the enforcement of exclusion also reminds us that the categorical distinction between corrupt, inefficient Chinese administrators and modern Western governance had yet to become entrenched. The administration of the U.S. government was as chaotic and corrupt as any.

Attempts to negotiate a treaty to formalize Zheng's suggestion failed, and attempts at unilateral enforcement within the United States continued. New legislation was enacted in 1884, 1888, and 1892, which included provisions for the registration of all Chinese resident in the United States. Administrative reform came to the forefront in 1900, when responsibility for Chinese exclusion was transferred to the Bureau of Immigration, led by the charismatic and controversial labor leader Terence Powderly. Claiming that exclusion was "merely an idle ceremony enacted at our seaports," Powderly and his successor, Frank Sargent, embarked on a thorough administrative reorganization.[19] Building from procedures and regulations that had been developed by the San Francisco collector of customs in the late 1890s, he established more intensive investigations and surveillance at ports and in the interior (widely criticized as "harassment"), extensive cross-referenced files, improved channels of communication between officers around the nation, aggressive prosecution of cases brought before the courts in which the Bureau claimed to have exclusive jurisdiction over immigrants, and a campaign against "erroneously" extending exempt status to "traders, doctors, lawyers, farmers, engineers, priests, clerks and the countless avocations bordering on manual labor."[20] Chinese registration records formerly held by Internal Revenue agents across the country and copies of newly produced documentation were centralized in Washington for arrangement into "systematic order."[21]

Powderly's efforts were capped by the Supreme Court's 1905 decision on *Ju Toy*, which asserted that Bureau of Immigration decisions were final even in cases of persons claiming U.S. citizenship. No appeal could be made to the courts except in cases of procedural error. By this time, however, the laws, decisions, and administrative measures and countermeasures surrounding exclusion had grown into an encrusted agglomeration of technicalities, contradictions, legal opinions, and customary practices that were navigable only by the most motivated and experienced individuals. Despite extensive procedures to weed out fraud, including interviews of as many as 600 questions, false merchant companies persisted and fraudulent families proliferated with multiple sons and brothers. The very existence of extensive, cross-referenced documentation within bureau files helped to make deception more predictable and systematic. The birth of nonexistent sons was a personal investment, which could be sold to potential new immigrants. These "slots" were sold along with coaching books that contained extensive family and personal histories, contracts stipulating a commitment of the migrant to give testimony when other "relatives" immigrated, and what the fees for such testimony would be. Schools were established in Hong Kong and San Francisco to help migrants memorize the data and teach techniques to pass immigration inspections.[22]

Most U.S.–based studies of Chinese exclusion wind down shortly after *Ju Toy*, which was the last major development of exclusion enforcement within the United States. Yet, at the turn of the century, it was just beginning to become clear that exclusion could not be effectively enforced within the boundaries of the United States. Migrants operated through transnational networks, far beyond the reach of U.S. laws and officials. The businesses and organizations that made up these networks were dependent on continued migration for profit and prestige. Every aspect of migration was commoditized. False papers, medical inspections, visas, witnesses who would claim to be uncles and brothers, paper families, and old ladies who knew applicants as babes in arms in San Francisco could be bought, sold, and exchanged around the Pacific. Enforcement had to be global as well, entangled in an ever-expanding web of encounters with officials, transportation companies, police, and lawyers around the world.

ENFORCEMENT IN CHINA

The U.S. consular service was also taken up in the spirit of reform in the first decade of the twentieth century. Before 1900, the Department of State was generally critical of the exclusion laws. Exclusion undermined its own priorities of cultivating friendly relations with China and promoting American commercial interests. The very idea of "exclusion" contradicted the "open-door" policy promoted by the United States in China at the turn of the century. Consuls also resisted the added duties of visaing section 6 certificates issued by the Chinese government to identify the "exempt" classes. The immediate impetus for greater attention to this duty at the turn of the century was the increasingly harsh charges by the commissioner general of immigration that consular officers were incompetent and corrupt in the execution of their duties. More generally, however, increased attention to the performance of routinized administrative duties was part of a general trend toward systematization, professionalization, and accountability within the consular service, a process that was eventually codified in the Consular Reform Bill of 1906.[23]

As early as the enactment of exclusion in 1882, Consul Moseby of Hong Kong wrote on behalf of trans-Pacific shipping companies to Minister Young in Beijing, asking him to inquire about provisions that the Chinese government had made for local officials to issue certificates to the exempt classes.[24] State Department officials told Young that this was purely the concern of the Chinese government. Young further asserted that he did not want to bring the issue up to Chinese officials, in order not to draw attention to a potentially sensitive issue, and because the "grave issue" of the treaty rights of foreigners in Chinese ports was much more important than the "minor questions" of Chinese migration.[25]

After the Chinese government stopped issuing certificates in 1883, the new exclusion law of 1884 required a consular visa on any section 6 certificate. Over the subsequent thirteen years, however, few migrants took any interest in this possibility. As was the case with many European governments earlier in the century, Chinese officials still saw emigrants primarily as a source of rebellion and humiliation. American consuls were happy to avoid any extra responsibilities and potential sources of friction. Even the relatively activist Consul Moseby resisted a Treasury Department circular of December 4, 1884, that allowed consuls to issue section 6 certificates in Hong Kong (where Chinese officials had no jurisdiction), complaining that it contradicted legislation and that the Treasury Department had no right to impose extra duties on him.[26]

The few certificates that were issued usually resulted in confusion or controversy. The Shanghai consul visaed twenty-nine certificates issued by the superintendent of customs and the *daotai* (circuit intendant) between October 1890 and July 1891. Collector Phelps in San Francisco rejected several of these certificates, and accusations of consular corruption appeared in California newspapers and official correspondence. After several rounds of recrimination, the basic problem turned out to be that the collector placed no faith in any certificate issued by the Chinese government, but the consul was convinced of the thoroughness of examinations by the *daotai* and Chinese Customs Service (manned mostly by foreigners) and believed that, in any case, he had no right to openly contradict official documents produced by those officials. The consul defended his own honor by asserting that he had virtually no contact with the individual applicants and thus no opportunity to be bribed.[27] As in 1883, the problem was laid to rest by a Chinese decision to stop issuing certificates.

Such incidents had little impact on institutional memories. In response to an 1896 inquiry about the number of section 6 certificates visaed in China since 1883, the American minister in Beijing reported that only four had been issued, under "special arrangement." This inquiry had been prompted by the Pacific Mail Steamship Company's desire to have an official in Guangzhou (Canton) authorized to issue section 6 certificates.[28] The Chinese government also had a growing interest in the facilitation of international trade and remittances through merchant migration. The provision of properly recognized section 6 certificates would also encourage recognition of China as an institutionally competent member of the "family of nations," as described by Reeves in this volume. By April 1897, certificates were issued by Chinese officials in Guangzhou and British officials in Hong Kong (for British subjects) on a regular basis, with a thorough consular examination of each case and multiple copies of reports sent to the Department of State and customs collectors. These procedures were maintained only erratically over the next several years, but it was the first time that southern China consuls were required to report regularly on routine work of any kind, other than accounting for expenditures. On the other hand, individual consuls unsystematically improvised actual procedures for the investigation and standards of evidence.

Almost no sooner were certificates regularly issued than customs officials and California newspapers accused the consuls, Chinese officials, and British officials of corrupt and irresponsible practices.[29] Chinese merchants soon entered the chorus, and no consulate on the south China coast would be free of such accusations over the next twenty-five years. Although sufficient evidence of corruption was found to discharge at least two consuls, much of the recrimination resulted from disagreements over proper procedure and interpretation. The 1897 response of Consul Wildman in Hong Kong to California accusations that he and the Hong Kong registrar general were issuing certificates indiscriminately can illustrate these differing expectations.[30] Wildman asserted that even though he believed he had no authority in law to deny a visa for a certificate issued by the registrar general in Hong Kong, he still checked each applicant carefully for the "marks of the coolie," which consisted primarily of shabby clothes and calluses on the shoulder from carrying poles and sedan chairs. He claimed to deny over half of all visa applicants on the basis of this examination, although he passed nearly all of those who came to his office in the company of bondsmen. He criticized public opinion and immigration officials in California for expecting merchants to wear "silken robes" and described Hong Kong as a "vast warehouse" with 65–85 percent of the residents engaged in some kind of merchandizing. The partners in these businesses were proprietors, workmen, and laborers all in one, and there was nothing in the law to stop them from picking fruit once they arrived in California. In other words, the Customs Service definition of a merchant was unrealistic in its narrow expectations, and unsuitable to Chinese realities.

In late 1903, Consul McWade at Guangzhou described the procedure by which he issued visas.[31] A potential migrant would tell his village elders that he wanted to go to the United States. The elders would contact a fellow villager doing business in Guangzhou, who would introduce him to a Guangzhou banker, and obtain a signed bond vouching for the truth of his statements. This banker would accompany the migrant to the superintendent of customs *(hoppo)*, who investigated his business and the validity of the bond and gave him an unsigned section 6 certificate. The banker then accompanied the applicant to the consul, who interrogated, fingerprinted, and stripped him to check his health and search for "signs of the 'coolie' class" and accepted another bond for $500. The migrant then returned to the *hoppo*, who ascertained that he was not involved in revolutionary activities, took a $100 application fee, and signed the certificate. Consul McWade only accepted applicants introduced by two bankers who were well known to him. In other words, men who could obtain section 6 certificates were those whose personal networks could get them into the offices of Chinese officials and the consul, had resources to obtain bonds, had no calluses on their shoulders, and could satisfy the Chinese government's demands for loyalty. Chinese social networks did the bulk of sifting for successful applicants.

McWade and Wildman largely devised their own procedures in conjunction with local Chinese and other officials. The State Department, still wary of routinizing a diplomatically touchy situation, issued no concrete guidelines. It remained relatively deaf to Bureau of Immigration concerns but did intervene in matters touching the discipline of the consuls, especially where the collection of fees was concerned. For example, in 1898, Consul Bedloe of Guangzhou made an agreement with the *hoppo* that both would accept initial applications for section 6 certificates. After initial investigation, each would pass the candidate along with his paperwork on to the other office for completion. Fifty dollars of the application fee would also be passed on, with the original office being allowed to keep whatever else it could get, up to a maximum of $90. The consul broke the arrangement when he found that most of the applicants were going to the *hoppo* first and started to issue fully visaed certificates on his own, at a price of up to $200 dollars. The *hoppo* responded with several letters to the consul and to Beijing demanding that Bedloe act in accordance with treaty and only visa certificates issued by a Chinese official. When the State Department got wind of the conflict, Bedloe justified himself by arguing that, if the department wanted to counter criticisms from San Francisco, it is "of paramount importance that the *hoppo* or other Chinese official authorized to grant permission to Chinese subjects to depart from China shall *not* decide as to who shall *enter the United States;* the corruption of Chinese officials being notorious."[32] Bedloe was criticized and the fee was reduced to one dollar, but Bedloe was not seriously reprimanded because of the lack of definite regulations on this point.

Chinese Enforcement

McWade's dependence on "bankers" suggest a relatively informal process of recommendation, and most consuls assumed that Chinese officials did little more than assign a clerk to accept the fee and sign any certificate that was presented to him. They indicated little awareness of the various formal arrangements made by Chinese merchants and officials for the provisions of certificates.

In 1899, shortly after the U.S. occupation of Manila, an organization called the *Baoshangju* (Commerce Protection Bureau) was established in Xiamen (Amoy, a city in Fujian province from which most emigrants to Manila departed).[33] It was organized by several local gentry *(shendong)* with the cooperation of Governor-General Xu Yingkui, who obtained an imperial edict permitting its activities. Its public goals included the protection of returned overseas merchants from the exploitations of port officials and local hoodlums, although in practice it also assisted in providing documentation required by the Americans at Manila. The success of this bureau soon led to an edict for the establishment of similar bureaus throughout the south coast. The edict stipulated that any cases of exploitation uncovered by the bureaus should be referred to local officials for investigation and proper action.[34]

In 1900, Governor Deshou of Guangzhou reported on his discussions with local gentry and the establishment of a *Baoshangju* in that city. The bureau would be self-supporting through migrant contributions, actively investigate abuses in labor contracting, and arrange it so that women and children would not be allowed to board ships without passports issued by the bureau. They also printed up blank passports that were sent to leading Chinese associations around the Pacific, to be issued with photographs to returning migrants. Upon return to Guangzhou, the document would be presented to the bureau so that they could better monitor abuses, collect fees, and distribute benefits. The governor proposed that the activities of the bureau should be publicized throughout China and to Chinese officials abroad as an effective model for the protection of overseas migrants abroad and in China. He also recommended that the director of the bureau be granted an official rank.[35]

Despite these auspicious beginnings, an investigation in Xiamen in 1903 by the newly formed Board of Commerce in Beijing revealed that things had taken a turn for the worse. Chinese in Penang, Singapore, and Manila complained that the gentry who had established the original bureau had turned the management over to hooligans and disreputable types. The bureau extorted fees from returning migrants, did not hold general elections, wasted money, and provided no useful services. It charged exorbitant fees for travel documents to Manila, many of which proved ineffective. A new edict insisting that officials go out of their way to protect returning merchants had recently been promulgated, but with little effect.[36]

The *Baoshangju* was reorganized in 1904, and its name was changed to *Shangzhengju* (Commercial Administration Bureau), but the same shadowy characters were left in charge as in 1903. In 1905 the Board of Commerce official Wang Qingmu consulted with local merchant-gentry, who confirmed the effectiveness of the *Baoshangju* in its early years. Wang was aware of edicts that charged him with personal responsibility for the welfare of returned merchants, but he also knew of the court's desire to promote commercial organization and attract the money of overseas merchants and of a recent interest in local "self-rule" as a critical aspect of reform. After careful reflection, he decided that the best way to attain all of these goals was to reorganize the bureau into a chamber of commerce under the leadership of the original founders of the *Baoshangju*. Quan Yongdao, a returned Manila merchant, was reinstated as director and would report directly to the *daotai*.[37]

THE RISE OF CONSULAR PROCEDURE

Although U.S. consuls were unaware of, or uninterested in, the activities of this bureau, by 1905 both Chinese and American officials had converged on a common explanation for the inefficiencies of migrant regulation: the interference of disreputable types who acted only in the service of their own profit. The strategy of blaming the corrupt actions of private individuals helped to consolidate government power over the right to confer legitimate identities.

The boycott of American goods that began in the summer of 1905 was a turning point, after which the United States took a firm grasp of migration procedure and excluded all middlemen from the identification procedure. The boycott started in Shanghai, in opposition to the exclusion laws, but was slower to gain momentum in the southern ports, from whence most of the migrants came. This is because the issues inspiring the boycott revolved more around national honor than practical migration concerns. Accordingly, only the most radical students challenged the basic right of the United States to exclude laborers. Most opposition to exclusion accepted the right of sovereign nation-states to regulate entry as they wished (an acceptance shaped by their own desire to rid China of extraterritorial treaties) and focused on the fact that Chinese were singled out from all immigrant laborers and on the harassment of merchants who should have been exempt. San Francisco newspaper editor Ng Poon Chew expressed this attitude succinctly: "Chinese laborers of all classes have been excluded from the United States by mutual agreement, and the Chinese themselves are not now asking for any change in this arrangement, but they do ask for as fair treatment as other nationalities receive in relation to the exempt classes."[38] Claimants to exempt status saw themselves as cosmopolitan businessmen and students, the representatives of a new, modernizing China, whose rights to move around the world with others of their class were guaranteed by international treaty.

Despite the limited goals, the extensive grass roots organization and virulence of the protests startled both American and Chinese officials. The initial response of the United States, formulated when the boycott was still only a threat, was to retreat into diplomatic tact. A State Department circular of June 26, prompted by direct orders from President Theodore Roosevelt, encouraged the visa of all properly filled section 6 certificates and promised that "any harshness in the administration of the Chinese exclusion laws will not for one moment be tolerated, and any discourtesy shown Chinese persons . . . by any of the officials of this Department will be cause for immediate dismissal of the offender from the service."[39] The gesture proved futile. Southern ports were soon riddled with anti-American placards, and the sale of American goods dropped precipitously. State Department officials were greatly disturbed by their lack of control over these events and suspected not only that Chinese officials were incompetent to repress the boycott, but also that they secretly supported the boycotters.

State Department officials also insisted that self-interested merchants, driven by the desire for personal profit from increased migration, instigated the boycott. A prominent victim of these accusations was Engracio Palanca Tan Kong, son of Carlos Palanca, one of the wealthiest and most powerful Chinese in late-nineteenth-century Manila. Engracio Palanca had purchased several Qing official titles and was appointed the first Chinese consul general at Manila in 1898. U.S. officials successfully demanded his removal from this post after a few months, in response to accusations of favoritism and corruption from other Chinese. In 1903, the Xiamen consul accused him of conspiring with Manila lawyers and the Xiamen *daotai* to sell section 6 certificates to prospective migrants. He was also believed to be a primary agitator in the 1905 anti-American boycott. They claimed he was bitter about maltreatment by Manila officials and manipulated the boycott movement to serve his own private interests. Such accusations flourished despite Engracio Palanca's defense of the Customs Service and his ownership of the Fujian Lottery Company, both of which were nearly burned down during the boycott disturbances by angry mobs complaining of corruption and extortion.[40]

The State Department eventually concluded that the proper response to the boycott was to demonstrate fairness in dealing with "exempt" Chinese migrants, but not to show weakness because the unruly Chinese needed to be taught a lesson. This meant that, if uprisings like these were to be brought under control and the scandals surrounding migration were to be suppressed, U.S. officials would have to ground migration procedures in an uncompromising rule of law and risk any diplomatic friction that might result.[41] The State Department began this process in November by asking consuls to describe their visa procedures in detail and circulating copies of Bureau of Immigration regulations. The consuls passed copies of the regulations on to Chinese officials and increasingly requested specific instructions from the State Department on how to interpret particular details.[42] State Department instructions of March 26, 1907, finally laid out the specific duties of the consuls in the issuance of section 6 certificates. As with most regulatory documents, this was a recognition of procedures already developed and implemented over the previous year and a half.

The consuls in Xiamen were quick to grasp the intentions of their superiors. As early as May 1905, Consul Anderson explained the stricter measures he had undertaken to exclude Manila lawyers from the section 6 process, "In view of the more or less extensive reputation Consulates hereabouts have had for looseness in such matters in the past, I am especially anxious to have these matters placed upon a strictly legal basis, known of all men."[43] In March 1906, Vice-Consul Lupton obtained an order of twenty-five bamboo lashes from the local mixed court for two migration brokers who had attempted to bribe his interpreter, reporting, "It is hoped that by this measure we will be able to get rid of the evil which seems to obtain in the Orient."[44] In April, Lupton told the *daotai* that no more certificates would be accepted that had been issued through the Xiamen Chamber of Commerce.[45] Whereas American consuls once felt they had no right to question the procedure by which such certificates were issued, Lupton now had no qualms in dictating terms.

The history of the Bo An Surety Company is most revealing about the new expectations surrounding section 6 procedure. In November 1906, Vice-Consul Hanna in Xiamen reported that the consul in Fuzhou (the capital of Fujian province) was visaing certificates that had been rejected by him. These applicants were trained and represented by a surety company, the ultimate object of which was "extortion and bribery."[46] A month later, Hong Zhaoxun, a representative of Bo An Surety Company in Fuzhou, walked through the front door of the Xiamen consulate, showed the company regulations to Hanna, and proposed to establish a similar company in Xiamen. Hong told Hanna that Li Cheng, founder of Bo An, had approached the Tartar-General of Fuzhou in late 1905 with a petition, which said, "We understand that the number of people entering [Manila] increases each year, and it is a pity that some persons not having any craft also devised means to enter that port and they have often committed crimes, etc. This is a disgrace to our nation. For this reason, the Government of Manila has begun to exclude Chinese of the inferior class. It is understood that our Government is to blame for allowing them to go instead of strictly cautioning them."[47] As a way to ensure that regulations concerning migration to Manila did not grow even stricter and to avoid delay for travelers, Li offered to form the Bo An Company to guarantee all migrants to the Philippines and make sure that certificates were issued only to men with good reputation and reliable recommendations. The custom of having merchants put up guarantees for potential emigrants as a way to ensure their loyal behavior when beyond the reach of imperial officials was a longstanding practice on the southeast coast, and the Tartar-General readily agreed.[48] The proposal was forwarded to Consul Gracey in Fuzhou, who suggested a few changes in the regulations to standardize fees, make the company more responsible for any false claims, and make it clear that the company guarantee was not conclusive and that migrants would still be subject to investigation and rejection by U.S. officials. The company rewrote its bylaws accordingly, and its plan was approved by Chinese officials all the way to Beijing. The Fuzhou superintendent of customs wrote that the proposal was a "convenient arrangement designed to discover unworthy classes" and promised to consider no applications not accompanied by a Bo An representative.[49]

Hanna's immediate reaction was to tell Hong that his plan was impractical because it was impossible to monitor the status of migrants after they arrived in the Philippines, that brokers were an unnecessary expense for the migrants, and that "any company, whose life depends on the number of Chinese it may be able to introduce to the Philippine Islands, and whose avowed purpose is such introduction, can only be viewed with suspicion by this Consulate."[50] As evidence of support of this plan by Consul Gracey and Chinese officials trickled in, however, Hanna doubted his original position and decided that the procedures used by the Fujian officials were not his concern so long as he was allowed to engage in his own independent examinations.[51]

Hanna's superiors were surer of themselves. Even before Hong had visited Hanna, Minister Rockhill in Beijing had told the Ministry of Foreign Affairs that he had learned that a Chinese official had delegated the proper investigation of section 6 certificates to a commercial company and that this action "destroys the confidence of my Government in the reliability of the statements made in the certificates granted by the said Viceroy. Suspicion is cast upon all such certificates, and this may work hardship to persons properly qualified to enter the United States." He went on to assert "that the motives of the company are wholly mercenary, that it is altogether untrustworthy, and that it ought to be suppressed."[52] In March 1907, the State Department praised Hanna for his "repressive attitude towards promoters seeking to establish a company designed to intervene in and make money out of the issuance of section 6 certificates."[53] It also criticized Consul Gracey for allowing bonds to take place of "scrupulous investigation," reminding him that bonding is a "useless if not objectionable practice."[54] Gracey wrote back, "I believed China in its waking up was taking on many foreign things, and as Guarantee Companies had proven to be very good in America I believed they might not be all bad in China. . . . I have now most thoroughly changed my mind, and believe [Bo An's] chief purpose to be 'graft', and its regulations only fine spun theories."[55] The company stopped business in January 1907, although section 6 papers with its seal continued to appear in Manila for months.

The State Department instructions of March 25, 1907, outlining procedures for section 6 visas, were strongly influenced by the Bo An incident. The instructions reaffirmed that applications accompanied by any middlemen or "interested parties" should be treated with suspicion and that the responsibility for investigation "can be shifted neither by confidence in the authorities issuing the certificates, who may or may not be thorough in their investigations or undeceived in their findings, nor by a delegation of the work of investigation to a subordinate."[56] The instructions went on to carefully define merchants, students, and travelers in the narrow senses preferred by the Bureau of Immigration. It also described the form for reports on each investigation and made stipulations for multiple copies to be sent to ports in China and the United States.

The instructions stopped short of specifying the form of the investigation and kinds of evidence to be accepted. Later, officials would even rebuke consuls if they felt their investigations were becoming too formulaic or they shared too much information about the procedure with Chinese. This was "to provide elasticity in the enforcement of difficult legislation" and make sure that Chinese could not prepare too carefully for the examination ahead of time.[57] Beneath all the procedure, the heart of the examination was still the direct encounter between government agent and applicant. As Hong Kong Vice-Consul Hope wrote in 1918, "So very much depends on the personal equation in these cases that the opinion of the examining officer is entitled to the utmost consideration."[58]

Proper determination of each case was possible only through direct, unmediated observation. Whereas bondsmen and personal recommendations had once been the best guarantee of a visa, they were now the best assurance of failure. An applicant had to be torn out of his social networks and judged on his "own" merits as to whether he was a "bona fide member of the exempt classes." Institutions and individuals suspected of "commercialism" and the Chinese government itself were tainted with the whiff of corruption, and assumptions of bad faith increasingly pervaded communications on Chinese immigration. Consuls took up the attitude of the commissioner general of immigration that, "no matter how trustworthy and honorable a Chinese merchant or laborer may be in the conduct of his daily business, he seems to have no compunction whatever in practicing deceit concerning matters in which the Government is interested."[59] Suspicion of the motivations of the Chinese government in immigration matters also became routine. As Consul Anderson in Hong Kong wrote in 1914, "It has been found by years of experience by many officers and with all forms of government in China that Chinese investigation of such cases cannot be relied on in the least."[60] In 1919, he simply stated that the Chinese system of signing certificates was "a system of extortion."[61] No Chinese contribution to the procedure was to be taken at face value, except the physical necessity of an official Chinese signature on the final document.

Not only were Chinese personal networks, commercial practices, and guarantors involved in immigration stigmatized as illegitimate operations, but so too was anybody who interposed himself in the investigation process. Lawyers of all nationalities had long been uniformly detested by immigration agents and were categorically excluded from all immigration hearings at consulates. Government agents argued that lawyers, brokers, and promoters of all kinds extorted unnecessary fees from ignorant migrants for useless services and that true students and merchants would migrate of their own volition. They also complained that brokers sullied the reputation of U.S. representatives by claiming their fees were necessary to bribe the consul and that they "are the first to cry 'boycott' when they find their business is being hurt."[62] Government officials even refused to cooperate with a number of missionaries and university professors who, after the 1911 revolution in China, worked with the Guangdong government to recruit students to study modern subjects in the United States in the hopes of contributing to the modernization of China. These individuals, whose "high-minded" goals were attested by letters of introduction from senators and university presidents, were criticized by consuls as promoters who selfishly "induced" migration to gain a commercial profit.[63]

Chinese moral and cultural inadequacies and the meddling of middlemen were basic explanations of the difficulties in enforcing exclusion. Bureaucratic rigor was the only acceptable solution. It was a solution that maintained a controlled distinction between government agent and applicant and standardized the characteristics that could qualify a migrant for admission. By the 1920s, ambitious young vice-consuls working on immigration matters curried approval from their superiors not by bragging of their understanding of the Chinese mentality, but by showing off their ability to manage complex filing and identification systems. For example, in 1931 Vice-Consul Jester of Hong Kong listed fifty-four improvements he had made in the section 6 routine and record keeping and developed a method of categorizing Chinese facial features.[64]

American consuls were not alone in their mistrust of middlemen. Chinese officials loathed the meddling of brokers, "litigation masters," and untrustworthy clerical staff with equal passion. The basic consular narrative of unscrupulous middlemen who preyed on the ignorance of simple peasants, goaded them into false claims, and devised cunning tricks to exasperate and deceive worthy but harried officials could have easily been cribbed from any number of Chinese bureaucratic memorials over the previous 800 years.[65] Chinese officials were perfectly willing to cooperate with American officials in providing proper certificates to deserving candidates whose qualifications were defined by mutual agreement. The most significant divide in exclusion enforcement was not necessarily Americans versus Chinese— although it was the most significant ideological divide—but officialdom versus the geographically mobile and socially resourceful. The American officials' constant reiteration of the basic differences in Chinese and American morality was less an explanation of their difficulties in monitoring Chinese migrants than an excuse that obscured the limitations of centralized state power. This excuse confirmed the hierarchical ordering of distinct nation-states and justified the consolidation of power by officials over isolated individuals. The organization of movement and profit through Chinese migrant networks was increasingly delegitimized and pushed underground.

CHINESE AND EXCLUSION

From our current perspective, the Chinese strategy of delegating the responsibilities of travel documentation to bureaus consisting of private merchants seems hopelessly naïve. At the time, however, they were a sensible reaction to widely perceived needs to develop more efficient administration, cultivate wider participation in governance through decentralized local "self-rule," and promote commercial activities.⁶⁶ In contrast, American reforms stemmed from a perceived lack of central coordination and struggled mightily to assert control over unruly private and individual interests for the perceived benefit of a larger national good. This commitment to a larger national good became inseparable from promoting the rule of law around the globe.

The shortcomings of Chinese reform meant that Chinese officials were ultimately unable to participate in any meaningful way in the production of travel documents, other than to maintain the formal appearance of equality between nations by affixing their signature to documents. International migrant networks, on the other hand, did continue to participate in the shaping of migration regulation, if only through the insistent production of "problems" and "fraud" that had to be resolved and exorcised through administrative action and reaction. Fraud was even made more systematic by centralized procedures, and Chinese continued to win innumerable day-to-day battles over the acquisition of travel documents. But the bureaucrats won the war. They defined the very categories of class, race, and nation that made up the playing field and the conditions under which conformance to the categories would be judged. The only legitimate way for a Chinese to assert his right to move around the globe was to present himself as an individual affiliated to nothing but the nation in which he was born and subject himself to official determination of his inclusion into the "coolie" or "exempt" classes. In the long run, despite the deceptions, the formal characteristics necessary to produce documentation became inseparable from the very identities of individuals who wanted to travel across the globe. The world traveler was firmly attached to the anchors of nation, race, and class that bound him.

NOTES

1. John Torpey, *The Invention of the Passport: Surveillance, Citizenship and the State* (Cambridge: Cambridge University Press, 2000).

2. Some of the more widely known studies of socially embedded institutions and institutionally embedded society include Pierre Bourdieu, *The Logic of Practice*, trans. Richard Nice (Stanford, Calif.: Stanford University Press, 1990); several essays in Mary Brinton, Victor Nee, and Robert Merton, eds., *The New Institutionalism in Sociology* (Stanford, Calif.: Stanford University Press, 2001); Mary Douglas, *How Institutions Think* (Syracuse, N.Y.: Syracuse University Press, 1985); and Michel Foucault, *Discipline and Punish: the Birth of the Prison*, trans. Alan Sheridan (New York: Vintage, 1979).

3. For example, Pierre Bourdieu, "Rites of Institution," in *Language and Symbolic*

Power (Cambridge: Polity Press, 1991), pp. 117–126, emphasizes how institutions separate groups and consecrate difference. In "On Symbolic Power," also in *Language and Symbolic Power,* p. 163, Bourdieu explicitly states that the "immigration of ideas" across culturally constituted institutions always damages those ideas.

4. A theoretical discussion of the expansion of institutional analysis to a global scale is Lauren Benton, "From World-Systems Perspectives to Institutional World-History: Culture and Economy in Global Theory," *Journal of World History* 7 (1996): 261–295.

5. International conferences in the 1920s to establish international standards for the regulation of migration foundered on the widespread assertion by receiving nations that effective regulations were already in place. Conferences on the standardization of passports merely ironed out the technicalities of an existing system. See Martin Lloyd, *The Passport: The History of Man's Most Travelled Document* (Phoenix Mill, U.K.: Sutton, 2003), pp. 120–130.

6. John Meyer, John Boli, George Thomas, and Francisco Ramirez, "World Society and the Nation-State," *American Journal of Sociology* 103 (1997): 144–181.

7. These claims about the significance of the exclusion laws are being developed in my forthcoming book, *Establishing International Identities: Asian Migration and Global Governmentality, 1868–1934.*

8. Aristide Zolberg, "The Great Wall: Responses to the First Immigration Crisis, 1885–1925," in Jan Lucassen and Leo Lucassen, eds., *Migration, Migration History, History: Old Paradigms and New Perspectives* (Bern: Peter Lang, 1999), pp. 308–309.

9. This section is based on Jane Caplan and John Torpey, eds., *Documenting Individual Identity: The Development of State Practices in the Modern World* (Princeton, N.J.: Princeton University Press, 2001); Lloyd, *The Passport;* Torpey, *Invention of the Passport;* and Aristide Zolberg, "International Migration Policies in a Changing World System," in William McNeill and Ruth Adams, eds., *Human Migration: Patterns and Policies* (Bloomington: Indiana University Press, 1978), pp. 241–286.

10. Torpey, *Invention of the Passport,* pp. 103–105.

11. Leo Lucassen, "The Great War and the Origins of Migration Control in Western Europe and the United States (1880–1920)," in Anita Böcker et al., eds., *Regulation of Migration: International Experiences* (Amsterdam: Spinkhuis, 1998), pp. 45–72.

12. There is a vast amount of scholarly work on the exclusion laws. Legal and institutional histories are Kitty Calavita, "The Paradoxes of Race, Class, Identity, and 'Passing': Enforcing the Chinese Exclusion Acts, 1882–1910," *Law and Social Inquiry* 25 (2000): 1–40; Sucheng Chan, ed., *Entry Denied: Exclusion and the Chinese Community in America* (Philadelphia: Temple University Press, 1991); Erika Lee, *At America's Gates: Chinese Immigrants during the Exclusion Era, 1882–1943* (Durham, N.C.: Duke University Press, 2003); Adam McKeown, "Ritualization of Regulation: Enforcing Chinese Exclusion, 1898–1924," *American Historical Review* 108 (2003): 377–403; and Lucy Sayler, *Laws Harsh as Tigers: Chinese Immigrants and the Shaping of Modern Immigration Law* (Chapel Hill: University of North Carolina Press, 1995). On the diplomatic aspects of exclusion, see Michael Hunt, *The Making of a Special Relationship: The United States and China to 1914* (New York: Columbia University Press, 1983); Delber McKee, *Chinese Exclusion Versus the Open Door Policy, 1900–1906* (Detroit: Wayne State University Press, 1977); and Shih-shan Henry Tsai, *China and the Overseas Chinese in the United States, 1868–1911* (Fayetteville: University Press of Arkansas, 1983). Documentary evidence of the early difficulties of enforcement is in Senate Document no. 62, 48th Congress, *Letters from the Secretary of the Treasury Transmitting in Compliance*

with Senate Resolution of the 7th Instant, Copies of All Papers Relating to the Subject of the Extension of the Act of May 6, 1882, to Execute Certain Treaty Stipulations Relating to Chinese (Washington, D.C.: Government Printing Office, 1884).

13. Christian Fritz, "Due Process, Treaty Rights, and Chinese Exclusion, 1882–1891," in Chan, ed., *Entry Denied,* pp. 29–30.

14. Owen Fiss, *History of the Supreme Court.* Vol. 8: *Troubled Beginnings of the Modern State, 1888–1910* (New York: Macmillan, 1993), pp. 298–322.

15. Senate Document no. 62, *Letters from the Secretary of the Treasury,* pp. 5–7, 14–15.

16. Dispatches from U.S. Consuls in Guangzhou, China 1790–1906 (hereafter CD), RG 59, Records of the Department of State, 31 Jan. 1884, no. 44.

17. Custom Case file no. 3359D related to Chinese immigration 1877–1891, entry 134, RG 85, NARA, Special Agent Herbert Beecher to Sect. of Treasury Manning, 23 Sept. 1885; Special Agent Horr to Sect. of Treasury, 4 Nov. 1882; and El Paso Collector Abner Tibbits to Sect. of Treasury, 15 Dec. 1883; Senate Document no. 62, *Letters from the Secretary of the Treasury,* pp. 23, 53–54, 75–78.

18. *Qingji waijiao shiliao* [Qing dynasty foreign relations documents] (Taibei: Wen Jai Chubanshe, 1964), 295 (79: 23a, in original edition).

19. *Report of the Commissioner General of Immigration* (hereafter *Report*) 1901: 46; *Report* 1903: 97.

20. *Report* 1905: 80.

21. *Report* 1904: 137, 141.

22. Madeline Hsu, *Dreaming of Gold, Dreaming of Home: Transnationalism and Migration Between the United States and South China, 1882–1943* (Stanford, Calif.: Stanford University Press, 2000), pp. 69–89. Copies of coaching papers are in U.S. Senate, *Chinese Exclusion,* v. 2, 122–124; General Records of Department of State, Visa Division, Correspondence Regarding Immigration, 1910–1939 (hereafter SDVD), entry 702, RG 59, NARA, 151.06/118; 151.10/360; and BISC 55452/385.

23. Wilbur Carr, "The American Consular Service," *American Journal of International Law* 1 (1907): 891–913.

24. Dispatches from U.S. Consuls in Hong Kong, 1844–1906 (hereafter HD), RG 59, NARA, 12 March 1883; and Dispatches from U.S. Ministers to China, 1843–1906 (hereafter MD), RG 59, NARA, 17 Oct. 1882, no. 42. Earlier, Moseby had been active in the enforcement of the Page laws against the immigration of prostitutes. See George Peffer, "Forbidden Families: Emigration Experiences of Chinese Women under the Page Law, 1875–1882," *Journal of American Ethnic History* 6 (1986): 28–46.

25. MD 27 Nov. 1882, no. 63. See also Senate Document no. 62, *Letters from the Secretary of the Treasury,* pp. 13–14.

26. HD 4 April 1885, no. 376; 15 April 1885, no. 379. On the repeal of this order, see Custom Case file 3359D, Cheng Tsao Ju to Sect. of State Bayard, 9 March 1886, and Wm. Morrow to Sect. of Treasury Manning, 18 March 1886.

27. Dispatches from U.S. Consuls in Shanghai, 1847–1906, RG 59, NARA, 21 July 1891, no. 141; 11 Aug. 1891, no. 144; 6 Oct. 1891, no. 156; 11 Nov. 1891, no. 166.

28. MD 26 June 1896, no. 2552; 24 July 1896, no. 2567. The official Chinese response to this inquiry hinted that arrangements to issue section 6 certificates had long been in place in Guangzhou, but was vague on details. See MD 7 Sept. 1896, no. 2596.

29. Such accusations became public record in U.S. Senate Commission on Immigra-

tion, *Chinese Exclusion,* vol. 2 (Washington, D.C.: Government Printing Office, 1902), pp. 315, 479.

30. HD 6 Oct. 1897, no. 13; 18 Nov. 1897, no 20; and 16 Feb. 1898, no. 38.

31. CD 3 Nov. 1903, no. 324; 9 Dec. 1903, no. 335.

32. CD 7 July 1898, no. 28 (emphasis in original).

33. Zhu Shoupeng, ed., *Guangxu chao dong hua lu* [Records of the Guangxu Court] (Beijing: Zhonghua Shuju, 1958), 4: 4365.

34. Ibid., 4: 4368.

35. Ibid., 4: 4476–4477.

36. Ibid., 5: 5001–5002, 5115–5116.

37. Ibid., 5: 5376–5378.

38. Ng Poon Chew, *The Treatment of the Exempt Classes of Chinese in the United States* (San Francisco: Chung Sai Yat Po, 1907), 14. On the boycott in general, see Hunt, *The Making of a Special Relationship,* pp. 235–254; Delber McKee, "The 1905 Boycott Revisited," *Pacific Historical Review* 55 (1986): 165–191; Guanhua Wang, *In Search of Justice: The 1905–1906 Chinese Anti-American Boycott* (Cambridge, Mass.: Asia Center, 2001); Wang Lixin, "*Zhongguo jindai minzuzhuyi de xingqi yu dizhi Mei huo yundong*" [The rise of modern Chinese democracy and the boycott against American goods] *Lishi Yanjiu* no. 1 (2000): 21–33; Wong Sin Kiong, *China's Anti-American Boycott Movement in 1905: A Study in Urban Protest* (New York: Peter Lang, 2002); Zhang Cunwu, *Guangxu sanshiyi nian Zhong Mei gongyue fengchao* [The 1905 political uprising against the Sino-American exclusion treaty] (Taipei: Academia Sinica, 1966); and boycott handbills and reports in CD 30 Oct. 1905, no. 86; 4 Dec. 1905, no. 95; and 6 Jan. 1906, report by Inspector Cheshire.

39. A copy is in BISC 51881/85.

40. Andrew Wilson, "Ambition and Identity: China and the Chinese in the Colonial Philippines, 1885–1912," Ph.D. dissertation, Harvard University, 1998, pp. 159–169; AD 25 July 1905, no. 39; 8 Aug. 1905, no. 41; 28 Aug. 1905, no. 47; 11 April 1906, Lupton to Rockhill; CD 19 Nov. 1903, no. 328.

41. AD 10 Oct. 1905, Anderson to Sect. of State Root; Hunt, *Making of a Special Relationship,* pp. 268–289; Sayler, *Laws Harsh as Tigers,* p. 165.

42. CD 26 Feb. 1906, no. 146.

43. AD 22 May 1905, no. 27.

44. AD 12 March 1906, no. 77; 13 March 1906, no. 79.

45. AD 11 April 1906, Vice-Consul Lupton to Minister Rockhill.

46. Numerical and Minor Files of the Department of State, 1906–1910 (hereafter SDNF), entry 192, RG 59, NARA 3121/9–1/2.

47. SDNF 8534/2.

48. Ng Chin-Keong, *Trade and Society: The Xiamen Network on the China Coast, 1683–1735* (Singapore: Singapore University Press, 1983), p. 171.

49. SDNF 3121/30. See also 3121/10–14; 8534/1.

50. SDNF 3121/10–14.

51. SDNF 3121/29, 31.

52. SDNF 3121/7–9.

53. SDNF 3121/14.

54. SDNF 3121/18.

55. SDNF 8534/1.

56. A copy is in BIA 12177/66.

57. SDVD 151.10/360, 905.

58. SDVD 151.10/487.

59. *Report* 1907: 107.

60. SDVD 151.10/215. For official Chinese efforts to protect against fraudulent certificates, see SDNF 803/60–62, and 88–90.

61. SDVD 151.10/531. See also SDVD 151/2; 151.08/12; 151.10/18–19, 26.

62. SDVD 151.10/101. See also SDVD 151.08/6, 12; *Report* 1907: 145; and 1910: 133.

63. SDVD 151.10/110. See also BISC 53775/245; SDVD 151.10/83, 90–98, 101–104, 113, 126, 143, 150, 185, 197, 216, 249, 278, and 292.

64. SDVD 151.10/1378, 1398, 1435, 1474; and 151.05/40.

65. Melissa Macauley, *Social Power and Legal Culture: Litigation Masters in Late Imperial China* (Stanford, Calif.: Stanford University Press, 1998); Bradley Reed, *Talons and Teeth: County Clerks and Runners in the Qing Dynasty* (Stanford, Calif.: Stanford University Press, 2000).

66. Roger R. Thompson, *China's Local Councils in the Age of Constitutional Reform, 1898–1911* (Cambridge, Mass.: Council on East Asian Studies, 1995).

EIGHT

Smuggling and Its Malcontents

Alan L. Karras

On June 17, 1999, a customs inspector at Atlanta's Hartsfield Airport impeded Columba Bush, Florida Governor Jeb Bush's wife, from returning home. Mrs. Bush was en route to Tallahassee after a short trip to France. While in Paris, she had spent $19,000 on clothing and jewelry. As anyone who has ever traveled on an international flight into the United States knows, the Customs Service asks every passenger for a dollar value of *all* the goods that they acquired abroad. Mrs. Bush declared that she had made $500 worth of purchases in Paris. By writing this fictitious number down and trying to evade paying duty on her goods, Mrs. Bush committed a crime.

She lied to the U.S. government. And she did so more than once. When customs officials found some French receipts in her purse, they gave Bush an opportunity to change her signed declaration. She refused to do so. Sticking to her story, she insisted that she was importing only $500 worth of new goods. The customs inspectors proceeded to search her bags, using her receipts as a guide. They discovered that her hidden treasure's worth was fully $18,500 more than she claimed. Florida's first lady then faced a fine of $4,100—three times the duty that she would have paid had she been honest with the government.[1]

U.S. Customs Service spokesman Patrick Jones clearly articulated the government's perspective: "Customs agents could have fined Mrs. Bush up to the full dollar amount of her purchases or confiscated the merchandise."[2] Because so many people daily fail to declare honestly their purchases, the Customs Service has resorted to a standard penalty to keep people moving through ports of entry; Jones dubbed the fee "the three-times-the-loss-of-revenue formula." The government designed the policy to "[g]et the [duty] revenue, get the penalty and get these folks on their way."[3] Notwithstanding the incontestable fact that Bush had violated commercial and customs law, the government's position toward her and others remained only mildly punitive. She was not arrested; indeed, paying the fine freed her from customs authorities.

The local media, while covering the story, generally misunderstood its significance. Although the story clearly illustrates how consumers ignore laws in their pursuit of rare or inexpensive goods, which is at least what *some* armed robberies are about, the media focused instead on Bush's political and social position. She is married to a local official—who just happens to be responsible for ensuring that the laws of a particular jurisdiction are implemented. The problem, like so many the media portray, became a political one rather than a moral or a legal one. According to the *St. Petersburg Times,* "[Governor] Jeb Bush['s] . . . wife misled U.S. Customs officials about $19,000 in new clothing and jewelry she brought into the country *because she didn't want him to know how much she had spent on her five-day Paris shopping trip."* [4]

Had the media thought about this half-baked reasoning, it would have become clear that this justification makes absolutely no sense. Only government officials in the airport's "sterile zone" can see the customs form, which travelers submit after landing. Because Jeb Bush was not present in the customs area at Hartsfield Airport, how would he have known how much his wife had spent in Paris? Although it is true that Mrs. Bush had the receipts with her, if she did not want her husband to know how much she had paid to French merchants, she could easily have discarded these pieces of paper in France, or on the plane, or at the Atlanta airport, or even somewhere in the state of Florida. Even if the governor found them, perhaps while checking pockets before doing the laundry, his wife could have—in a Lucille Ball moment—told them that her total was 19,000 francs, and not 19,000 dollars. Or that the exchange rate of francs to dollars was 10,000 to 1.

That being said, Jeb Bush could still have learned how much his wife spent in Paris simply by reading his monthly credit card and bank statements, assuming the couple maintains a joint account. (And if they do not have a joint account, then why would the governor care a bit about his wife's profligate spending?) In other words, smuggling goods, and then lying to the government about it after getting caught, is by no means required to hide expensive purchases from one's spouse, even if he happens to be a millionaire and a government official. Columba Bush's legal run-in was not, as the governor claimed and the media allowed, a private affair: "I love my wife more than life—she is my comfort and I am very proud of her. . . . What she does with our money is our business—she can deal with that with me." [5] In fact, the money in question was not Bush family money at all. This was legal revenue to which the U.S. government was duly entitled, under "the rule of law." Columba Bush was guilty of defrauding the U.S. treasury; she is a tax evader. But because cheating on import duties and customs declarations is so widespread, government officials have adapted by levying fines on the spot and then getting "people on their way."[6]

Rather than treating incidents like Mrs. Bush's Atlanta experience as yet another political embarrassment for her husband, we ought to consider them as lenses through which we can view the operation of the global economy, along with its strengths and weaknesses. Columba Bush was unlucky enough to get caught, but many more people routinely, and successfully, violate the customs laws as they traverse national boundaries. Nor is this a phenomenon peculiar to North America; the *India Tribune* published an editorial soon after Mrs. Bush's escapade that discussed the regularity with which the subcontinent's wealthy routinely evade government rates.[7] The fact that governmental authorities have a strategy designed to keep cheaters moving through the airport suggests that they have entered into a tacit negotiation with the public about the degree to which such criminal behavior can be tolerated.

Nor are smuggling and its prevention confined to individuals passing through international airports. We do hear, from time to time, about grand-scale clampdowns in distant places. For example, on March 6, 2000, the *New York Times* reported that, "after years of tolerance, China is waging a desperate war on the smuggling that has long helped enrich the country's prosperous Southern provinces at the expense of central government coffers—often with the cooperation of local officials."[8] In effect, China's central government cracked down on corrupt local officials who, witnesses reported, disappeared from their jobs overnight. Fines were levied; the most egregiously complicit officials were executed. Smugglers saw their income diminish, and many of them went out of business. Their patrons, as well, found life to be significantly more difficult. Large numbers of people became unemployed, taxi drivers could not get fares, and clothing factories that had depended upon illegally imported textiles declared bankruptcy. The Chinese government had gone to the other extreme from the U.S. Customs Service. By eradicating smuggling and punishing its participants (as opposed to its much larger base of beneficiaries), the Chinese central government created economic havoc in a region that had come to depend upon contraband for its material standard of living.

But smuggling à la Bush or on the scale of Shantou, China, should not be viewed as a problem that our contemporary views created. Indeed, the global economy that allowed individuals such as Columba Bush and thousands of Chinese residents the opportunity to violate national law, the same global economy with which politicians and social scientists everywhere (along with the media) are so preoccupied, is nothing new. The Indian Ocean economy, for example, largely dominated by Chinese merchants, had developed and evolved beginning perhaps as early as the twelfth century.[9] Along with its growth and operation came not just increasingly widespread trade—and more access to consumer and luxury products, but also the imposition of duties—and the evasion of those very same tariffs. In some instances, we could characterize impost evasion as smuggling; in other instances, piracy seemed more aptly to characterize the situation.[10]

This general pattern of emerging international trade, followed by the imposition of regulations and the resulting evasion of these regulations, also appeared widely across the eighteenth-century Caribbean region, along with the rest of the Atlantic World. Although piracy was certainly on the wane after 1720, it did periodically reappear.[11] Smuggling, however, generally remained widespread and, in some places at some times, became an accepted if not quite legitimate form of mercantile activity. Because every country and its colonies had distinctive commercial rules and regulations, not to mention inadequate and irregular enforcement mechanisms, the threat of detection of illegal activity did not pose much of a deterrence. Just as with the contemporary examples, the resultant benefits to most individuals from evading customs far outweighed any potential costs.

But this is not necessarily the best way to consider this problem. Rather, it seems to me that, to understand the meaning of smuggling in any given political economy, the benefits of tax evasion for any *individual* need to be weighed against the costs, not just to the individual, but rather to the *state* (or government) itself.[12] Smuggling and other forms of illegal trade clearly undermine the "rule of law" about which we have been hearing so very much of late. While we, or the Chinese in Shantou, might expect certain authorities to refrain from violating the laws that they have been instructed to enforce, we must also remember that they have more and easier opportunities to violate the law. On another level, we expect that governmental officials should simply put aside their own individual needs to consume in order to make sure that legal restrictions, often designed to reduce or control societal consumption, are uniformly applied. Altruism does not always win out. The ideal Weberian bureaucracy has never historically existed, nor, as our examples have shown us, is it now in place.[13]

Though record keeping has become more systematic and consistent over the past several centuries, it is still impossible to speak of this subject as anything other than the sum of anecdotes. We are, after all, dealing with subterranean activity. For every Chinese businessman or Columba Bush who is identified, there are many hundreds or thousands more who get away with their illicit endeavors. We should not, therefore, overly concern ourselves with the precise scale of this kind of fraud; any estimates at which we arrive will certainly be incomplete and incorrect. We should instead focus on the banned behavior's meaning in order to expose the nature and function of such prohibited behavior in societies and economies around the globe. Doing so strongly suggests that many of the new supranational institutions (for example, the World Trade Organization), like earlier empires, designed to regulate and systematize the flow of goods around the planet do little to eradicate pernicious extralegal behavior. Smuggling, after all, is more than simple tax evasion. It is virtually unregulated trade in a market place; it relies simply and easily on the principles of supply and demand or, as Adam Smith termed it, "abundance and scarcity."

But before advancing further with such a contemporary argument, I would like to explore, at least anecdotally, a historical example. I will use the eighteenth-century Caribbean area, and by extension the Atlantic world, as the principal geographic region and chronological period. That being said, readers with greater expertise than I in other geographic areas or temporal periods should easily recognize the kinds of examples I use and will probably conjure similar illustrations from their own bailiwicks.

The Seven Years' War between Britain and France (and, eventually, Spain), as well as between their respective American colonies, ended in 1763. King George III shortly thereafter ordered that smuggling was to be eradicated as much as possible in the hemisphere.[14] In response, Grenada's new British governor claimed that smuggling "is what I have always assiduously endeavoured to restrain."[15] The governor, however, hastened to add that there was little smuggling to eliminate, except for some small amounts of coffee. He proposed eradicating this contraband by stationing more British troops and faster British ships around the island—an expensive proposition, to be sure.

Just over a month later, the British admiralty revealed that Governor Scott had underestimated the degree to which smuggling took place under his watch. French residents of nearby Martinique and Guadeloupe shipped their islands' sugar to Grenada for reexport to Britain.[16] In other words, the French transported their sugar crop in French ships to a non-French island, violating French laws. Residents of newly British Grenada imported these sugars to their island in non-British bottoms, thereby violating *their* country's laws. Passing French sugar off as British, and shipping it to the United Kingdom as British produce, compounded this crime. Neither imperial administration, in Paris or in London, could sanction this behavior. But, although their tempers flared, the high costs of enforcement ensured that nothing would be done to make interisland commerce impossible. In effect, the island residents had negotiated new rules for themselves, simply by violating the statute books.

Complicating the illicit connection between the French islands and Grenada, a group of English merchants settled in Grenada after it became a British territory in 1763. They attempted to develop regular trading networks with Britain, by use of existing mercantile law; they quickly found themselves extremely frustrated. Grenada's formerly French colonists continued to import their consumer goods from France—using the same channels that they used to import French sugar and pass it off as British produce. The British traders became aware of this only when they imported consumer goods and found that there were no buyers. "The French never buy English goods, when they can buy French nor [do they] trade with any Englishmen when they can be supplied by their own countrymen."[17] In other words, like Columba Bush, French residents of Grenada believed that the British laws under which they resided did not fully apply to them. Unlike the U.S. Customs Service, however, London ordered the navy to clamp down on Grenada's errant ways.

It did no good. The trade between the three islands continued largely unimpeded. Although several small vessels each year were seized, many more eluded detection. Moreover, capturing only a few vessels a year allowed local officials to claim that they were vigorously acting to uphold the laws; in no ways should it be seen as a full-on attack against contraband. In the contemporary Chinese example described earlier, the government crackdown was significant precisely because it was sustained for longer than three months, the previous limit. Just as the Chinese state wondered how long they could keep up the pressure, the eighteenth-century British state began to see that the long-term costs associated with exacting legal compliance outweighed any short-term benefits of exerting state authority. Even so, after several years of trying—half-heartedly and with limited resources—to eradicate smuggling from this part of the Caribbean, it became clear to the admiralty, at least, that "some of the first people in those islands are concerned in this unlawful trade."[18]

Indeed, the very group of people who requested that the laws of trade be applied when they moved to the island found themselves participating in smuggling. The situation had become so bad that by 1766 many naval officers were so harassed whenever they tried to stop commercial fraud that they gave up attempting to do so altogether. The British government now faced the "most destructive, and pernicious of any kind of illicit trade that can be devised."[19] The British even contemplated having Grenada's residents, along with those of the other ceded islands, ship their produce to other regional British territories so that they might establish a quarantine zone around the islands. (In that way, no foreign ship could have any legitimate business within the zone.) That plan never took off; its cost was prohibitive. Once again, a local population of illegal traders and their consumers successfully forced a major state to reconsider the way laws were applied.

One of the main problems impeding rapid and systematic eradication of smuggling around the region can be found by considering the positions of those charged with upholding the law. Such people were, and still are, consumers whose interest is to accumulate as much product as possible with as little expenditure as possible. Such conflicting interests allowed local officials to become either indifferent to their obligations as preventative authorities or corrupt, looking askance at those who violated the laws, so long as they were amply, and personally, enriched. Then, as now, smugglers were not the only ones to violate established laws of trade. In the eighteenth century, some officers and crews embezzled part of cargoes that they had captured; others accepted bribes to release seized shipments. Low wages, or wages that were dependent on seizures—or condemnations, in the cases of judges—provided ample opportunities for those who wished to violate the law or even their instructions of employment.[20] Moreover, their actions often had unanticipated consequences—most prominently the diminution of government in the eyes of its population.

One example will have to suffice here; there are dozens more like this within existing records. In 1784, Jamaica's receiver general, "Mr. Fitch," was accused of buying two British-built ships "as agent to and on account of Lieutenant Colonel Miranda, Aide de Camp to . . . Governor of the Island of Cuba."[21] In this case, not only were the allegations accurate—for Fitch did buy ships for the neighboring colony's governor—but the Spanish actually used these British-built ships in their war against the British.[22] Customs collectors in every European colony in the Americas were regularly, if discreetly, accused of embezzling funds—and choosing personal gain over professional duty. So, too, were sailors, who had been directed to stop others from smuggling, found guilty of stealing goods, which might otherwise have been sold at auction, for their own personal enrichment.[23] It seems clear that in an international or "global" economy in which individual countries still maintained their own trading policies, allegiance to the state could in no way be guaranteed. (That assumes, of course, that we can claim that adherence to a particular government's laws indicates some sort of state allegiance.)

Just as it is possible to demonstrate that individual consumer needs came before any sort of loyalty to government, even among officials employed specifically for that purpose, it is also possible to observe that individuals of every nationality and from every economic class cooperated for a common, if legally subversive, aim. The Spanish port of Monte Christi, on the northern coast of Hispaniola, enjoyed celebrity in the western Atlantic, all the way from New England to South America's Caribbean coast. Just as there are duty-free zones and offshore banking centers in the world today, so did they exist in the eighteenth-century Americas. What happened at Monte Christi was illegal from just about any country's perspective; it nevertheless allowed American colonists ample opportunity to "truck, barter, and exchange" without much fear of government intervention. This should in no way suggest that the region's governments and officials were unaware that smuggling, illegal trading, and money laundering regularly took place in the port. Indeed, this is further evidence that an unspoken negotiation took place between governments and those who lived under their rule. We know about Monte Christi because some people got caught trading there and articulated the commercial process to imperial officials.

Rhode Island mariner William Taggart was one of them. His description of what happened in Monte Christi allows a glimpse of entrepreneurial activity in the eighteenth century. Approximately a hundred Spanish residents populated the settlement, near the border with French St. Domingue, in 1760.[24] As Taggart elucidated it, the stream of commerce had many opportunities for bribes and big profits. English ships (from Britain, the North American colonies, or neighboring Caribbean islands), along with those from other European nations, would dock in the harbor, pay the Spanish governor *cash*, and be given a Spanish license to enter the port. (Non-Spanish ships were not allowed in Spanish colonies; the Spanish governor of Monte Christi broke the law.) Traders would also pay the Spanish governor a fee, usually a piece of eight, for every hogshead of molasses that the British wanted to sell to the French on the other side of the frontier. In exchange for this consideration, the governor overlooked the Spanish residents who would unload British cargoes and transport them to the French colony. Moreover, molasses was not the only product so handled; British goods of all sorts, including munitions, could easily be exchanged. Spanish sailors had no trouble selling foreign goods to the French and earning a profit. But they, too, had to pay their own governor a fee to overlook their breaking the laws that he had been sworn to enforce. In just such a fashion, hundreds of ships were able to unload their cargoes and trade with the French in a relatively short time.[25]

In return, the English and other foreign traders received Spanish money and French luxury goods, as well as French sugars, molasses, and other tropical produce—such as coffee. These crops could then enter the European marketplace as British produce. Presumably tropical products fetched higher prices in protected British markets than in French ones; that is, at least, the logic of engaging in such exchanges.[26] English and French colonists (along with other European residents of the hemisphere), who were often at war during the eighteenth century, therefore managed to engage in commercial activities, directly contravening their governments' orders. Residents of this far-flung Caribbean area effectively formulated their own laws, while developing a trading system that was much more "free market" or "global" than anything then officially permitted. (The same argument could be made about modern examples: travelers have wide latitude to skirt many commercial regulations.) The hazard of getting caught was not any greater in 1760 than it is today. British officials reckoned that somewhere between 400 and 500 foreign ships called annually at Monte Christi. During the twenty-three days that William Taggart visited the town, he claimed that more than 100 ships landed or were waiting near the harbor for an opportunity to land. Because 100 poor Spanish settlers could not likely afford to buy the products from 100 ships, something else—illicit trade—must clearly have been transpiring.[27]

We know about Monte Christi because the British government at this particular moment became interested in closing down opportunities for contraband commerce. Whitehall had surmised, and I think that ministers were very probably correct in their reasoning, that the North Americans shipped not only molasses through Monte Christi to the French colony at Saint Domingue, but that they also sold gunpowder and naval stores to King Louis's subjects. The French, in turn, used this military materiel in their battles and skirmishes with the Royal Navy. British colonists—in pursuit of their own individual profit—effectively armed their national government's enemies. They had successfully, if not exactly maliciously, undermined the authority of the very government that had been charged with protecting them. Individual residents of the Atlantic world thus gained the upper hand in their negotiations with state authority.

Illicit commerce at the port continued unabated, if occasionally harassed, through the 1760s and 1770s. At the start of the American Revolution, North Americans knew that they could purchase gunpowder at Monte Christi. The explosive that could be purchased there came not only from France—which actually supplied it openly later in the war—but also from Britain's nonrebellious Caribbean colonies. These colonies brought military supplies to Monte Christi in exchange for French sugars, which the British then reexported to Europe, passing them off as British produce. In fact, British Caribbean residents made significant profits on this sugar; they did not seem even slightly bothered that their commercial exchanges prolonged a costly war against the very country whose protected markets allowed them to profit in the first place.[28] The situation becomes a little more complex when we consider that the colonists in the Caribbean constantly claimed that they had neither the cash nor the requisite supplies necessary to defend themselves against armed attack. Although these shortfalls might in part be explained by planter stinginess against imperial determination to pass defense costs on to the defended, another explanation can be found in the illegal trade with Monte Christi. Once again, personal profit came before any sort of strict legal obedience.

But perhaps I paint too monochromatic a picture. It is important to realize that the state itself shares culpability. After all, at some moments it encouraged its colonists to violate another country's laws.[29] Indeed, a case could even be made that states entered comfortably into negotiations with their citizens in order to avoid losing control over areas more important than commerce. Going back to Mrs. Bush's example, the state let her off with only a fine, despite having the ability to do more. She knew the risks of getting caught were small; customs officials knew they would not impose its maximum legal penalty. (Incarceration is generally used only for those who smuggle with the intention of selling their imports.)[30] Neither position was clearly articulated and widely disseminated; so too was that the case in the eighteenth century.

In 1752, for example, Attorney General John Gambier of the Bahamas wrote to the colony's governor that "some of our vessels that go to the Windward [within the government of the Bahamas] to cut Wood have been chased by some Spanish . . . *Guarda Costas.*" He brought bad news, he thought, when he reported that "some of them have been absolutely taken."[31] The attorney general did not much like the idea that Spanish boats could get away with harassing British ships in British waters. He sought action. Governor Tinker forwarded Gambier's complaint to the board of trade in London, which, in turn, transmitted it to the secretary of state.[32]

At first glance, it might seem odd that British records contain no evidence that a diplomatic remonstrance was lodged with the Spanish court. Gambier's complaint, if true, accused the Spanish of piracy during peacetime—grounds for protest if ever they existed. To understand why nothing more was made of the report, it becomes necessary to reconstruct how the two colonies' ships came to be in the same area. Doing that makes it apparent that the Bahamians were not likely blameless. As a result, complaints from London to Madrid could well have fallen on deaf ears. On the one hand, the British government overtly encouraged a trade with the Spanish, which they knew directly to contravene Spanish law. Had the British officially complained, Spanish authorities might have learned that their own American residents were in British waters, which was forbidden. Or, Spanish officials might have surmised that the British ships, laden with prohibited European goods in demand by Spanish residents, regularly entered Spanish waters. Ignoring cries from British subjects in the Bahamas over their Spanish-seized property, the London government likely assumed that this seizure was the price of doing business outside the normally proscribed trading patterns. It should therefore be thought of as a short-term sacrifice for long-term benefit.[33] But what really happened?

The area to the windward of Nassau includes much of the Bahamian archipelago, as well as the Turks and Caicos Islands. Extending several hundred miles southeast from New Providence, these small islands became home to pirates and smugglers alike.[34] As important, Monte Christi was also to the windward of Nassau. British ships could easily have been on their way to or from this port when they were seized. The *"guarda costas"* about whom colonial officials such as Attorney General Gambier complained might detain and seize ships with which they had recently engaged in contraband trade.

To return to the specifics of Gambier's 1752 case, one of two scenarios likely took place. The Spanish *guarda costas* could easily have been engaged in a contraband trade within Bahamian waters. They seized their trading partners in an effort to cover their tracks and escape detection, coincidentally not paying for the goods that they had just received. The second, and probably more likely, possibility was that the British ships were not just cutting wood within the Bahamas. Rather, they were trading at Monte Christi and managed to run into Spanish *guarda costas* on their way either to or from Hispaniola. The Spanish sailors could be neither bribed nor otherwise deterred from capturing the ship and sharing in the prize. Or, perhaps the British crew did not have enough money or goods to ransom their ship. What *is* clear is that, if the British government had made a diplomatic exchange or protest in defense of its ship, the Spanish could well have paid more attention to Monte Christi than they already did. Protesting the loss of one ship had to be weighed against the continued availability of goods and crops that would otherwise remain forbidden.

And so, we are left with this. Local officials inconsistently enforced and erratically reported laws prohibiting commerce between different countries. Both island and mainland residents flaunted trading restrictions that diminished their ability to consume. European governments knew about this and only infrequently decided to intervene. In this way, individuals got the better of their governments.

We might characterize this regional pattern as a forerunner to what the contemporary media has dubbed "globalization." In the modern version, supranational organizations have replaced the old national empires. We now have World Trade Organization, European Union, North American Free Trade Agreement, Association of Southeast Asian Nations, Caribbean Community, Organization for African Unity, and International Monetary Fund policies, to name only a few such entities. Designed to ensure "free trade" and consistent policies between member countries, policies and rulings are often ineffective because they do not adequately consider diverse local conditions and needs. What happens when affected individuals choose to ignore the rules of these organizations? We are finding out only slowly— but the answer to emerge, at least so far, is that individual members of the public possess the power to directly determine consumption patterns by ignoring or undermining those policies that they believe favors others more than themselves. Strict enforcement of these laws—without a dedicated police authority—is virtually impossible.

In this light, Columba Bush's actions were not startling at all. And, although I have chosen to begin and end my chapter with her, I could easily have selected many less prominent people who have been in the identical situation. Mrs. Bush and other individuals are involved in rewriting what the law means by ignoring laws that are inconvenient. Like many others before her, her actions argue loudly against government regulation. And like many others before her, she will eventually discover that undermining the authority of the government in the commercial sphere goes a long way to delegitimating it in many other areas, some of which are far more important than regulating consumer behavior. Individuals who cheat the government of money to which it is entitled deprive government of the means to fulfill many of its basic political economy missions. What remains is a state with far less power than individuals ever recognize. Though this has always been the case, continued erosion of state authority and responsibility must result in a near complete inability of any government to carry out its most basic functions.

NOTES

1. I have relied on the *St. Petersburg Times*'s version of this event; many other newspapers, mostly in Florida, carried the story. See Jo Becker, "Bush: Wife Meant to Hide Shopping Spree from Me," *St. Petersburg Times,* June 22, 1999. Also see Rick Bragg, "Governor Explains Wife's Lie to Customs," *New York Times,* June 22, 1999, p. 14; Judy Hill, "Well, at Least She Has the Clothes," *Tampa Tribune,* June 25, 1999; Andrew Marshall, "Bush's Wife Is Caught Smuggling Clothes," *Independent* (London), June 25, 1999; Charles Rabin, "Customs: First Lady Declined a Chance to Amend Declaration," *Miami Herald,* June 20, 1799, p. 1B.

2. Becker, "Shopping Spree."

3. Ibid.

4. Ibid (emphasis added).

5. Ibid.

6. Only Jane Wolfe, in "The Hazards of Trying to Sneak it in," *New York Times,* June 11, 1999, sec. 3, p. 8, manages to have a full discussion of the problem, the degree to which it is widespread, and the ways in which the Customs Service has responded to the increase in smuggling. Carl Hiaasen, in "First Class Faux Pas," *Miami Herald,* June 27, 1999, p. 1B, also understands the basic problem. He argues, "Columba Bush's brush with customs was no invasion of privacy. A law was violated, albeit clumsily, by the wife of a well-known, up-and-coming, political figure."

7. See A. Balu, "Nothing to Declare," *India Tribune,* September 22, 1999, www.tribuneindia.com/99sep22/edit.htm#4.

8. Elizabeth Rosenthal, "China's Fierce War on Smuggling Uproots a Vast Hidden Economy," *New York Times,* March 6, 2000, A1, A10.

9. See Warren I. Cohen, *East Asia at the Center* (New York: Columbia University Press, 2000), esp. p. 114. See also K. Chaudhuri, *Asia before Europe: Economy and Civilisation of the Indian Ocean from the Rise of Islam to 1750* (Cambridge: Cambridge University Press, 1990), p. 147.

10. Carl A. Trocki, in *Prince of Pirates: The Temeriggongs and the Development of Johor and Singapore, 1784–1885* (Singapore: Singapore University Press, 1979), discusses the role of trade and piracy in the transformation of regional governments and dynasties (p. 6 ff.). A discussion of the suppression of piracy can be found on pp. 56–59, 67–72. For the purposes of this chapter, however, it generally can be assumed that smuggling was usually nonviolent evasion of commercial law while piracy was a more direct and often violent seizure of goods for the purposes of moving it across national or imperial frontiers.

11. For one example, see Gilbert Fleming to the Lords of Trade, December 22, 1750, CO 152/41, Public Record Office (hereafter PRO).

12. Of course, doing this will require an extensive consideration of the nature, origin,

and development of *civil society*. Doing so here is beyond the scope of this chapter, but the reader should be careful to consider the relationship of any individual who smuggles to other individuals and the government that creates the laws under which they live. This is clearly a problem for those interested in the workings of civil society.

13. See Max Weber, "Bureaucracy," in H. H. Gerth and C. Wright Mills, eds., *Max Weber* (Oxford: Oxford University Press, 1946), pp. 196–244. This is a translation from *Wirtschaft und Gesselschaft,* pt. 3, chap. 6.

14. The British government repeatedly sent policy statements and directives to its overseas minions. An example of the kinds of orders that circulated to all of the colonial governors can be found in George Scott to Lord Egremont, November 7, 1763, CO 101/9, p. 157, PRO.

15. Ibid.

16. Joseph Partridge to Richard Tyrell, December 24, 1763, CO 101/9, p. 198, PRO.

17. See Richard Tyrell to Admiralty Board, December 13, 1763, and Robert Paul to Richard Tyrell, November 22, 1763, ADM 1/308, PRO. This kind of behavior is also discussed in Andrew O'Shaughnessy, *An Empire Divided: The American Revolution and the British Caribbean* (Philadelphia: University of Pennsylvania Press, 2000), esp. chap. 3.

18. Richard Tyrell to Philip Stephens, May 6, 1765, ADM 1/308, PRO.

19. Copy of Part of a Letter from Mr. William Conner, Collector of the Customs at Grenada to William Pue, dated the 12th January 1767, ADM 1/308, PRO.

20. Ship's crews divided up shares of captured cargo, with one share being given directly to the state for auction and the other to the judicial official (or judge) who condemned it. This meant that both judges and a ship's crew had a personal financial interest in every cargo. There were, therefore many opportunities to divide up the proceeds in a way that was not legally prescribed. Moreover, judges were paid more for condemnation then for acquittal. As a result, any concerned party could offer a judge extra money to get the smuggled goods released. Acquittal could thus become more financially beneficial to a corrupt judge.

21. James Campbell to Archibald Campbell, April 8, 1784, CO 137/49, PRO.

22. Ibid. This will be a recurrent theme; the British government often fought wars against enemies that used British arms, British ships, or British gunpowder, all of which were illegally sold to them through established smuggling ports and routes.

23. For several examples of this, see Samuel Clarke to Captain Lavie, January 31, 1797, ADM 1/320, and Captain John Dilkes to William Harvey, July 6, 1797, ADM 1/320, PRO.

24. William Taggart's Declaration, April 21, 1760, CO 152/46, p. 267, PRO.

25. See also Thomas Shirley to William Pitt, August 1, 1760, CO 152/46, p. 265, PRO, and for the list of fees and prices current, Shirley to Pitt, April 10, 1760, CO 152/46, p. 269, PRO.

26. See also O'Shaughnessy, *An Empire Divided,* pp. 61–62.

27. William Taggart's Declaration, April 21, 1760, CO 152/46, p. 267, PRO. Thomas Shirley reported the 400–500 figure in his letter to William Pitt, August 1, 1760, CO 152/46, p. 265, PRO.

28. The Governor of Jamaica, Basil Keith, put forward the idea that the colonists in rebellion were not buying their gunpowder from Jamaica, as the British suspected, but rather were procuring it in Monte Christi. He did not mention, of course, that Monte Christi got

its gunpowder from the British West Indies. See Basil Keith to Lord George Germain, March 27, 1776, CO 137/71, f. 81, PRO.

29. For one example, see a legal opinion in Sir William Godolphin to the Earl of Arlington, May 10–20, 1672, Granville Papers, PRO 30/29/3/1, PRO.

30. See Wolfe, "Hazards," for a discussion of what the Customs Service reported to the press about its different levels of handling fraud.

31. *Guarda costas* were often private individuals who had been commissioned to serve in this capacity by local authorities. They shared with the state any prizes that they recovered. Extract of a letter from John Gambier to Governor Tinker, April 7, 1752, CO 23/15, p. 60, PRO.

32. See Extracts from the Board of Trade, July 9, 1752, CO 23/15, p. 58, PRO.

33. In other words, the British government probably chose to exclude Gambier's presentation of Spanish villainy from the realm of the possible. If it were true that the Spanish ship was in British waters, a diplomatic protest would have required the Spanish to explain their position. It would likely then be revealed that they were there as traders. And if that were suggested as an explanation, the British government's policy of encouraging the Spanish to ignore Iberian statutes might be exposed, plunging the crown into a potentially hostile situation. Indeed, it was better to say nothing, write off the loss, and continue with business as usual.

34. Non-Bahamians, including those living in Bermuda and on Hispaniola, Cuba, and occasionally Jamaica, frequently came to these low-lying islands to fish and to rake for salt. Pirates had earlier used some of these places as bases from which to carry out their own occupation, which principally required them to stop bullion-filled, European-bound ships from the Spanish territories.

NINE

Cartographies of Connection
Ocean Maps as Metaphors for Interarea History

Kären Wigen

Recent years have witnessed a veritable sea change in the practice of history in the English-speaking world. Where most historians traditionally studied stable national cores, today more and more find themselves drawn to the mobile and the marginal. Impatient with the space-time grid of their professional training, a growing group of scholars identifies with a thematically defined agenda: one concerned with the global circulation of people and ideas, money and microbes, social movements and institutional responses. What all these phenomena have in common is their transnational geography. None can be satisfactorily investigated within the bounds of a single state, and most spill across even the macroregions of area studies.

Collectively, the ascendancy of such topics has begun to configure a new field of inquiry, one that might be termed *interarea history*. In fundamental ways, interarea history troubles the foundational categories of the discipline, for areas and states constitute not only the intellectual apparatus through which we think about the world, but also the units in which we organize our curriculum and train our students. Investigating far-flung connections is thus a daunting project, both professionally and conceptually, and has prompted a searching conversation about the origins, uses, and limits of received geographies.[1]

If that conversation has taught us anything, it is that ours is not the first generation to confront a bewildering new world with an outmoded map. As historians today set about bending, bridging, and otherwise improvising on inherited categories to accommodate new findings and new questions, we might be well advised to look to an earlier moment of cartographic improvisation, when another group of thinkers was forced to bend and stretch their inherited metageographical framework to accommodate new findings and new questions.

The precedent that I have found most instructive is the mapping of the world's oceans in the early modern era. Starting in the late fifteenth century, as every schoolchild learns, European navigators discovered continents that had been previously uncharted. But they also made simultaneous discoveries of vast sea-spaces. The process of mapping water-bodies may not have drawn as much attention as the assimilation of new landmasses into the medieval continental scheme. But conceptually, the challenge of maritime cartography was more complex—for reasons that go to the heart of our current predicament.

Like the global connections that draw our attention today, the ocean is a crossroads, a site of interaction—a space of passage, rather than a place to settle and control. By its nature, sea-space has to be shared. This, in turn, makes its geographical identity hard to fix; the usual rules of geopolitical nomenclature—naming by claiming—do not readily apply. Moreover, ocean-space has few clear boundaries. Winds and currents might organize the earth's waters into various subsystems, but all of them are connected, and fixing their limits in any durable, objective way has proved impossible. As a result, oceans have posed a conceptual challenge very similar to that of transnational history: neither one can be carved up definitively into discrete, bounded domains. Atlas makers since the early modern period have thus faced a conundrum similar to our own: how does one go about mapping a global commons? By what principles might areas be delimited in an interconnected, interstitial, interarea domain?

The answers to those questions have been a long time coming. As Martin Lewis has documented, European maritime geography effectively remained in flux for almost half a millennium. Between 1450 and 1950, Western cartographers experimented with four fundamentally different models for mapping ocean space: national seas, maritime arcs, bounded basins, and a single global ocean.[2] It is my contention that each of these four ocean schemes constitutes a useful metaphor for a specific paradigm in the emerging field of interarea history.

To the extent that scholars of transnational phenomena can be thought of as explorers in a similarly borderless, interstitial domain, revisiting these early oceanic geographies might help us to see broader patterns in the way that new scholarship is "mapping" interarea history. Accordingly, the remainder of this chapter fleshes out these four paradigms, drawing on an earlier cartography of interactive sea-space to shed light on the emerging geographies of connective history. Most of the literature discussed here consists of scholarly articles and monographs, where the new transnational approaches first appeared. But in recent years, connective perspectives have begun to reshape textbooks and reference works as well. The final section of this chapter focuses on one particularly promising, pioneering new work, the Dorling Kindersley (DK) *Atlas of World History.*

NATIONAL SEAS

The first way that European cartographers attempted to apprehend ocean-space was by carving it up into national seas. In this early model, maritime territory was essentially appropriated as an extension of national territory; coastal waters were simply named after the states that abutted them. Thus, maps of the North Atlantic might show a "British Ocean" and a "Scottish Ocean"; the western Pacific was typically labeled a "Chinese Sea"; and the waters off the coast of South America were routinely segmented into a "Sea of Peru," a "Sea of Chile," a "Sea of Brazil," and so on. Not surprisingly, enterprising mapmakers in Western Europe tended to extend European national claims conspicuously farther than the rest. A map from 1553 by Pierre Desceliers, for instance, represents the North Atlantic as a striking succession of horizontal bands, projecting a "Sea of France," a "Sea of Spain," and a "Sea of the Antilles" thousands of miles into open waters.[3] (See figure 1.)

This kind of cartography serves as a useful metaphor for our most venerable interarea fields, diplomatic and imperial history. Operating in the same way as the toponyms on Desceliers's map, labels such as "Spanish Empire" or "American diplomacy" effectively extend a national claim over a big swath of transnational space. The resilience of this kind of categorization can be seen not only in higher education, but also in the publishing industry that supports it. Consider the organization of a recent catalogue from Penguin Books. According to Penguin, the spice wars in the Indian Ocean—featured in a recent paperback called *Nathaniel's Nutmeg*[4]—constitute an episode in "British history." Likewise, a reprint of *The Voyages of Captain Cook* is also identified as a book about Britain rather than as a work of Pacific studies (a category that Penguin does not yet recognize) or "world history" (a category that appears to include only developments in Asia and Africa). These cases reveal a common paradigm, in which transnational entanglements are framed in national terms.

This model obviously has its limits, and many historians in the past few years have made a strong case for the need to go beyond the perspectives of traditional imperial and diplomatic historiographies. But it is worth noting that the habit of identifying great swaths of world history as de facto "national seas" has its uses. If nothing else, this habit can serve to alert national historians to transnational concerns. Such is the case in British history, where the past decade has given rise to a whole new body of scholarship, focusing less on the British Empire than on "imperial Britain." Bringing imperial history back home, as it were, this scholarship documents in case after case how developments in the metropole were profoundly shaped by the needs, the resources, and the lessons of the colonization project.[5]

Similar stirrings are afoot in my own field of East Asian history. In new work on China, Korea, and Japan, diplomatic and imperial relations are being recast, not as peripheral concerns suitable for separate specialties, but as central concerns and crucial preconditions for the assertion of state legitimacy.[6] The same is true for the premodern era. Where comparative sociologists argued in the 1980s for "bringing the state back in," Tokugawa and Ching historians in the same years began bringing the *world* back in to the history of the nation-state.[7] To be sure, many textbooks still reflect an older perspective (describing the Tokugawa period as "an era of seclusion," for instance, and segregating discussions of empire from chapters on domestic

Figure 1. World map showing national seas, by Pierre Desceliers. Note the horizontal toponyms extending westward from the Eurasian continent into the Atlantic ocean (to read these labels, orient the map with south at the top). From Die Weltkarte des Pierre Desceliers von 1553, *reproduction published in 1924 by the Vienna Geographical Society. From the American Geographical Society Collection, University of Wisconsin–Milwaukee Library.*

development), but a new emphasis on the interconnectedness of East Asia has already begun to reshape the materials through which historians teach about this region.[8]

OCEAN ARCS

Just as diplomatic and imperial paradigms are not the only way to approach interarea studies, however, so national seas are not the only way to conceptualize sea-space. During the European Enlightenment, French cartographers developed a new model, embedding national seas in long ribbons of water that might wrap around or between whole continents. The result was a two-tier configuration, incorporating local seas into longer *ocean arcs*. (See figure 2.)

Figure 2. World map showing ocean arcs, by Nicolas Sanson. From Sanson's "Mappe-monde geo-hydrographique, ou description generale du blobe terrestre et aquatique, en deux plans-hemispheres" (Paris: Hubert Iaillot, 1719). From the American Geographical Society Collection, University of Wisconsin–Milwaukee Library.

A 1719 map by Nicolas Sanson shows this new principle at work. Like his predecessors, Sanson identified a dozen national seas, bordering the coastlines of every continent. But further from shore he demarcated a single "Occidental Ocean," curving from northern Europe around the horn of Africa; its counterpart, the "Indian or Oriental Ocean," was shown as flowing from the Bay of Bengal to the Banda Sea. Between these two, he identified a "Meridional or Ethiopian Ocean" that wrapped around the entire southern half of Africa. Similar ribbon-like arcs (some with the same names) can be seen on a 1696 map by Jacques-Dominique Cassini. Cassini, however, also added a dramatic, sinuous "Sea of the North," extending all the way from the Caribbean Sea to the North Pole and beyond, linking up with the Pacific in the vicinity of Kamchatka. (See figure 3.)

Although it is not entirely clear how these ocean arcs were derived, it appears that they were meant to mark pathways of interaction. Both Cassini's and Sanson's "oceans" roughly denote trading circuits in the age of sail. Their Indian, or Oriental, Ocean, for instance, corresponds to the old segmentary trading system that extended from the Swahili coast to the South

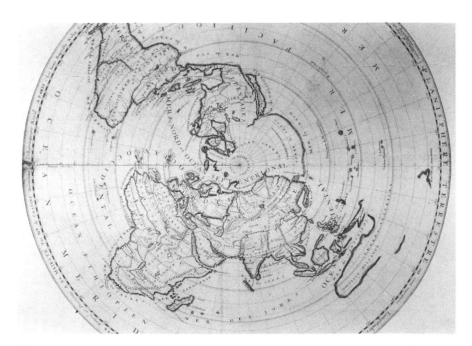

Figure 3. Polar projection showing ocean arcs, by Jacques-Dominique Cassini. Detail from the Cassini world map of 1696. From the American Geographical Society Collection, University of Wisconsin–Milwaukee Library.

China Sea. Likewise, their Occidental arc approximates the first leg of the triangular trade in the North Atlantic, which was already well established when their maps were published at the turn of the eighteenth century. Finally, their Meridional, or Ethiopian, Ocean denotes the hazardous passage around the Cape of Storms, where European ships braved the hazardous Agulles Current to forge a direct link between the Indian Ocean and the Atlantic world.[9] Cassini's "Sea of the North" is a more fanciful projection, but even here the intended implication may be that this stretch of sea, too, marks a *potential* pathway of interaction (the elusive "northwest passage" that the French, in particular, were so eager to find).

For whatever reason, ocean arcs had a relatively brief life on European maps, and their very existence is mostly forgotten. Yet their contours remain provocative, inviting us to think about pathways of connection as demarcating meaningful "areas" within the wider expanse of the sea. That sensibility, I would argue, has a clear counterpart in interarea history today: the study of *transnational networks*. Like Cassini, the network historian starts from the geography of interaction, framing an area on the basis of historical human linkages. Such an approach can illuminate an enormous variety of associations, from feminist sisterhoods to Sufi brotherhoods, from governmental bodies like the Dutch East India Company (VOC) to nongovernmental bodies such as the Red Cross.[10] But of all the transnational networks on the planet, the one with the greatest grip on our profession's imagination at the moment is undoubtedly the diaspora.

Considered from a geographical standpoint, diaspora scholarship has a compelling feature: it effectively creates new domains for historical research. In methodological terms, what is novel about this approach is the way it has allowed scholars to frame fields on an ad hoc basis, crossing conventional borders in pursuit of particular patterns of interaction. The prototype here is Paul Gilroy's famous *Black Atlantic*.[11] Notably, Gilroy did not propose to study one empire; nor did he tackle all of Atlantic history or did posit an "African Atlantic"—a colonial inversion of the "national seas" paradigm. Instead, he identified a cultural archipelago as his area, stretching his frame to include all black people and their cultural forms, on whatever side of the Atlantic he might find them.

This is a fascinating way to think about areas, and one that has clearly struck a deep chord. In the last few years, diaspora scholarship has rocked the academic world. Its burgeoning scholarship, headlined in the new journal *Diaspora* (but spilling over into area- and discipline-specific journals as well), propelled a five-year Ford Foundation initiative called "Crossing Borders" and has issued a profound challenge to the institutional and pedagogical segregation of ethnic and area studies.[12] Indeed, it is worth pondering why this approach has gained such a following at this historical moment. What social forces might be converging to make the diaspora paradigm so compelling to Anglo-American academics in the late twentieth century? Certainly, the reactivation of global diasporas as important economic and political forces in our time, following the liberalization of U.S. immigration laws in the 1960s and the tremendous surge of migration worldwide in subsequent years, has played a crucial role.[13] The growing power of diasporic identities in our own classrooms has unsettled our mental maps of the past.

For all their power, however, networks and diasporas are not the only new principles for mapping world history, just as ocean arcs were not the final answer for mapping the world's seas. Over the course of the twentieth century, both national seas and ocean arcs largely gave way to a third paradigm, that of the discrete ocean basin.

OCEAN BASINS

By the 1950s, most atlases and geography textbooks recognized only three "true" oceans—the Atlantic, Pacific, and Indian. These labels were not new in themselves; all three toponyms had appeared on European maps since at least the 1400s. What was novel was the way they were deployed. Rather than sharing space with national seas and maritime arcs, the Atlantic, Indian, and Pacific Oceans now extended right up to the shoreline. A true ocean had come to be defined as a bounded body of water, vast in scale, abutting the surrounding landmasses on most sides. This remains our normative ocean prototype today. (See figure 4.)

For those who seek to reconfigure areas in history, the basin paradigm might at first seem hopelessly retrograde. After all, discrete, bounded oceans are the conceptual counterpart to discrete, bounded land areas—the very grid that interarea history is trying to transcend. But I would submit that, when extended to sea-space, this paradigm undergoes a subtle but important shift. At sea, it functions to frame interstitial spaces of passage as autonomous places with their own names. Giving such spaces an independent identity marks them as worthy of study in their own right.

In this sense, the basin model is a useful metaphor for yet a third approach to interarea studies—the study of contact zones, frontiers, and borderlands. The essence of this approach is to focus on interstitial places, zones of particularly intensive cross-cultural exchange, including not only conquest and assimilation, but also translation and creolization, cosmopolitanism, and hybridity. What makes this approach distinctive is that, while shifting attention away from national cores, it retains a primary emphasis on place. Empires and diasporas, fortune-seekers and pilgrims, germs and ideas might pass through, but in this approach, the geographical frame is fixed, and the perspective is resolutely regional.[14]

The Interactions conference featured two different manifestations of this approach that, together, help convey both its breadth and subtlety. John Mears, reflecting on borderlands as a comparative analytical category, makes the important point that "borderlands" have been historically made into "bordered lands" by the actions of nearby states. Stephen Rapp, focusing on the Caucasus, turns the same point around, insisting that, if we want to understand places like Caucasia in their own terms, we must view them through local eyes as a "crossroads" rather than as someone else's frontier or periphery. A similar point has been made by geographers Palmira Brummett and Lydia Pulsipher, who zoom in even closer. Focusing on individual islands and port cities, they show that maritime cities often serve simultaneously as nodes in a wider system of exchange and as the locus of complex, cosmopolitan communities in their own right, with distinctive and durable identities that mark them off (sometimes starkly) from the nations that surround them.[15] Together, these essays not only show the promise of crossroads/border studies, but also make a very important methodological point, namely, that scale of analysis is not a given that can be read off from historical processes but, rather, is a critical scholarly choice. Because interarea

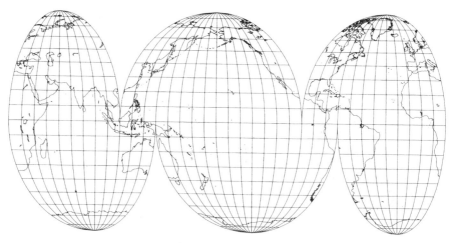

Figure 4. World map showing one global ocean, by Athelstan Spilhaus. From Atlas of the World with Geophysical Boundaries, Showing Oceans, Continents and Tectonic Plates in Their Entirety *(1991). Reprinted with permission of the American Philosophical Society, Philadelphia.*

interactions manifest themselves at every scale, from the micro to the macro, teaching about such interactions calls for both flexibility and care in choosing the lenses for our lectures.

THE GLOBAL OCEAN

The final metaphor for interarea studies might be seen as either a refutation or a transcendence of the earlier models. This is the approach where national seas, ocean arcs, and maritime basins are subsumed into a single global ocean. Both Elisée Réclus and Carl Ritter, two of the nineteenth century's most systematic geographical thinkers, insisted that the earth's oceans were really one great, globe-girdling water mass, dominating the Southern Hemisphere (just as the bulk of Eurasia and North America dominated the Northern Hemisphere). From this perspective, the Atlantic, Pacific, and Indian Oceans are merely giant embayments of a single, interconnected sea. (See figure 5.)

This vision of a single ocean readily serves as a metaphor for a fourth paradigm in transnational history: the global approach. This can take a number of forms. On the one hand, global historians can trace the path of a particular mobile entity, whether a germ, an idea, or a commodity. This biography-of-things approach has given world history some of its most powerful, vivid material for classroom use, bringing home to students in a concrete way the extent to which globalization pervades their daily life.[16] But globalists can also take other tacks. For instance, they might focus on *responses* to mobility: attempts by situated actors (whether workers or consumers, states or local communities) to regulate, channel, or disrupt global flows. French historian Matt Matsuda, for instance, has drawn attention to the tremendous levels of energy that modern European states had to invest in a system of identification designed to keep track of the movements of their increasingly mobile citizens, workers, and outlaws.[17] Adam McKeown's new book adopts a similar focus, documenting the enormous and unwieldy institutions designed either to control or to facilitate Chinese immigration across the Pacific.[18] Both of these recent works effectively answer Lauren Benton's call for a new "institutional world history."[19] So, too, does the work of Charles Bright and Michael Geyer, represented in this volume in a provocative chapter on regimes of world order in the twentieth century.[20]

Nor does this exhaust the possibilities of the global paradigm. A third way to do global history is to identify a moment in time and take a truly catholic interest in everything that happened in the world during that moment. The temporal slice might be as wide as a century or era, or as narrow as a single year.[21] Although a narrow slice may be the only manageable one to tackle in scholarly writing, more expansive units of time can clearly be productive frameworks within which to organize courses, conferences, and scholarly journals.[22] And then, for those who desire a truly panoptical view across eras, as well as areas, there is yet another way to do global his-

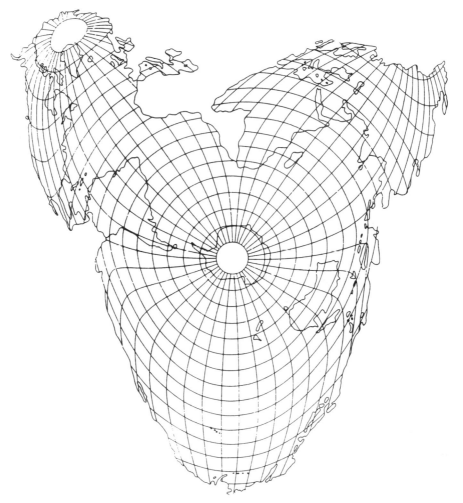

Figure 5. World map highlighting individual ocean basins, by Athelstan Spilhaus. Spilhaus notes that this "interrupted Mollweide projection cuts all continents to show oceans to best advantage." From Atlas of the World with Geophysical Boundaries, Showing Oceans, Continents and Tectonic Plates in Their Entirety *(1991). Reprinted with permission of the American Philosophical Society, Philadelphia.*

tory, namely, to analyze the shifting kinds, degrees, and registers of globalization over time.[23]

This brief inventory suggests at least four ways to do global history: tracking specific flows, analyzing responses to flows, taking a slice of time, and narrating successive modalities of globalization. Admittedly, these are disparate studies to group under one paradigm. But what unites them is their truly global reach. To the extent that historians working in this vein are analyzing processes rather than places and dealing with truly globe-spanning regimes, they effectively take us beyond interarca to "panarea" history.

In short, just as cartographers after 1492 conceptualized sea-space from four very different perspectives, so historians have approached interarea connections in four corresponding ways—as extensions of national history, through transnational networks, by focusing on contact zones, and by analyzing global flows or processes. Each of these approaches generates a different metageography for interarea history, so in a sense we have four competing models for organizing this emerging subfield. But I would insist that there is no need to privilege one of these approaches over another. All four models can and should be retained and deployed simultaneously for different sorts of projects. To go back to the ocean metaphor, national seas are useful frameworks of analysis for some purposes; grouping them into ocean arcs or basins will reveal other sorts of processes and dynamics; and these in turn need to be combined conceptually for still other analytical purposes into a single global framework.

BRINGING THE WORLD TO STUDENTS

The foregoing discussion brings us finally to the pedagogical issue that is at the core of this collection: how is the new interarea perspective being incorporated in curricular materials? How are teachers who are excited by this new research bringing transnational perspectives into the classroom?

One answer, of course, is to incorporate interarea perspectives into the national history surveys that constitute our bread-and-butter courses. This is being done in a wide variety of ways across the discipline, often through subtle but powerful shifts in the nature of assigned readings.[24] A bolder option, being explored on many campuses, is to develop new courses that tackle a wider canvas: diasporic spheres, ocean basins, or indeed world history as a whole. Indeed, the last decade has seen a burgeoning of such courses across the United States and a parallel profusion of textbooks and teaching aids for their instructors and students.[25]

A hallmark of this new literature, and one of the most promising publications of the decade, is a new historical atlas edited by Jeremy Black, published in London as the DK *Atlas of World History*.[26] The first notable thing about the DK *Atlas* is its novel organization. The book is divided into two roughly equal parts, with elaborate cross-referencing between the two. Part 1, "Eras of World History," maps the world as a whole from prehistory to the present, taking successive temporal snapshots that illustrate a variety of themes (agricultural origins, urban growth, organized religion, oceanic exploration, trade and biological diffusion, empire, migration, and the like). This is followed by an equally substantive part 2, "Regional History," which slices the subject along a different axis altogether. This section devotes conscientiously parallel treatment to developments in eight areas: North America, South America, Africa, Europe, West Asia, South and Southeast Asia, North and East Asia, and Australasia and Oceania. Black has previously published sharp critiques of the ethnocentric worldviews represented in national atlases.[27] That background has served him well here, judging from the remarkably evenhanded way in which the DK *Atlas* represents the globe. Every regional section, for instance, follows the same sequence, beginning with a two-page spread titled "Exploration and Mapping." This reveals exploration to have been a truly global project, placing the familiar charts of European discovery alongside equally detailed treatment of non-European voyages, and showing a tantalizing sample of premodern maps from every world region.

Complementing the novel organization of this atlas is its creative cartography. The maps are visually stunning, with sharp graphics, subtle colors, unusual projections and scales, and innovative framing tailored to the themes at hand. Not surprisingly, those themes correspond closely to the various paradigms of interarea history discussed above. Prominently featured are transnational flows (whether of peoples, languages, religions, or biota), commercial and social networks (including criminal syndicates), and transoceanic diaspora (including a variety of slave migration streams). Overall, the coverage is less weighted toward wars and geopolitics than that of most previous atlases, with greater amplification of economic, social, and cultural developments. But even in the geopolitical domain, clever use of overlays and shading allows unusually subtle mapping of boundaries and frontiers. In light of the level of detail and the relatively affordable price ($50), it is likely that this atlas will be used, not just in world history courses, but to contextualize regional histories as well.

Taken together, the DK maps reveal that, although locations on the globe may endure, the human configurations that we call "places" effectively come and go. If thriving centers can be turned into backwaters under a new regime, peripheries too are subject to inversion, and a cultural "middle ground" of the kind identified by Richard White is highly vulnerable to chance and change.[28] These examples drive home geographer Doreen Massey's point that the localities we inhabit are temporally, as well as spatially, delimited; all places, at whatever scale, are temporary "envelopes of space-time."[29] By my reading, this message increasingly underlies college-level history pedagogy across the United States, in virtually every subfield of the discipline.

CODA

Inevitably, the recent turn to interarea history raises challenges for historical practice. To paraphrase Jeff Wasserstrom's recent manifesto in *Perspectives Online*, historians may increasingly want to "read globally," but we still need to "write locally."[30] One question this poses is how do we operationalize this in training the next generation? What configuration of fields best prepares an apprentice historian for pursuing grounded yet globally minded research? A second question has to do with incorporating indigenous voices into our work. Inasmuch as "one person's periphery is another person's homeland," part of the project of interarea studies must be a critical analysis of location from many different perspectives. As a recent University of Chicago report puts it, "world regions" are also "regional worlds," places from which local people articulate their own worldviews.[31] In other words, "areas" are not just objects but also active participants in knowledge production. This too has implications for historical practice. I suspect that taking this insight seriously may entail changing the way we work; in particular, it points toward collaborative research with scholars in the areas we study. But this, in turn, raises logistical questions: how can such collaborative work be supported? What are its difficulties? And, if it is indeed worthwhile, how can we get it recognized by tenure and promotion committees?

A final challenge is that of making world history truly inclusive. By dint of their training and professional pressures, practitioners of U.S. and European history (at least in my country) tend to focus their lenses more narrowly than do those of Asia, Africa, and Latin America. Perhaps as a result, they tend to be underrepresented in conversations about global history. Yet historians who operate at a microscale are everywhere revealing local evidence of hybridity and multiculturalism—the outcomes and engines of the very global interactions charted in works like the DK *Atlas*. Surely, "local" historians working near home and "global" historians studying distant lands are both viewing similar processes, just at a different scale of resolution; we may be using different ends of the telescope, but we are all looking at the same interactive world. Both of these perspectives are needed, and specialists from *all* areas must be in on the conversation if this field is to move forward. Otherwise, the "world" of world history may end up rather like the world of world music: a truncated category produced by the marketing department, rather than an inclusive intellectual domain.

NOTES

This chapter first appeared in Hanna Schissler and Yasemin N. Soysal, eds., *The Nation, Europe, and the World: Textbooks in Transition* (Oxford: Berghahn Books, 2004).

1. Martin Lewis and Kären Wigen, *The Myth of Continents: A Critique of Metageography* (Berkeley: University of California Press, 1997).

2. Martin Lewis, "Dividing the Ocean Sea," *Geographical Review* 89:2 (April 1999): 188–214.

3. For reproductions of these and other maps discussed in this essay, see Lewis, "Dividing the Ocean Sea."

4. Giles Milton, *Nathaniel's Nutmeg; or, the True and Incredible Adventures of the Spice Trader Who Changed the Course of History* (New York: Penguin Books, 1999).

5. For examples, see parts 1 and 2 of Frederick Cooper and Ann Laura Stoler, eds., *Tensions of Empire: Colonial Cultures in a Bourgeois World* (Berkeley: University of California Press, 1997).

6. For a review of this literature, see Kären Wigen, "Culture, Power, and Place: The New Landscapes of East Asian Regionalism," *American Historical Review* 104:4 (October 1999): 1183–1201; See also Peter J. Katzenstein and Takashi Shiraishi, eds., *Network Power: Japan and Asia* (Ithaca, N.Y.: Cornell University Press, 1997), and Andre Schmidt, "Colonialism and the 'Korea Problem' in the Historiography of Modern Japan," *Journal of Asian Studies* 59:4 (November 2000): 951–975.

7. Peter Evans, Dietrich Rueschemeyer, and Theda Skocpol, eds., *Bringing the State Back In* (New York: Cambridge University Press, 1985). See also Kären Wigen, "Bringing the World Back In: Meditations on the Space-Time of Japanese Early Modernity," Research Papers in Asian/Pacific Studies, Asian/Pacific Studies Institute, Duke University, 1995. An expanded version of this paper, under the title "Japanese Perspectives on the Time/Space of 'Early Modernity,'" was presented at the Nineteenth International Congress of Historical Sciences, Oslo, Norway, August 7, 2000. The paper is available at www.oslo2000.uio.no/english/index.htm (under "Major Themes 1a, 'Is Universal History Possible?'").

8. Two excellent works that synthesize the new perspectives in a manner suitable for introductory college-level courses include Mark J. Hudson, *Ruins of Identity: Ethnogenesis in the Japanese Islands* (Honolulu: University of Hawai'i Press, 1999), and Tessa Morris-Suzuki, *Reinventing Japan: Time Space Nation* (Armonk, N.Y.: M. E. Sharpe, 1998).

9. For information on the difficulties of navigating in this region (and much else on oceans and seafarers in the early modern period), see the fascinating "Latitude" web site created by Patricia Seed of Rice University (http://www.ruf.rice.edu/~feegi).

10. Papers on these and other network topics were presented at the "Interactions"

conference on February 1–3, 2001, at the Library of Congress. A complete program, with abstracts, is available at http://www.historycooperative.org/proceedings.interactions/index .html.

11. Paul Gilroy, *The Black Atlantic: Modernity and Double Consciousness* (Cambridge, Mass.: Harvard University Press, 1993).

12. For how these trends have affected Asian-American studies, see *positions: east asia cultures critique* 7:3 (winter 1999), a special issue on "Asian Transnationalities." On related developments in African-American studies, see Christopher Shea, "A Blacker Shade of Yale: African-American Studies Takes a New Direction," *Lingua Franca* 11:2 (March 2001): 42–49. For more on the Ford Foundation's "Crossing Borders" initiative, see http://www .fordfound.org/publications/recent_articles/crossingborders.cfm.

13. Ethne Luibheid, "The 1965 Immigration and Nationality Act: An 'End' to Exclusion?" *positions: east asia cultures critique* 5:2 (fall 1997): 501–522. More broadly, see Arjun Appadurai, *Modernity at Large: Cultural Dimensions of Globalization* (New Brunswick, N.J.: Rutgers University Press, 1996).

14. An important subfield where this perspective has been worked out is the "new Western history" of the United States. Leaders in this field include Patricia Limerick, William Cronon, and Richard White.

15. For an abstract of the essay by Palmira Brummett and Lydia Pulsipher, see the "Interactions" web site (note 10).

16. See, for instance, Alfred Crosby, *Ecological Imperialism: The Biological Expansion of Europe, 900–1900* (New York: Cambridge University Press, 1983); Arjun Appadurai, ed., *The Social Life of Things: Commodities in Cultural Perspective* (New York: Cambridge University Press, 1981); and Craig Clunas, "Modernity Global and Local: Consumption and the Rise of the West," *American Historical Review* 104:5 (December 1999): 1497–1511.

17. Matt K. Matsuda, "Doctor, Judge, Vagabond: Identity, Identification, and Other Memories of the State," *History and Memory* 6 (1994): 73–94. A revised version is reprinted, with illustrations, as chap. 6 of Matsuda's later book, *The Memory of the Modern* (Oxford: Oxford University Press, 1996).

18. Adam McKeown, *Chinese Migrant Networks and Cultural Change: Peru, Chicago, Hawaii, 1900–1936* (Chicago: University of Chicago Press, 2001).

19. Lauren Benton, "From the World-Systems Perspective to Institutional World History: Culture and Economy in Global Theory." *Journal of World History* 7 (1996): 261–296.

20. See also Michael Geyer and Charles Bright's earlier collaboration, "World History in a Global Age," *American Historical Review* 100:4 (October 1995): 1034–1060.

21. For a lively example of the latter, see John E. Wills, Jr., *1688: A Global History* (New York: Norton, 2001).

22. On the latter point, see the journals *Eighteenth Century Studies* and *Early Modern History,* both of which strive for global representation within a temporal frame.

23. This is the approach taken by C. A. Bayly in his truly magisterial essay for the Interactions conference mentioned above; see the web site identified in note 10.

24. On resources for this kind of pedagogical innovation in the Japan field, see note 8, above.

25. An excellent gateway to these resources for world history is the web site of Northeastern University's World History Center (www.whc.neu.edu). For an experiment in ocean-centered research and pedagogy, see the Oceans Connect project at Duke University (www .duke.edu/web/oceans).

26. Jeremy Black, ed., *Atlas of World History: Mapping the Human Journey* (London: Dorling Kindersley, 2000).

27. Jeremy Black, *Maps and History* (New Haven, Conn.: Yale University Press, 1997).

28. Richard White, *The Middle Ground: Indians, Empires, and Republics in The Great Lakes Region, 1650–1815* (New York: Cambridge University Press, 1991).

29. Doreen Massey, "Places and their Pasts," *History Workshop Journal* 39 (1995): 182–192.

30. Jeffrey Wasserstrom, "Eurocentrism and Its Discontents," *Perspectives Online*, January 2001, www.theaha.org.

31. "Regional Worlds: Transforming Pedagogy in Area Studies and International Studies," The Globalization Project, University of Chicago Center for International Studies, 2000. Available at http://regionalworlds.uchicago.edu/pub.html.

TEN

Chronology, Crossroads, and Commonwealths
World-Regional Schemes and the Lessons of Caucasia

Stephen H. Rapp, Jr.

Most people are fascinated by frontiers, and, if ever there was a frontier, it is the Caucasus—the great mountain barrier stretching from the Black Sea to the Caspian, dividing Europe from Asia, West from East, Christendom from Islam.
—Sir Fitzroy Maclean, *To Caucasus: The End of All the Earth*

Adventurer Sir Fitzroy Maclean, member of the British parliament and diplomatic service, and the reputed inspiration for Ian Fleming's James Bond, was neither the first nor the last to draw attention to the remarkable geopolitical position of Caucasia. The ancient Greeks imagined the two Iberias, one in Europe, the other in Asia (that is, in Caucasia), to be the very edges of the earth. Others emphasized the enormous cultural diversity of this Eurasian crossroads. Arabs thus conceived of Caucasia as "the mountain of languages." In light of Caucasia's intermediate position, a practical question arises: how does one study the region in Eurasian and even world perspective? Like many of the small number of Caucasian specialists trained in North America, I initially approached the region's history and culture through university programs devoted to Russia, the Soviet Union, and Eastern Europe. Although incorporated politically into the Russian empire and then USSR from the nineteenth century, Caucasia was one of those extraordinary arenas of intense cultural interplay nestled at the juncture of "civilizations" that have attracted attention but have eluded definition and study on their own terms. As world historian Marshall G. S. Hodgson perceptively observed, "It would be hard to place such peoples as Georgians and Armenians unequivocally within any one major 'civilization.'" [1]

This chapter locates Caucasia within a vibrant belt of encounter and communication extending from the Mediterranean to the Caspian and Red Seas, the Persian Gulf, and, only more recently, northward to Russia. Over the length of its history, Caucasia's social, cultural, and political orientation has tended to be southerly, toward the Near and Middle East, than westerly, toward the Mediterranean and Europe. Nevertheless, two of Caucasia's most prominent peoples, the Georgians and the Armenians, today insist that they have constituted the far eastern edge of Europe since antiquity.[2] Consequently, as the eastern terminus of "European civilization," Caucasia has been an integral part of the (immanently progressive) "West" from primordial times. The isthmus not only was the physical point of contact between Europe and Asia, so the argument goes, but also occupied a unique position—indeed, was destined—to assume the role of cross-cultural mediator.[3] In this capacity, Caucasia initiated and mediated dialogue between East and West and also guaranteed the preservation of European civilization by diverting the Eastern menace in its various manifestations and, in particular, Islam.[4]

Caucasia's concurrent association with multiple political and sociocultural enterprises, in addition to the constantly shifting imperial and cultural hegemonies cast over it, urge us to reconsider the world-regional and the related area-studies scheme at the heart of non-Western studies at universities in the United States.[5] Although Caucasia may very well constitute a "special case"—an unusual and spectacular example of a distinctive cultural area profoundly affected by overlapping empires, civilizations, and world regions, its intense cross- and multicultural condition throws valuable light on the manner in which scholars have deployed models of large-scale history and geography.

My principal research interest is late-antique and medieval Caucasia, especially the Georgian and Armenian communities whose interlocking Christianizations occurred after the conversion of their respective monarchies in the first half of the fourth century.[6] Owing to space limitations, and because I have drawn heavily upon my current work, several peoples have not received the attention they would deserve in a comprehensive treatment: the peoples of the Caucasian far east, for example, the Azeris and the extinct Caucasian Albanians (whose modern-day relatives would seem to be the Udins of Azerbaijan); peoples the mountainous north, including the Alans, Daghestanis, Ossetians, Ingushes, and Chechens; and many others, among them Abkhazes, Kurds, Jews, Arabs, and Greeks, not to mention considerable numbers of Russian and German migrants. Though the primary self-orientation of today's Christian Caucasians is toward Europe, Muslim Caucasians, who are concentrated in the east and north, tend to have more in common with the sociocultural traditions of the Iranians, Turks, and Arabs. This chapter, then, considers representative examples and vignettes from the Georgian and to a lesser extent the Armenian communities of Caucasia in an exercise to rethink the world-regional scheme and an intriguing revision on three specific points: first, chronology and change in existing world-regional schemes; second, the centrality of crossroads, which have usually been treated as peripheries or frontiers by great powers and modern scholar-ship; and third, the commonwealth as a primary classification of large-scale history alongside empire, civilization/culture, and world region.

A QUESTION OF TIME

In their insightful 1997 monograph *The Myth of Continents: A Critique of Metageography*, geographer Martin Lewis and historian Kären Wigen metic-ulously probe the origin and evolution of the study of large-scale geography, "the set of spatial structures through which people order their knowledge of the world."[7] Having examined the creation and utility of basic metageo-graphical categories, including continents, they conclude that "the global geographical framework in use today is essentially a cartographic celebration of European power. . . . Implicitly, this was a geography of power."[8] Lewis and Wigen devote special attention to the world-regional scheme, the basic organizational principle of American academic programs involving the non-Western world. It, too, was inextricably bound to global imperialism, colo-nialism, and hegemony, and especially the interests and military policies of the United States and the countries of Western Europe. Despite its check-ered past, the authors persuasively affirm the validity of world regions as historical-geographical units, though they advocate an improved version by removing privilege and exceptionalism so far as possible.[9]

The refined scheme diverges from the standard system in three cru-cial ways. In the first place, Lewis and Wigen endeavor to avoid "defining regions in terms of specific diagnostic traits, focusing instead on historical processes." Second, political and ecological boundaries have been "ignored . . . giving primacy instead to the spatial contours of assemblages of ideas, practices, and social institutions that give human communities their distinc-tion and coherence." Finally, the refinement seeks to express not only the distinctiveness of cultures, but also large-scale interplay, "for one region's identity has often coalesced only in confrontation with another."[10]

This undertaking is as grand in conception as it is worthy of praise, yet Lewis and Wigen's revision is not without shortcomings.[11] Despite the explicit assertion to the contrary, some units retrace political boundaries, and decidedly modern ones at that. Three examples leap from the page. The modern border of Mexico and the southern United States, the Rio Grande, plainly separates "North America" and "Ibero-America." The demarcation of "Western and Central Europe" from the massive "Russia—Southeast Europe and the Caucasus" (hereafter "Russia—SEEC") complex replicates the borders of modern nation-states.[12] Finally, the northern boundaries of modern India, Pakistan, and Iran divide "Central Asia" from "Russia—SEEC."

The revised scheme, just as its predecessor, is plagued by presentism, the privileging of the modern period to the detriment of preceding eras and marked by a neglect or unwillingness to see the past on its own terms so far possible. Of course, presentism's grip reaches far beyond world historiography to the larger historical discipline and academia as a whole. Existing world-regional models single out modern realities and experiences, including the concept of nation-states, as a guiding metageographical consideration for all periods.

Though Lewis and Wigen do not expressly restrict their refined world-regional scheme to modern times, their ten "principles of critical metageography" hold that "world regions do not constitute timeless entities (and . . . therefore *a good regionalization scheme will not be applicable across all historical periods*)."[13] Although the authors sometimes address premodern history and geography (a focused discussion of which appears in their concise section "Cultures and Contacts in the Premodern Era"), their proposed model, graphically summarized by a single map, nevertheless features certain modern concepts and experiences, ones shaped in many ways by global forms of dominance and interconnection linked to Western Europe and the United States.[14] Unwitting readers may well apply it to all periods of human history.[15] Quite obviously, however, the relevance of modern political boundaries for earlier epochs is often negligible if not altogether absent. A political map reflecting the world as it existed in, say, 751 A.D., would look quite different from one drawn from the perspective of the twentieth or twenty-first century. In addition, the refined zones are meant to enhance the representation of large-scale spheres of interaction, and in many cases they do, yet these for the most part have also been temporally frozen in the post-1500 era. "African America" and "Ibero-America" are appropriate categories for the early modern and modern periods (though an integrated Atlantic World is conspicuously missing), yet the indigenous peoples and cultures of the pre-Columbian "New World" are passed over in deafening silence.[16] This representation comes precariously near to the curious three-page passage in *The Rise of the West* in which William McNeill rationalizes the almost complete absence of the precontact Americas and Pacifica on the grounds that they did not participate in sufficiently intense, long-distance, cross-cultural exchanges prior to the advent of global imperialism and colonialism.[17] Seeing areas like the Americas and Pacifica on their own terms is as necessary as illuminating large-scale dynamics involving them.

That political boundaries constitute an improper category around which to construct world regions will surely win widespread support, yet Lewis and Wigen have not always abided by the rules governing their own metageographical universe. Furthermore, like the standard world-regional schemes before it and the closely related area-studies organizational model in the United States, the revised vision showcased in *The Myth of Continents* does not convey the march of time and gives an unfair advantage to the modern epoch. Despite the authors' good intentions, disenfranchisement of human history before circa 1500 is the inevitable consequence. If the backbone of history is chronology and if change is an essential feature of the historical profession, then the refined scheme—like its precursor—ultimately represents only a slice of the world's total past. Though an admirable refinement, and as elegant and as straightforward as it may be (as is, to be fair, surely one of the goals of such a difficult project), Lewis and Wigen's model inadvertently perpetuates the regrettable trend of turning a blind eye toward chronology and hence to change in the interests of simplicity. Attempts to satisfy the overwhelming thirst for a single elegant scheme have so far resulted in a critical flaw: temporal preferencing.[18]

As central a problem as this "freezing of time" might be, a solution is elusive. If a multiple-map approach is adopted, how many maps ought there be?[19] Perhaps two, dividing the premodern and modern eras? But how should we define "modern" and "premodern," especially should we wish to avoid the perpetuation of Eurocentric chronologies? Periodization can be a useful device, yet it is also notoriously problematic and itself prone to projections of power and privilege.[20] Perhaps maps should be drawn at intervals of a millennium at, say, 1000 B.C., 0, 1000 A.D., 2000 A.D. But can a conscientious world historian really justify the introduction of a Christian system of dating for the thousand-year intervals, no matter how convenient or how deeply entrenched this particular system of dating happens to be? A similar problem results with the adoption of other calendrical systems, say, the Islamic system based on the *hijra*. Perhaps a computer should be programmed to select "random" dates and intervals. But this is a dreadful solution that dehumanizes the past. It may very well be that one map is preferable in particular circumstances to an approach incorporating several. But what must be readily apparent in any world-regional scheme is that choices have been made (a particular strength of the text of *The Myth of Continents*) and that the last two or three centuries of human experience be privileged to the detriment of premodern history.

CROSSROADS CAUCASIA

Inability to represent change over time is a chronic problem of existing world-regional schemes. Another nagging puzzle is what to do with peoples, cultures, and zones not fitting neatly within a single region.[21] In Lewis and Wigen's revised scheme, Ethiopia and the Horn of Africa (and one might extend this to the southern Arabian peninsula) is one such zone. Although it has been located within "Sub-Saharan Africa," the "Ethiopian Zone" has been singled out. The other example is the region of "Central Asia," which Lewis and Wigen divide into two, a "Lamaist Zone" bifurcated by an "Islamic Zone."[22] Yet another special-case area is Caucasia, which does not constitute a separate world region in the refined scheme, but its unusual quality has been acknowledged by the addition of its name to the "Russia—SEEC" unit.[23]

Caucasia is an area—perhaps better identified as a subregion, or "zone," with respect to existing world-regional schemes—that would be but a blip on the Western scholarly radar if it were not for the sizeable Armenian diaspora in Europe and the Americas, the prospects for extracting oil from Azerbaijan and the planned construction of the Baku-T'bilisi-Ceyhan (BTC) pipeline terminating in Turkey, and the ongoing conflict in Chechnya.[24] Although impossible to justify, this deficit of attention and interest is not difficult to explain. The mountainous ribbon of land separating the Black from the Caspian Sea that is Caucasia is a small place when viewed from orbit: on the basis of current political boundaries it occupies some 400,000 square kilometers and boasts a highly multicultural population in excess of 20 million. Second, with the noteworthy exception of the Armenians and certain peoples like the Meskhian Turks exiled to Central Asia by the Stalinist regime, the vast majority of the indigenous Caucasian peoples still reside in the region. Most ethnic groups based in Caucasia do not have large diaspora communities in the United States and Western Europe, which, in the unusual case of the Armenians, have both sparked international interest and generated substantial controversy and intraethnic division. Finally, in the nineteenth and twentieth centuries Western scholars tended to regard the isthmus as an exotic appendage, a frontier, of, first, the Russian empire and, then, the Soviet Union.[25] The area's non-Slavic character was more often than not seen as an aberration, and its distinctive history was downplayed in favor of relatively recent linkages with Slavic-dominated Russia, a view also taken up by Russian and Soviet ideologies.

While in some respects Caucasia's association with Russia is appropriate, before the early nineteenth century the region had a stronger affiliation with political enterprises and cultures situated to its south and west, not with the north. A few specific examples from the history of the various Georgian peoples prior to their incorporation into the Russian empire in the early nineteenth century illustrate this point.

Connections among Georgians and Eurasian peoples to the south and west are vividly attested in one of the earliest surviving Georgian-language histories. The ninth-century *Life of the Kings (C'xorebay k'art'velt'a mep'et'a)* elaborates the legendary ethnogenesis of the major Caucasian peoples, its anonymous Christian author contending that these diverse populations were biologically related through common descent from Togarmah, a direct relative of Noah, who is featured in the Hebrew Bible/Old Testament, the ultimate Judeo-Christian source for the origins of peoples.[26] The Caucasian eponyms, cloaked in the epic Iranian-like imagery of hero-giants and fixed within an ancient Hebrew genealogy, struggled against the biblical Nimrod, the first king of the world and an Iranian. Having defeated Nimrod, the eponyms established the major Caucasian peoples. Although newly founded Caucasia shared the culture of Iran, Nimrod's successors continued to make war upon Georgia, Armenia, and northern Caucasia. Later, when the successors of Nimrod (that is, the Achaemenid Great Kings) were defeated by Alexander "the Great," some of the Caucasians took advantage of the situation: it was at this time that indigenous kingship was actually established among the eastern Georgians, that is, the K'art'velians, the Asiatic "Iberians" of the Greeks and Romans/Byzantines.[27]

This legendary account was consigned to writing in the early ninth century, by which time eastern Georgia had been thoroughly Christianized. It is therefore to be expected that biblical genealogies would have been exploited. Although Nimrod is a biblical figure, the infamous "mighty hunter" before the Lord (Genesis 10:9), the medieval Georgian tradition expands his identification: he was not only the world's first king, but was Iranian by ethnicity. So a tradition appropriated from the Hebrew Bible was imbued with Iranian imagery. This is significant because after Nimrod, *The Life of the Kings* features several ancient Iranian hero-kings who are also attested in the eleventh-century *Shāhnāma* by the Iranian poet Ferdowsī, for example, Ap'ridon (Ferdowsī's Farīdūn), K'ekapos (Kay Kāvūs), K'aixosro (Key Khusrau).

Indeed, the historical context and the intertwined heroic, royal, and social imagery dominating the Georgian *Life of the Kings* are decidedly Iranian, or better yet, Iranian-like or Iranic. Put another way, its anonymous writer, like other Georgian historians of the time, connected his community's history to that of the Iranian world and the Near East. Thus, the very name of the semilegendary first indigenous monarch of eastern Georgia, P'arnavaz, features the Iranian root *farnah/farr*, which signifies the royal radiance of legitimate rulers in pre-Islamic Iran.[28] In fact, among the ruling elite of eastern Georgia personal names based upon Iranian were dominant down through the eighth and early ninth centuries, several hundred years after the initial Christianization of the local monarchy.[29]

The provenance of the Caucasian peoples, like origins generally, has generated intense controversy. But the picture becomes considerably clearer at the end of the first millennium B.C., at which time we have ample evidence for the close affiliation of the Caucasian peoples with the Iranian commonwealth. Achaemenid and subsequent Sasanid inscriptions explicitly name Armenia and eastern Georgia. Individual Iranians could deliberate whether Caucasians were full members of the commonwealth, but on the whole Iranians regarded the isthmus as a cultural and social outpost of greater Iran. And some, as is evidenced by the inscription of Shāpūr I carved near Persepolis circa 262 A.D., explicitly counted eastern Georgia as an integral part of Iran proper, that is, the "Aryan" empire.[30] Armenian, Georgian, and the languages of northern Caucasia are replete with words having direct correspondences in Old and Middle Iranian as well as Avestan and Parthian.[31] Iranian and Iranian-like epic traditions circulated throughout premodern Caucasia; they were transmitted orally by *gōsāns*, "minstrels." Zoroastrianism, the faith promoted by the Sasanid dynasty, and other Mazdaic religions were practiced throughout Caucasia.[32] The Aramaic script, used extensively by the Iranian bureaucracy, was also employed by the eastern Georgian and Armenian elite before the invention of local scripts in the late fourth/early fifth century A.D.[33] And, finally, the social structure prevalent throughout ancient and medieval Caucasia reflected that of Iran: powerful noble houses dominated the countryside, while kings attempted to construct an all-pervasive central authority. Along these lines, *The Life of the Kings* states in no uncertain terms that King P'arnavaz organized his government by "imitating the kingdom of the Persians."[34]

Nina Garsoïan, James Russell, and others have investigated various aspects of Armenia's opulent Iranian heritage.[35] In medieval Armenian literature, the connection with Iran and Iranians is especially conspicuous in the anonymous fifth-century *Epic Histories*.[36] For their part, when present-day Georgian academics have explored Georgia's historical linkages to Iran, they have tended to highlight connections to Islamic Iran, especially to the early-modern Safavid empire.[37] My own work, however, has extended many of Garsoïan's findings about Armenia's antique and medieval Iranian heritage to neighboring Georgia. Furthermore, although it has garnered relatively little attention from Western specialists, many of the diverse tribes of northern Caucasia were also part and parcel of the Iranian commonwealth. In cultural terms, nomadic peoples such as the Scythians, Cimmerians, Sarmatians, Alans, and Ovsis (compare the modern Ossetians) shared a great deal with Iran. Almost a century ago, M. Rostovtzeff demonstrated the extensiveness of Iranian influence among peoples who lived in what is now southern Russia and Ukraine.[38] More recently, C. Scott Littleton and Linda Malcor have provocatively argued that the Iranian-like culture of the northern Caucasians was by no means geographically limited to west-central Asia.[39] In their view, nomadic mercenaries originating from northern Caucasia conveyed the core legend of the tradition of Arthur and the Knights of the Round Table to the western and northern provinces of the Roman empire. Littleton and Malcor draw special attention to the settlement of the Iazyges in Roman Britain around 175 A.D. and then that of the Sarmatians and Alans in Gaul in the fifth century. The so-called Nart Legends, stories of heroic giants having numerous parallels throughout the Iranian commonwealth, are still preserved among some of the northern Caucasians and were instrumental in tracing the connection.[40] If the authors are right, then the Caucasus region played a vital role in the development of medieval European literature. Furthermore, owing to its geographical position, it is entirely possible that Caucasia was an intermediary in the transmission of the Iranian/Parthian idea of the armored knight to Byzantium, through which it penetrated Western Europe.

Simply put, from the time that they clearly emerge on the historical stage in the first millennium B.C., Caucasia's sedentary and nomadic populations were intimately associated with the Iranian commonwealth.[41] Notwithstanding, this enduring circumstance is not at all discernable in Lewis and Wigen's revised scheme or in the previous world-regional model. It is also worth noting that the special "Islamic zone" of "Central Asia" largely fell within the Iranian cultural orbit in the long pre-Islamic period, as did the steppes of what is now southern Russia and Ukraine. This, too, is invisible in the revised model. Thus, the example of the massive Iranian commonwealth draws attention to the static nature of existing world-regional models and their strong predilection for the recent. Again, it may be that several maps are needed in order to reflect historical dynamism, and within such a series the Iranian commonwealth certainly belongs.[42] If total elapsed time were a primary determinant for identifying units within a regional paradigm, Caucasia would undoubtedly fall within the same sector as Iran.

Yet such a map would itself prove deceptive by obscuring the constantly shifting and contested orientations of Caucasia over time or even at a given moment. Although the many cultures of Caucasia were affiliated with the Iranian commonwealth in antiquity, the penetration of Greco-Roman culture was by no means insignificant.[43] It was particularly evident along the Black Sea littoral, where Greek colonies were established as early as the seventh century B.C. Greek myth recollects the exotic character of distant Caucasia, believed to be perched on the very edge of the Earth, in the stories of Jason and the Argonauts and Prometheus. The Armenian court was Hellenized "under the influence of its queen, Cleopatra of Pontus, and Greek rhetoricians and philosophers were welcomed as guests and advisors of the royal family" in the first century B.C. The classical writer Plutarch reports the reading of the *Bacchae* of Euripides at the wedding of the Armenian sovereign's sister to the Parthian heir.[44] Greek influence in Caucasia attained an unprecedented level during the Hellenistic kingdoms, particularly through connections with the Seleucid dynasty in Mesopotamia.[45] Greek inscriptions from the period have been unearthed throughout Caucasia, including inland districts and areas in the far north. The Hellenistic concept of the divine king was adopted—and adapted—by the newly formed dynasties in Armenia and eastern Georgia. Despite the upsurge of Hellenic and Hellenistic cultural influence, and Roman after them, Iranian-like cultural and social patterns persisted, and locals regarded these as an integral part of Caucasian identity, not as foreign imports.

This is not the picture normally painted by scholars who approach premodern Caucasia through the lens of classical—that is, Greco-Roman—or Byzantine studies. Before the conversion to Christianity of the Armenian and eastern Georgian monarchies in the fourth century, the most detailed contemporary evidence for the region is provided by Greco-Roman authors, many of whom had no firsthand knowledge about it. To the Romans, like the Greeks before them, Caucasia was the limit of their authority and influence; it often constituted the far eastern rim of their empire. It is hardly surprising that the nature of surviving sources (not to mention the structure and priorities of modern-day academia) has led some scholars to construct a rather skewed image of premodern Caucasia. In his important synthesis *Georgia in Antiquity*, David Braund, historian of the classical Mediterranean and Black Seas, acknowledges Caucasia's intimate connections to Iran —and for this he is to be applauded—but nevertheless fixes Georgia's history primarily within a Greco-Roman and Hellenistic framework.[46] Most disquieting is Braund's almost complete dismissal of medieval Georgian texts, many of which locate Caucasia (and not just Georgia) within an Iranian/Near Eastern context. Braund's depiction of Georgia reflects his training, interests, and perspective as a classicist, and this is hardly unusual: many scholars continue to study Caucasia as an unusual yet integral part of the Hellenic, Hellenistic, and then Roman enterprises. Significantly, even these cultural and political entities are divided among three of Lewis and Wigen's refined areas. Because of their modern and static qualities, these transregional, cross-cultural phenomena are imperceptible.

Despite their preeminence, Iranian and Iranian-like cultures did not monopolize Caucasia. According to the early-ninth-century *Life of the Kings*, the cosmopolitan character of eastern Georgia was manifest by the tradition that six languages were commonly spoken there in antiquity: Armenian, Georgian, Khazar (an anachronism!), Syrian, Hebrew, and Greek.[47] Despite the absence of its languages from this (later) passage, Anatolian[48] (Hurrian, Hittite, and so forth) influences waxed strong throughout Caucasia. In a series of brilliant researches Giorgi Melik'ishvili has exposed the deep influence of Anatolian religious beliefs among the Georgians and Armenians.[49] The Zoroastrianism practiced by many Caucasians incorporated not only local practices and beliefs, but also select elements of indigenous Anatolian religions. Indeed, to some degree, Georgian religious ideas appropriated and combined Iranian and Anatolian concepts. Though many scholars have been tempted to identify the god Armazi in the Georgian tradition with the Zoroastrian Ahura-Mazda, Michael Tsereteli has argued that Armazi is actually a Mesopotamian deity of the sky and storms, the Hurrian Teshub.[50] On the other hand, Michael Tarchnishvili has linked the Georgian Armazi to a Mesopotamian lunar deity; in the Luvian language, *arma* denotes the moon.[51] Whatever Armazi's ultimate inspiration, scholars concur that Armazi was associated with the moon. Ivane Javaxishvili has shown that the lunar attributes of Armazi were transferred to the Christian St. George, known in Georgian as *t'et'ri Giorgi*, "White George."[52] As late as the nineteenth century, Georgians could envisage the power of St. George as exceeding that of Christ himself. The characteristics of the chief "pagan" deity Armazi were thus projected onto the Christian figure of St. George, resulting in a new, syncretic figure.[53]

Scholarship not infrequently presents the Christianization of the Armenian and eastern Georgian monarchies as the single most important episode in premodern Caucasian history. In the early fourth century, perhaps around the year 314, Trdat III of Armenia embraced the Christian God through the intervention of Gregory "the Illuminator." King Mirian III of the eastern Georgian kingdom of Kʻartʻli followed suit a few decades later, around 337. These events corresponded with an upsurge of Roman, and then Byzantine, political and military influence. At the end of the third century, the Sasanids of Iran had been forced to cede hegemony over Caucasia to the Romans. Thus commenced a ferocious competition between Rome/Byzantium and Iran/the caliphate over the strategically crucial isthmus. In addition, Caucasia was emerging as a thriving conduit for long-distance trade. Routes through Armenia and Georgia linked the fabled Silk Roads to the Black Sea; one route terminated at the Black Sea port of Phasis.[54] Although contemporary hagiography suggests otherwise, most scholars have suggested that the acceptance of Christianity by Trdat and Mirian was a deliberate ploy to connect their kingdoms with the Roman empire and thus to strike a balance between the Roman and Iranian imperial competitors. Countless modern observers have assumed an instantaneous and absolute alliance with Christian Byzantium brought about by the royal conversions.[55] What is abundantly clear from contemporary Armenian and Georgian sources, however, is that, although elites began to be Christianized, the well-established Iranian-like culture and social structure remained largely intact. For example, the celebration of hero-giants and the Christian affiliation of eastern Georgia were combined in the fifth- and sixth-century King Vaxtang Gorgasali, who is depicted by his medieval biographer as a Christian *bumberazi*, champion duelist.[56] This imagery, for the most part, would have been alien to a contemporary Greek from Byzantium but circulated widely throughout Christian Caucasia. Local Christian clerics labored to conceal the region's rich Iranian heritage by simply omitting it from their works or censuring things Iranian. The Zoroastrian Iranians were, after all, producing martyrs. The bottom line is that the conversion of Armenia and eastern Georgia did not entail an immediate reorientation toward Byzantine civilization, but the potential for an association had been greatly enhanced.

Tensions between Sasanid Iran and Byzantium assumed a sharp religious flavor by the start of the fifth century. Iranian elites increasingly identified Christianity as a sign of Roman affiliation, whereas their Roman counterparts associated Zoroastrianism with Iran and Iranians. It was in this context that both empires jockeyed for control over the strategic territory of Caucasia. The contemporary Byzantine historians Procopius and Agathias describe the strained situation, their focus on Caucasian affairs demonstrating the isthmus's significance to Constantinople. The Armenians' situation was especially precarious, their kingdom having been partitioned by the great powers at the end of the fourth century. Although it might have seemed natural enough for the Christian Armenians to rally behind an alliance with Byzantium, this was not the case. The theological controversies of the fifth century and the failure of Byzantine troops to aid the Armenians during a disastrous uprising in 451 brought distrust and division. By the seventh century, many Armenians eventually united under the banner of their church in opposition to the christological pronouncements of the Fourth Ecumenical Council, held at Chalcedon.[57] Although some Armenians would accept Chalcedon and "Byzantinize" to varying levels (persons of Armenian background and ethnicity advanced to the highest levels of the imperial government and even occupied the imperial throne), most eventually subscribed to a version of Christianity that did not accept Chalcedon.[58] In fact, these Armenians were part of the so-called Monophysite branch of Eastern Christianity, which united such disparate peoples as the Armenians, Syrians, Copts, and Ethiopians in a faith quite distinct from that of the imperial church.[59] Eastern Georgians remained in communion with the Armenians at first but then broke ranks and accepted Chalcedon in the first half of the seventh century. The christological rift contributed to the division of Christian communities Caucasia, and, partly as a result of it, the newly Chalcedonian Georgians were rapidly drawn deeper into a Byzantine religious and cultural orbit. Here it is worth noting that christological orientation was by no means restricted to the ecclesiastical sphere. It also had political overtones, for acceptance of Chalcedon often went hand in hand with political allegiance to Byzantium.

As this split was institutionalized, the Arabs invaded Iran and brought down the Sasanid dynasty once and for all in 651. Within a few decades much of Caucasia was occupied and colonized by the Arabs. It was at this time that Islam was implanted in eastern and northern Caucasia, where it remains prominent to this day.

It was during the Islamic occupation of eastern Caucasia that a branch of the Bagratids, an old Irano-Armenian family, seized political authority in the southwestern Georgian domains. Under Byzantine tutelage, the Georgian Bagratids seized power in 813, restored kingship in 888 (it had been in abeyance since the Sasanids had dismantled it in the sixth century), and then assembled the first all-Georgian kingdom in 1008. One indication of the reorientation toward Byzantium was the replacement of the traditional Syro-Palestinian liturgy practiced in Georgia with that of Constantinople in the ninth/tenth centuries.[60] Significantly, various sites in the Byzantine empire, well beyond Georgian territory, became the leading Georgian literary centers of the period. Especially noteworthy are the scriptoria of the Iveron (literally "of the Georgians") Monastery on Mt. Athos, St. Catherine's Monastery on Mt. Sinai, the Monastery of the Holy Cross in Jerusalem, and several monastic foundations in the vicinity of Antioch in Syria.[61] Yet another sign of contemporary Georgia's reorientation toward the west is the Byzantine-inspired images of royal authority adopted by the Bagratids, ones that are especially evident in not only contemporary art, but also in royal biographies that drew heavily upon Byzantine concepts of imperial power.[62] Prior to Bagratid rule, eastern Georgian kings had been portrayed in a manner consistent with the royal imagery of Iran, but this changed by the eleventh century.

The Bagratids and the Georgian elite were deeply affected by Byzantium in this period, and although deep connections with the Middle East remained intact, it would be appropriate to include the contemporary Georgian crown and the culture promoted by it within the Byzantine sphere.[63] This orientation also applies to much of Caucasia, for in the eleventh and twelfth centuries almost all of Caucasia, including Armenia, was brought under Georgian rule, and zeal of the Crusades affected the Georgian armies, which sought to extricate the Arabs and Turks (especially Seljuqs) from it. It should be noted, however, that the Cilician Armenian realm was established in southeastern Anatolia at the end of the eleventh century. In Lewis and Wigen's scheme, these two Armenias are partitioned between different units, and this is not entirely unfair owing to the unprecedented contacts of Armenians in Cilicia with Catholic Europe. But this exemplifies another universal problem with world-regional schemes: diasporas and other "divided" communities are rendered invisible.[64]

But in the thirteenth century, following the death of the powerful Queen T'amar in 1213, Georgia was governed by inept rulers whose positions were further eroded by the Mongol conquest. After the breakup of the single Mongol empire of Chenghis Khan, Caucasia was incorporated into the Mongol ilkhanate based in Iran. Byzantium was not in a position to assist, for Constantinople itself had been sacked during the Fourth Crusade, in 1204. The central Byzantine government never fully recovered. In the fourteenth century, Caucasia was invaded several times by the armies of Timur. At the same time Islam was further solidified in the eastern and northern domains of the isthmus. The lack of a strong local authority also explains the inroads other confessions and religions made among the Georgians. Perhaps the most notable example is Catholicism. In 1329 the Roman Catholics established a bishopric in the Georgian capital, but their sustained drive to establish Catholicism in Caucasia was initiated considerably later by the Congregatio de Propaganda Fide, itself established in 1622. This push entailed the dispatch of a Theatine mission to western Georgia from 1626 to around 1700 and the establishment of a Capuchin mission house in T'bilisi from 1661 to 1845. The fall of Constantinople to Mehmed II in 1453, the consolidation of the Ottoman enterprise, and the revival of Iran under the Safavid dynasty brought about a renewed wave of Islamic influence in Caucasia. Indeed, the Ottomans and Safavids regularly clashed in the Caucasian arena. The treaty of 1555, which had partitioned Georgia between the Ottomans and Safavids, was repeatedly violated beginning in 1602. Some Christian Caucasians, and Orthodox Georgians in particular, began to look to the Russian empire for aid, but the Georgian elite also pinned their hopes on the papacy and governments of Western Europe. Sulxan-Saba Orbeliani's mission to Western Europe in 1713 exemplifies the flourish of diplomatic activity between Georgia and France in the eighteenth century.[65]

This brings us back to Caucasia's historical connections with Russia. Notwithstanding Caucasia's customary inclusion within the Russian unit in world-regional schemes, we still observe no close association with Russia in the fifteenth century. There had been occasional contacts before this, such as those enabled by the establishment of Armenian colonies in Crimea, Ukraine, and Poland in the mid-thirteenth century. Although a small number of Armenian merchants settled in Moscow in the fourteenth century, it was only in the sixteenth century that Armenian commercial activity intensified as a consequence of Russian expansion to the south, toward the Caspian Sea.[66] A regular, sustained relationship between Caucasia and Russia can be traced only to the second half of the sixteenth century, when the Armenian commercial presence in Russia was greatly expanded and the Russian government and the Bagratid kingdoms of eastern Georgian began an exchange of official embassies.[67] As they had done with Byzantium before, Orthodox Georgians increasingly pinned their hopes on the Russian tsar, and this was in accordance with Russia's depiction of itself as a, or even the, legitimate successor of Byzantium. In 1783 the eastern Georgian monarch Erekle II signed a treaty with Russia that legally made his realm a "protectorate" of the empire. Then, beginning in 1801, the Russian empire unilaterally annexed Christian Caucasia.[68] The submission of the peoples of northern Caucasia, many of whom were Muslim, was not completed until later in the century. The Russian *Zakavkaz'ia*, "Transcaucasia/Transcaucasus," entered common usage in this period. Denoting "across the Caucasus [mountains]," the term imparts a distinctly Russian imperial perspective and as such is irrelevant for the earlier periods. And it was under Russian rule that Georgian and Armenian nations were first made.[69] When the Russian empire came to an end, Armenia, Azerbaijan, and Georgia were united into a single Transcaucasian Federation and subsequently, in 1918, splintered into three sovereign countries. By 1921 all three had been conquered by the Red Army, thus enabling their forced incorporation into the Union of Soviet Socialist Republics. All three retained union republic status until the dissolution of the USSR in the early 1990s. Although ties to the Russian Federation and the Commonwealth of Independent States remain strong, Near/Middle Eastern influence is again on the ascendancy in Caucasia. In recent years economic and cultural encounters with Turkey and Iran have (re)gained momentum.

EURASIAN COMMONWEALTHS

In light of the preceding discussion, the wrong question to ask is to which particular unit or region Caucasia belongs. Nevertheless, this is precisely the kind of question inspired by existing world-regional schemes, which, whether it is their architects' intent or not, offer a chronologically frozen snapshot of the past and do not satisfactorily reflect the wide range of connections existing between and among regions, however they might be defined.[70]

I have already mentioned Lewis and Wigen's wise decision to salvage the world-regional model. Yet their vision, like the original, poses a number of problems insofar as chronology, crossroads, and frontiers (as viewed from some center) are concerned. Those large-scale units in which Caucasia has been and could be situated must now be reexamined.

The "Russia—Soviet Union" Complex

Both the standard and refined schemes incorporate Caucasia within the "Russia—Soviet Union" unit. For the nineteenth and twentieth centuries, this makes a great deal of sense. Georgia, Armenia, Azerbaijan, and other Caucasian entities were annexed to the Russian empire and then Soviet Union. In fact, Lewis and Wigen's "Russia—SEEC" complex is really a zone of Slavic domination and could be interpreted as a representation of the Soviet Union and the Warsaw Pact. It might also be argued that "Russia—SEEC" also represents the world of Orthodox/Eastern Christianity (see further).

Even for the nineteenth and twentieth centuries, however, as we have seen, Caucasia's association with "Russia—SEEC" is not without its difficulties. From a cultural perspective, the Caucasian peoples remained in many ways separate and distinct from the Soviet center in which the Slavic, and especially the Russian, idiom dominated. What is not indicated in either scheme is that sustained contacts between Caucasia and Russia originated in the sixteenth century. Thus, the greater part of Caucasian history has little, if anything, to do with Russia or the Soviet Union. Looking to the future, it is not at all certain that post-Soviet Caucasia will remain within the Russian sphere at all. The government of the Republic of Georgia, for instance, has forged a new relationship with that of the United States and seeks admission into NATO and the European Union. For their part, Azerbaijani leaders have cultivated relations with neighboring Turkey and Iran.

The Idea of Commonwealth

Although Lewis and Wigen's refinement of the world-regional scheme deserves applause, the refinement itself can be further enhanced. One improvement might involve the idea of commonwealth.[71] For the history of Caucasia, two studies about commonwealths are especially pertinent. In his landmark *Byzantine Commonwealth*, Dimitri Obolensky broadly defines commonwealth as encompassing peoples who share "a common cultural tradition," by which he really seems to have in mind "civilization." For the Byzantine commonwealth this entailed the profession of a single religion—Eastern Christianity, especially Orthodoxy—recognition of the special status of both the Byzantine Church and emperor based at Constantinople, acknowledgment of the "norms" of Romano-Byzantine law, and, significantly, "the belief that the literary standards and artistic techniques cultivated in the empire's schools, monasteries were of universal validity and worthy of imitation."[72] Though contemporaries were not always conscious of the bonds of the Byzantine commonwealth, Obolensky attributes to its members a "rich cosmopolitan experience" to which non-Byzantines belonged and contributed.[73] In particular, Obolensky argues for the existence of a Byzantine commonwealth from the mid-ninth to the fifteenth century that was characterized by the Byzantino-Greek core and the various Slavic peoples of Central and Eastern Europe. Although he is most concerned with the Slavs, the author nevertheless acknowledges the inclusion of non-Slavic elements, including the Christians of Caucasia.[74] Indeed, this is one of the weaknesses of Obolensky's otherwise splendid attempt to take a "long view." The Byzantine commonwealth of any period was hardly restricted to Slavic lands. In the period reviewed by him, roughly 500 to 1453, Christian Caucasia was an essential component of that cultural world, though its physical distance from Constantinople (compare the Balkans) somehow left it less essential in Obolensky's eyes. Caucasia's greater geographical distance from Constantinople is insufficient grounds for disqualifying it from a study of the Byzantine commonwealth. Indeed, one of the fundamental qualities of commonwealths is that their limits tend to be blurry and overlap with other cultural zones, perhaps more so than the way in which civilizations are normally defined.

Elaborating upon Obolensky's definition, Garth Fowden has adopted a more theoretical and Afro-Eurasian approach.[75] In *Empire to Commonwealth*, Fowden investigates the ideas of universal religion, monotheism, and "world empire" in antiquity and the transformation of *some* empires in late antiquity into commonwealths. In particular, Fowden examines the first Iranian empire of the Achaemenids, the restored Iranian empire of the Sasanids, the first Byzantine commonwealth (especially from the late fifth to the ninth century), the second Byzantine commonwealth (which corresponds to Obolensky's commonwealth of the Slavs of Eastern Europe), and, finally, the Islamic "world empire" (the only one actually attained in late antiquity) and its eventual transformation into a commonwealth.[76] Central to Fowden's definition is the marriage of monotheism and monarchy. Imposition of a strict "orthodoxy" (Greek *orthodoksos;* literally "right belief") in each monotheism necessarily entailed the idea of dissent, "heresy." Indeed, it is the acquisition by the so-called heretics of "stable, non-clandestine structures and hence of political potential and actual power" that transmuted empire into commonwealth.[77] In other words, a vital prerequisite for commonwealth in late antiquity was the identification/imagining of a substantial, organized opposition, that is to say, "heresy" and "heretics." Polytheism lacked the inherent exclusivity—could we call it unity?—necessary for the creation of this manner of dissent.

Despite their starkly different approaches to the premodern commonwealth, both models have their merits. Although the consequences of monotheism are of enormous import on the Afro-Eurasian and world stages, and this is seen repeatedly in Fowden's treatment, I favor Obolensky's more flexible definition of a commonwealth in which basic cultural, political, religious, social, and other patterns were shared while, simultaneously, enormous diversity could exist. As both authors have rightly contended, commonwealths are closely associated with the idea of empire, and with this formulation I concur. Fowden stresses this idea when he writes, "There could be no commonwealth without a preceding empire." Yet, he continues, not every empire could spawn a commonwealth, but only empires guided by rigid political monotheism seeking control of the "Fertile Crescent," namely, the region contemporaries considered to be the center of things (that is, this "Fertile Crescent" was *the* "world"), could evolve into commonwealths.[78] One of the exciting implications of Fowden's thesis is that Iran, the Near East including Mesopotamia and Caucasia, the Roman and then Byzantine worlds, and the Islamic world together constituted a single historical unit stretching from Inner Asia to northern Africa.[79] For late antiquity—which the author defines as the period from the second to the ninth century A.D.—Fowden's definition makes a great deal of sense so far as the Christian Caucasian experience is concerned. As the northern sector of Fowden's central "Fertile Crescent" Caucasia belonged to the "center" coveted by would-be "world empires," and this accounts for the Eurasian influences in the isthmus.

Can there be commonwealths without monotheism, without the concomitant orthodoxy and heresy, and without the striving for and occasional attainment of a "world empire"? For Fowden the answer would seem to be a resounding no, at least for the period up through the ninth century. Fowden has put forth a compelling case for the formation of certain commonwealths in late-antique times as a direct political consequence of monotheism. He has, however, identified only a particular variety of commonwealth. It might be argued that Achaemenid and then Sasanid Iran are an example commonwealth not involving monotheism, though in the Sasanid case, at least, a unifying religion (Zoroastrianism) played a prominent role.[80] In my view, the Iranian cultural world under the Achaemenids and Sasanids is really one and the same, a veritable commonwealth, whose nucleus survived the initial shock of Alexander's conquest and the subsequent Hellenistic/Seleucid and Parthian "successor states." Sedentary peoples like Georgians and Armenians belonged to this Iranian commonwealth. Similarly, nomadic and seminomadic peoples—including the Alans, Sarmatians, and Scythians—could also claim membership, though, as Obolensky has observed for the Byzantine commonwealth, these peoples may not have consciously thought about this affiliation. Zoroastrianism, and Zoroastrian ideas—along with the wider Mazdaic faith, could be found among all these peoples, but that is not to suggest that all or even most of the Georgians or the Sarmatians, for example, venerated Ahura-Mazda. Among the sedentary populations belonging to these two closely related Iranian commonwealths, the social landscape was typically divided among powerful aristocratic houses. Historical traditions and especially heroic myths and legends about remote history were shared among the commonwealth's members. Independent rulers, often not subordinate to the Great King, could be found among the non-Iranian peoples, especially in Caucasia and to the north of the Caucasus Mountains. Clearly, this is something beyond empire. Achaemenid and Sasanid Iran together constitute a different kind of commonwealth, one still associated with empire, but one not built upon a rigid monotheism. It is, in other words, a commonwealth of the more generic, cultural variety described by Obolensky—a federation of kingdoms and other political enterprises, of varying degrees of autonomy, linked by common interests, experiences, and, in a broad sense, culture.[81]

CAUCASIA AND THE COMMONWEALTHS OF CENTRAL AND WESTERN EURASIA

As defined here, the Byzantine commonwealth encompassed not only the Byzantine empire centered at Constantinople, but also the various non-Greek peoples and kingdoms of the expansive *Oriens christianus*. This is not to say that all Eastern Christians were happily and forever united, or, as we have seen, that all of them consciously thought about the existence of the commonwealth. For example, Eastern Christians came to be divided into several "national" churches based upon dominant linguistic and ethnic groups. "National" churches distinguished "Eastern" Christians from their medieval "Western" (European) counterparts. The hierarchies of the autocephalous (internally independent) "national" churches often clashed, and not only on an intellectual plane. Even more divisive was the theological and especially christological discord, that is, controversies about the human and divine natures of Christ—indeed, it was the formal organization of these heresies that, to Fowden's mind, led to the creation of the Byzantine commonwealth. Monophysitism/anti-Chalcedonianism and Nestorianism were just two of the more prominent groups declared heretical by the Orthodox churches, though it must be said that Monophysites and Nestorians saw themselves as perfectly "orthodox" (note the use of "O" and "o"). Notwithstanding such divisions, Eastern Christians were bound by several core ideas, namely that ethnically based "national" churches were a legitimate way for Christianity to be organized; the Eusebian Theory, monotheistic sacral kingship, properly defined the nature of Christian kingship (though the fourth-century bishop Eusebius and his hero Constantine "the Great" had not intended it, this notion was routinely adapted by Eastern Christian rulers other than the emperor proper); and that the Byzantine emperor, down to the fall of Constantinople in 1453, held a special political position within all Christendom—though what that status was and what prerogatives it might have entailed were matters of debate.

One of the contributions of Lewis and Wigen's refined world-regional scheme is the enlargement of the "Russia—SEEC" complex to encompass more of the territories and peoples that had for several centuries fallen within Eastern Christendom, a region in which the Byzantine commonwealth played a central role. In the standard model, Greece is normally assigned to Western Europe; the Balkans, Caucasia, and Russia to the Soviet Union/Eastern Europe sector; and Asia Minor, the Near East, and northeastern Africa to the Middle East. Thus, the thousand-year transregional Byzantine commonwealth is hopelessly divided between three major regions.[82] Lewis and Wigen rectify this deplorable circumstance by locating Greece and the Balkans within the Russian area, yet Asia Minor, Egypt, and the Near East, regions that for centuries belonged to the Byzantine/Mediterranean world, are included within the Southwestern Asia—Northern Africa complex. The more recent Islamic affiliation of these regions has been given precedence over the earlier orientation.

Through their adjustments, however, Lewis and Wigen nevertheless demonstrate the association of Russia, Eastern Europe, and Caucasia with the Byzantine commonwealth. It is curious though that the word "Russia" has been incorporated into the unit's label. "Russia" has virtually nothing to do with Siberia and northeastern Asia prior to the Russian conquest of the seventeenth century. If the names of empires and nation-states are incorporated into the names of world regions, it might be argued that "Byzantine" belongs in the "Russia—SEEC" complex: why privilege the Russian achievement over the Byzantine one? Is it really enough that a Russia has survived down to our own times and a Byzantium has not? To be fair, choices must be made, and whether we like it or not, we write and conduct research from our own temporal perspective, but does it make historical sense to give precedence to a modern name simply because of chronological proximity to us?

Caucasia's affiliation with Byzantium is in some respects appropriate and logical. For the scholars of the Caucasian isthmus, the Byzantine empire/commonwealth has been the perspective of choice at least so far as the Christian period is concerned. But as we have seen, much of Caucasia remained within the Iranian cultural world for hundreds of years following the royal conversions of the fourth century. From this time, down to the ninth or tenth century and beyond, it could legitimately be argued that the bulk of Caucasia belonged to both the Byzantine and Iranian commonwealths simultaneously. This cultural plurality corresponds to the political and military struggle to control Caucasia on the part of the Romans/Byzantines and Sasanid Iranians.

As has been hinted throughout this chapter, one of the "big losers" in both the standard and refined schemes—and in world-historical literature generally—is the Iranian commonwealth. Indeed, this is indicative of a larger trend within world history to ignore pre-Islamic Iran altogether.[83] As they do in so many other instances, both schemes give precedence to the modern state of affairs: thus pre-Islamic Iran—built around the Achaemenid empire, Parthia, and the Sasanid empire—is entirely subsumed (and rendered invisible) within the core Islamic unit, southwestern Asia/northern Africa in the refined map. Nevertheless, in terms of geographical extent, cultural influence and stunning achievements, and chronological span, the Iranian commonwealth was every bit as grand as, say, Byzantium, the Roman empire, or China under the Han dynasty. At its height, the Iranian commonwealth stretched from eastern Asia Minor in the west to Inner Asia, northern India, and the western border of China in the east; from Caucasia and the southern steppes of what would become Ukraine/Rus'/Russia in the north to Arabia and even northeastern Africa in the south.[84] Indeed, both the Iranian and Byzantine commonwealths were of a size comparable to some of the units of the refined scheme, for example, southern Asia.

Of course, it can be persuasively argued that Caucasia—or at least pieces of it—also belonged to other sociocultural and geopolitical entities. For centuries Caucasia was also affiliated with the Islamic commonwealth.[85] Eastern Caucasia was occupied and colonized by the Arabs already beginning in the second half of the seventh century. Substantial numbers of Caucasians converted to Islam (a process that continued well into the eighteenth and nineteenth centuries), while others maintained their Christian affiliation, though they lived under the nominal rule of the caliph and his governors. Azerbaijan and Daghestan later became hotbeds of sufism and a major base for the Naqshbandiyyah order in particular.[86] The Ottomans and Safavids controlled parts of Caucasia, and local peoples participated in both courts; the Safavid royal bodyguard was dominated by Georgians, while Armenian merchants based in New Julfa directed a great deal of the overland transcontinental trade.[87] As is well known, large numbers of Armenians lived within the Ottoman domains, and they eventually became the target of genocide in 1915. Other external Islamic entities had direct contacts with the peoples and lands of Caucasia. After the breakup of the unified Mongol empire of Chenghis Khan, Caucasia was claimed by the Mongol ilkhanate in Iran. After the conversion to Islam of the Īlkhans beginning in the waning years of the thirteenth century, the Mongols began to favor Islam within Caucasia. Later, Timur (Tamerlane) led no fewer than three campaigns into the Caucasian heartland. It might plausibly be argued that Caucasia belongs to Inner Asia, the refined scheme's "Central Asia." Were the Volga and the Caspian really such impenetrable barriers? Future research may in fact extend the hybrid "Central Asian" complex to the Black Sea, a water-based region that holds enormous scholarly potential yet today still awaits its Braudel.[88]

It might also be asserted that Caucasia belongs to the period and zone of late antiquity.[89] In their edited collection *Tradition and Innovation in Late Antiquity* (1989), Frank Clover and R. S. Humphreys cogently argue that late antiquity does not simply represent a single century or two of the Mediterranean experience.[90] Instead, they propose the period from around 400 to around 900 as encompassing late antiquity. It was marked not by the collapse of Rome but by its transformation into the Byzantine empire (with its fulcrum in the eastern Mediterranean, Greek language and culture, Christianity) and was further characterized by urban life and client states. Significantly, early Islam is portrayed as a continuation of late antiquity in the Near East; the period 600–900 witnessed the laying of the foundations of Islam, whereas after 900 "a distinct and integrated Islamic culture began to develop, one which would generate its principal problems and solutions from within itself."[91] As we have seen, Fowden similarly depicts late antiquity as extending from the peak of the Roman empire in the second century A.D. to the onset of the "decline" of the Islamic "world empire" in the ninth century. For him, the period is best characterized by empires promoting various forms of monotheism, the attempt to establish "world empires" (only the Arabs were successful), and the appearance of several commonwealths as a direct consequence of monotheism. One criticism of these important (re-)formulations of late antiquity is the absence of the pre-Islamic Iranian commonwealths.

All this begs an important question: how much elapsed time is necessary for a toponym/ethnonym to qualify as a label for a world region (assuming such designations should be used in naming world regions in the first place)? Or is temporal proximity to the present the overriding factor? The concepts of late antiquity, Iranian commonwealth, and Byzantine commonwealth are, as they are articulated here, by definition multiethnic, multicultural entities, sometimes but not necessarily dominated by a centralizing political authority. Late antiquity was not simply a period: it was also a sociocultural phenomenon, a zone of cultural interaction whose arteries were the Mediterranean, Black, and even Red Seas. Though it was sustained for at least half a millennium, it is not represented in existing world-regional models. Even more perplexing are the absences of the Iranian and Byzantine commonwealths, both of which, it could be argued, endured for more than a millennium each. Should these entities have been part of the early modern or modern eras, we can presume that they would have been conspicuously represented.[92]

No Way Out?

Tiny Caucasia has thus raised big questions about world-regional models. First, both the standard and refined paradigms reflect a rather severe temporal prejudice favoring the last several hundred years and certainly the period after 1500. Lewis and Wigen's refinements are a welcome enhancement, yet in the smoldering residue from the original system a central problem stubbornly clings to life: history and culturally constituted zones of sharing and interaction before the early modern era are often indiscernible.[93] Second, as a consequence, both models ignore several prominent premodern commonwealths, yet in some ways these may prove to be an appropriate way to engage the large-scale history of a substantial proportion of premodern Eurasia. Finally, the continued use of a single map with more or less definite boundaries obscures the sense of change over time. Though Lewis and Wigen have improved the standard model by redefining Central Asia and Ethiopia as hybrid regions, their vision falls somewhat short in this regard. The historical experiences of Caucasia demonstrate the existence of cultural reorientations, sometimes rapid and dramatic. And more than that, at a given time affiliation to one cultural zone, commonwealth, civilization, world region/system, or other classification of interactivity/cultural sharing was by no means exclusive. If boundaries must be drawn, why not allow for and indicate overlap in the map itself?[94] The Georgians and Armenians of Caucasia are a case in point: although both belonged to the Iranian commonwealth, they also became integrated into the Byzantine commonwealth and at the same time came to play a prominent role in and to be affected by the Islamic commonwealth. Within this fluid and ever-changing cosmopolitan environment—one teeming with negotiation and coexistence, confrontation and conflict—the Caucasian peoples created their own distinctive identities and cultures. Cosmopolitanism, and the myriad contacts with the Eurasian world, in so many ways define the pan-Caucasian experience. Very little of this can be discerned from either regional scheme, and in any case to privilege one of these cultural affiliations/influences at the expense of the others would be unjustified as it would yield only a slice of a considerably richer and more dynamic cross-cultural system.

Lewis and Wigen are mindful of the enigma of Caucasia: "Though home to a singularly dense patchwork of peoples and languages, the Caucasus remains effectively invisible in most schemes, having been designated not a region in its own right but a borderland between Europe, the 'Middle East,' Inner Asia, and the Russian sphere."[95] Their solution is to add the designation "Caucasia" to a particular world region, and in their refined scheme we thus encounter "Russia—Southeast Europe and the Caucasus." Caucasia has been singled out (a "borderland" redefined?), as in some manner it should be, yet its coupling to Russia and Southeastern Europe is disputable especially when a long view is taken. Although Lewis and Wigen's proposed scheme is a giant leap ahead, Caucasia should be shaded in their map, indicating its status as a distinctive subregion/crossroads. It should not, however, be included within any single world region. Similarly, Ethiopia is entitled to crossroads status. In the map of the refined model, Ethiopia has been shaded, yet it is clearly included within "Sub-Saharan Africa." It, too, should not be comprehended within any single region. Yet another similar case is "Central Asia," though owing to its sheer size (and perhaps for other reasons) Lewis and Wigen have shaded the entire region and have divided it into two zones. Surely there are yet other attractive candidates for crossroads status within Africa and Eurasia—and beyond.

This brings us back to the static mapping characterizing existing world-regional models. Although the bureaucracies of higher education, the news media, my students, and countless other constituencies may appeal for a single elegant map to divide the globe into a number of historical zones, a series of maps may more effectively illustrate historical change and transformation over time. To illustrate the need for multiple maps, one might think of a cartoon. Existing world-regional schemes with their single map essentially show us only the final frame of the cartoon, or, at least, a frame near the end. Adding a frame at the beginning is an improvement but still obscures the dynamism between start and finish. But a new assortment of complicated dilemmas emerges. How many maps? Which time periods should they represent? The ancient-medieval-modern sequence for European history poses many problems when applied globally, no matter how convenient it may be. How should the regions themselves be defined? Whether or not the multiple-map arrangement is endorsed, we must acknowledge that any map is necessarily an approximation. In the particular case of existing world-regional schemes, the single map effectively arrests the past in a manner privileging historical realities of the early modern and modern eras. If premodern eras are to be represented, as I believe they must, the integration of commonwealths into the regional scheme alongside exciting chronological and cultural reformulations of late antiquity (which is really an integrated Mediterranean world and western Asia, from the Caspian to the Straits of Gibraltar) may prove a fruitful approach. Finally, we must seek to see all peoples and cultures on their own terms and in dynamic relation to others, not exclusively as, say, peripheries or frontiers of a few privileged centers. Caucasia has long been and continues to be a preeminent Eurasian and now global crossroads, and this status makes it not only a center in its own right, but also a center of a very special kind.

NOTES

This essay is dedicated to the memory of my student Paul McMillan. Georgian is transliterated according to the Library of Congress system in which the symbol ʻ indicates the aspiration of the preceding consonant. Georgian *c* is roughly equivalent to English/Russian *ts*, and Georgian *x* to *kh* (like *ch* in loch).

1. Marshall G. S. Hodgson, *The Venture of Islam: Conscience and History in a World Civilization* (Chicago: University of Chicago Press, 1973), 1: 33.

2. These two peoples have been predominantly Christian since the fifth century. Several post-Soviet scholars in the Georgian Republic have alleged longstanding and enduring links of Western Europe and Georgia/Caucasia, for example, the recent publications of Tʻedo Dundua, a specialist of antiquity: *Christianity and Mithraism: The Georgian Story* (Tʻbilisi: Meridian, 1999) and *North and South: Towards the Question of the NATO Enlargement,* underwritten by NATO and available on its web site, www.nato.int/acad/fellow/99-01/f99-01.htm; accessed January 2001. In an interview with the BBC's "Talking Point," broadcast on January 18, 2004, Georgian president-elect Mikhail Saakashvili emphasized that Georgia's historical development, the "nature" of the Georgian people, and the recent "Rose Revolution," are all indications of Georgia's longstanding inclusion in Europe. This sentiment also featured prominently in Saakashvili's inaugural address: *Sakʻartʻvelos respublika* 20 (January 26, 2004). More balanced on Georgia's historical connections with Western Europe is D. L. Vateishvili, *Gruziia i evropeiskie strany: ocherki istorii vzaimootnoshenii XIII–XIX veka,* vol. 1/1–2 (Moscow: Nauka, 2003), with English summaries, "Georgia and European Countries: Historical Essays on [Their] Relations, 13th–19th Centuries." On account of the human remains dating to 1.8 million years ago found at the Dmanisi site in southern Georgia, Western European scholars have joined their Georgian colleagues in making Caucasia the far eastern edge of Europe, thus classifying the Dmanisi remains those of the earliest *Europeans:* Ann Gibbons, "Jawing with Our Georgian Ancestors," *Science,* January 24, 1992, p. 401.

3. Caucasia as the boundary between Europe and Asia, "West" and "East," has its provenance in the Classical and Byzantine Mediterranean/Near East: Otʻar Lortʻkʻipʻanidze (Lordkipanidze), *Phasis: The River and City in Colchis,* Arrian Tchanturia, trans., *Geographica Historica,* vol. 15 (Stuttgart: Franz Steiner, 2000), pp. 23–26.

4. Compare U.S. policy toward Georgia in the early twenty-first century (note 28 below). In his ninth-century biography, the Georgian King Vaxtang I Gorgasali (reigned 447–522) is described as having the unique capacity of mediating lasting peace between Iran and Byzantium. This tradition was taken up and injected with modern political overtones by Zviad Gamsaxurdia, first president of the restored Republic of Georgia, who claimed that Georgia had been chosen by the Christian God to mediate the two spheres (elaborated in his *Sakʻartʻvelos sulieri misia,* translated into English by Arrian Tchanturia as *The Spiritual Mission of Georgia* [Tʻbilisi: Ganatʻleba, 1991]). See also Martin W. Lewis and Kären E. Wigen, *The Myth of Continents: A Critique of Metageography* (Berkeley: University of Cali-

fornia Press, 1997), p. 235, note 97, but here the tradition's medieval roots are not acknowledged.

5. In addition to this volume's introduction and chapters, see Lewis and Wigen, *Myth of Continents,* pp. 157–169; and Patrick Manning, *Navigating World History: Historians Create a Global Past* (New York: Palgrave/Macmillan, 2003), esp. chap. 8, "Area Studies," pp. 145–162.

6. In this essay "Caucasian" denotes an inhabitant of the Caucasus region and not the modern racial category first articulated by Johann Blumenbach in the nineteenth century.

7. Lewis and Wigen, *Myth of Continents,* p. ix.

8. Ibid., pp. 189–190.

9. Compare Edward Said, *Orientalism* (New York: Knopf/Vintage, 1978), p. 45: "Can one divide human reality, as indeed human reality seems to be genuinely divided, into clearly different cultures, histories, traditions, societies, even races, and survive the consequences humanly?" Said's *Orientalism* offers no viable alternative; compare Lewis and Wigen's refined scheme.

10. Lewis and Wigen, *Myth of Continents,* p. 188 (these approaches mesh well with the notion of commonwealth explored below); compare p. 14: "The various area studies complexes . . . sometimes encourage a certain insularity in scholarship, making it unnecessarily difficult for scholars to investigate processes that transcend conventional world regional boundaries."

11. Ibid., pp. 14, 19, 192–194, et passim, for the refined model as a work in progress.

12. In addition, it is worth noting that the authors have (consciously?) lessened the distance between "Western and Central Europe" and "North America" by making those two units adjacent to one another.

13. Ibid., p. 198, emphasis added, though, significantly, the italicized text appears within parentheses; compare p. 155: "The stripped-down view of civilizational realms, while truly foundational for world history, *is not the best framework for contemporary global geography. It is too focused on the past, has too little to say about large areas of the globe, and tends to overstress elite cultural features. For those seeking to understand the modern world, the most comprehensive heuristic metageographical framework is that of world macroregions*" (emphasis added). If the authors are right, then 1500 really symbolizes a revolution in human history. Consequently, one might wonder whether premodern specialists really belong in existing area-studies centers (surely we do!). While chapter 5 ends with the last quote, chapter 6 begins with the chronologically unspecific remark that "the burden of our argument to this point has been to show that received metageographical categories, from continents to civilizations, are inadequate frameworks for global human geography." See note 93 below for Lewis and Wigen's suggestion that the modern era properly begins with the Mongols.

14. Ibid., pp. 142–146.

15. See, for example, ibid., 130.

16. Compare ibid., pp. 199 and 204–205. Thus, Lewis and Wigen's refined paradigm is an improvement insofar as *early modern* period is concerned.

17. William McNeill, *The Rise of the West: A History of the Human Community* (Chicago: University of Chicago Press, 1963), pp. 414–416, and compare his "*The Rise of the West* After Twenty-Five Years," *Journal of World History* 1:1 (1990): 1–21, esp. p. 7, for a single medium-sized paragraph about Sub-Saharan Africa. See now J. R. McNeill and William H. McNeill, *The Human Web: A Bird's-Eye View of World History* (New York: W.W. Norton, 2003). For the pre-Columbian Americas, compare Jerry Bentley, *Old World Encounters: Cross-*

Cultural Contacts and Exchanges in Pre-Modern Times (Oxford: Oxford University Press, 1993), pp. 25–26.

18. Though my own chronological specialization is premodern, I would certainly not advocate a single metageographical scheme advantaging, say, late antiquity.

19. Consider Lewis and Wigen's own observation: "[T]he foregoing examples demonstrate that global human geography is not reducible to any single one-dimensional schema" (*Myth of Continents*, pp. 154, 198–199).

20. An example is the ubiquitous application of "ancient," "medieval," and "modern" (including in this chapter), terms that most appropriately describe the historical self-identity of Western Europe.

21. Indigenous Caucasian scholars are perfectly aware of this issue. For a recent attempt by a local specialist to explore Georgia as a crossroads in light of Western and Russian/Soviet literature, see Nino Ch'ikovani, "Sak'art'velo c'ivilizac'iat'a gzajvaredinze," in *Saistorio shtudiebi* (T'bilisi: Ena da kultura, 2001), 2: 160–171, with English summary, "Georgia on the Crossroad of Civilizations," pp. 170–171. For the acknowledged fuzziness of metageographical categories, including world regions, see Lewis and Wigen, *Myth of Continents*, pp. 14, 102, and 150–155.

22. Lewis and Wigen, *Myth of Continents*, pp. 179–181. "Unlike Southeast Asia, Central Asia forms a highly ambiguous world region in contemporary geographical discourse, one whose boundaries are contested by almost all parties. Like Southeast Asia, it is also ambiguous in terms of its cultural constitution. . . . [A]n overriding regional heritage never took shape in Central Asia, and the area has been deeply split for centuries between Islam and Lamaist Buddhism, with shamanism persisting until recently along its northern fringe" (p. 179).

23. Although Lewis and Wigen have not indicated Caucasia's status as a "special case" in their revised paradigm, the authors are aware of it: ibid., pp. 28, 35, 177, 203 (quoted below), and 217 (note 49).

24. On the Caucasus as a region, see ibid., p. 203, for Caucasia as an "interstitial zone" (others named are Ethiopia and Tibet). But "interstitial" would seem to make Caucasia a periphery/frontier. Caucasia was no mere periphery; it was a part of several adjacent and overlapping regions and formed a connective tissue among them. When thought about in this way, Caucasia was a Eurasian center. And now, there is the alleged presence of al-Qaeda in Pankisi Gorge in the Georgian Republic and Georgia's membership in the "Coalition of the Willing." Surprisingly few scholars have investigated the notion of Caucasia as a coherent historical unit, let alone the idea of Caucasia's place within a larger Black Sea world. Cyril Toumanoff emphasized a single "Christian Caucasian" civilization, which, significantly, excluded the various peoples of northern Caucasia and non-Christian communities. See *Studies in Christian Caucasian History* (Washington, D.C.: Georgetown University Press, 1963). See also Nina G. Garsoïan and Bernadette Martin-Hisard, "Unité et diversité de la Caucasie médiévale (IVe–XIe s.)," in *Il Caucaso: Cerniera fra Culture dal Mediterraneo alla Persia (Secoli IV–XI)*, Settimane di Studio del Centro Italiano di Studi Sull'alto Medioevo 43:1 (Spoleto: Sede del Centro, 1996), pp. 275–347.

25. The same applies to contemporary Russian observers: Susan Layton, *Russian Literature and Empire: Conquest of the Caucasus from Pushkin to Tolstoy* (Cambridge: Cambridge University Press, 1994); and Austin Jersild, *Orientalism and Empire: North Caucasus Mountain Peoples and the Georgian Frontier, 1845–1917* (Montreal: McGill-Queen's University Press, 2002).

26. *Life of the Kings*, in Robert W. Thomson trans., *Rewriting Caucasian History: The Medieval Armenian Adaptation of the Georgian Chronicles, the Original Georgian Texts and the Armenian Adaptation* (Oxford: Oxford University Press, 1996), pp. 2–84. For the Old Georgian text, see Simon Qauxch'ishvili, *K'art'lis c'xovreba* (T'bilisi: Saxelgami, 1955), 1: 3–71, reprinted as Stephen H. Rapp, Jr., general ed., and with a new introduction, *K'art'lis c'xovreba: The Georgian Royal Annals and Their Medieval Armenian Adaptation*. Vol. 1 (Delmar, N.Y.: Caravan Books, 1998).

27. Despite the claim of *The Life of the Kings*, Alexander never visited eastern Georgia. See Giorgi Leon Kavtaradze, "Caucasica II: The Georgian Chronicles and the *Raison d'ètre* of the Iberian Kingdom," *Orbis Terrarum* 2 (2000): 187–195.

28. Mzia Andronikashvili, *Narkvevebi iranul-k'art'uli enobrivi urt'iert'obidan* (T'bilisi: T'bilisis universitetis gamomc'embloba, 1966), 1:496–499, and English summary, "Studies in Iranian-Georgian Linguistic Contacts, I," pp. 547–571. Caucasians later applied a Christianized version of *farnah* to their saints. For the Armenian *p'ark'*, see Nina G. Garsoïan in her translation of *The Epic Histories Attributed to P'awstos Buzand (Buzandaran Patmut'iwnk')* (Cambridge, Mass.: Harvard University Press, 1989), p. 552.

29. For example, Saurmag, Mirvan, Arshak, Amazasp, Rev, Vach'e, and Bakur. See also Rapp, "Imagining History at the Crossroads: Persia, Byzantium, and the Architects of the Written Georgian Past." 2 vols. Ph.D. dissertation, University of Michigan, 1997, pp. 164–165.

30. André Maricq, ed., "Res Gestae Divi Saporis," in *Classica et Orientalia* (Paris: Librarie orientalists, 1965), pp. 47–49, 78.

31. Andronikashvili, *Narkvevebi;* and Joct Gippert, *Iranica Armeno-Iberica: Studien zu den iranischen Lehnwörten im Armenischen und Georgischen*, Österreichische Akademie der Wissenschaften, Philosophisch-Historische Klasse, Sitzungsberichte, vol. 606/1–2 (Wien: Verlag der Österreichischen Akademie der Wissenschaften, 1993).

32. James Russell, *Zoroastrianism in Armenia* (Cambridge, Mass.: Harvard University Press, 1987), and "Pre-Christian Armenian Religion," in *Aufsteig und Niedergang der römischen Welt [ANRW]* (Berlin: W. de Gruyter, 1990), 18:2679–2692; Michel van Esbroeck, "La religion géorgienne pré-chrétienne," in *ANRW* (Berlin: W. de Gruyter, 1990), 18: 2694–2725; Rapp, "Imagining History at the Crossroads," pp. 287–308; and Kaka Kimshiashvili and Goderzi Narimanishvili, "A Group of Iberian Fire Temples (4th Cent. B.C.–2nd Cent. A.D.)," *Archaeologische Mitteilungen aus Iran* 28 (1995–1996): 309–318.

33. The origin of the Georgian script has aroused considerable debate. For its contextualization within the development of other scripts developed by Christians, see Thomas Gamkrelidze (T'amaz Gamqrelidze), *Alphabetic Writing and the Old Georgian Script: A Typology and Provenience of Alphabetic Writing Systems* (Delmar, N.Y.: Caravan Books, 1994), translated from the 1989 Georgian edition.

34. *The Life of the Kings*, Thomson trans., p. 35.

35. See, for example, Nina G. Garsoïan, *Armenia between Byzantium and the Sasanians* (London: Variorum, 1985) and *Church and Culture in Early Medieval Armenia* (Aldershot: Variorum, 1999); and Russell, *Zoroastrianism in Armenia*, "Some Iranian Images of Kingship in the Armenian Artaxiad Epic," *Revue des études arméniennes* n.s. (1986–1987): 253–270, and "The Scepter of Tiridates," *Le Muséon* 114:1–2 (2001): 187–215. See also Nina G. Garsoïan and Jean-Pierre Mahé, *Des Parthes au Califat: Quatre leçons sur la formation de l'identité arménienne,* Travaux et mémoires d'histoire et civilization de Byzance. Vol. 10 (Paris: Centre de recherche, 1997), p. 36. See note 32, *supra.*

37. See now *Encyclopedia Iranica,* Ehsan Yarshater, ed., vol. 10/5 (New York: Biblioteca Persica, 2001), pp. 460–497.

38. See, for example, M. Rostovtzeff, *Iranians and Greeks in South Russia* (New York: Russell and Russell, [1922] 1969).

39. C. Scott Littleton and Linda Malcor, *From Scythia to Camelot: A Radical Reassessment of the Legends of King Arthur, the Knights of the Round Table, and the Holy Grail,* rev. ed. (New York: Garland, 2000).

40. See John Colarusso, *Nart Sagas from the Caucasus: Myths and Legends from the Circassians, Abazas, Abkhaz, and Ubykhs* (Princeton, N.J.: Princeton University Press, 2002).

41. Peter Golden has identified four periods of relations between the sedentary and nomadic peoples of Caucasia: (1) Hunno-Khazar, fourth–ninth century; (2) Seljuq-Qipchaq, the middle of the eleventh–thirteenth century (this period includes the Turkicization of Azerbaijan); (3) Mongol, thirteenth–fourteenth century; and (4) Ottoman-Safavid, middle of the fifteenth–early sixteenth century. See Golden, "Cumanica I: The Qipchaqs in Georgia," *Archivum Eurasiae Medii Aevi* 4 (1984): 45–87, esp. p. 46 for this periodization; "The Turkic Peoples and Caucasia," in Ronald G. Suny, ed., *Transcaucasia, Nationalism, and Social Change: Essays in the History of Armenia, Azerbaijan, and Georgia,* rev. ed. (Ann Arbor: University of Michigan Press, 1996), pp. 45–67; and *An Introduction to the History of the Turkic Peoples: Ethnogenesis and State-Formation in Medieval and Early Modern Eurasia and the Middle East* (Wiesbaden: Otto Harrassowitz, 1992). These periods also connect Caucasia to the so-called Turko-Iranian ecumene, for which see below.

42. Indeed, to have a single map for a single pre-1500 period and another for 1500 and after would in its own way privilege the modern era by equating its 500 years with the numerous millennia that preceded it! Compare the "East"/"West" dichotomy.

43. See, for example, Otʿar Lortʿkʿipʿanidze (Lordkipanidze), "Vani: An Ancient City of Colchis," *Greek, Roman, and Byzantine Studies* (summer 1991): 151–195. Roman and early Byzantine influences were mostly confined to fleet stations along the shore of the Black Sea. For these stations and a reinterpretation of Irano-Roman conflicts in the Near East to the sixth century A.D., see Benjamin Isaac, *The Limits of Empire: The Roman Army in the East,* rev. ed. (Oxford: Clarendon Press, 1992), pp. 42–50 and 229–235, for Caucasia.

44. Nina G. Garsoïan, "The Emergence of Armenia," in Richard G. Hovannisian, ed., *The Armenian People from Ancient to Modern Times* (New York: St. Martin's, 1997), 1:57.

45. For the Hellenistic period, see the overview by Stanley M. Burstein, *The Hellenistic Period in World History: Essays on Global and Comparative History* (Washington, D.C.: American Historical Association, 1996).

46. David Braund, *Georgia in Antiquity: A History of Colchis and Transcaucasian Iberia, 550 B.C.–A.D. 562* (Oxford: Oxford University Press, 1994). To be fair, Braund does give some attention to Georgia's association with Iran—for example, chaps. 4 and 8—but the overall picture is unbalanced in favor of the classical Mediterranean.

47. *The Life of the Kings,* Thomson trans., p. 23. It is extremely curious that Iranian is not included in this list. By Syrian, *asuruli* (literally "Assyrian"), the medieval author might actually intend Aramaic, the written language of the Iranian court. Significantly, several Aramaic inscriptions have been found in eastern Georgia, and some reflect a local dialect that scholars call Armazic after the ancient Georgian capital city Armazi-Mcʿxetʿa. Armazi is also the name of one of the ancient Georgian deities, for which see further. For the use of Aramaic/Armazic in Caucasia, see the essays by Konstantine Ceretʿeli (Tsereteli) collected

in his *Semitologiuri da k'art'velologiuri shtudiebi* = *Semitological and Kartvelological Studies* (T'bilisi: Logosi, 2001).

48. Anatolia corresponds to Asia Minor.

49. Giorgi Melik'ishvili, *K istorii drevnei Gruzii* (T'bilisi: Izdatel'stvo Akademii Nauk Gruzinskoi SSR, 1959).

50. Michael Tsereteli, "The Asianic (Asia Minor) Elements in National Georgian Paganism," *Georgica* 1:1 (October 1935): 28–66.

51. Michael Tarchnishvili, "Le Dieu Lune Armazi," *Bedi Kartlisa* 11–12 (1961): 36–40.

52. Ivane Javaxishvili, (Dzhavakhishvili, Dzhavakhov), "St. George the Moon-God," M. Tseretheli trans. *Quest* 3:3 (April 1912): 528–545. For the identification of Mithras as the forerunner of St. George, see G. Tsetskhladze, "The Cult of Mithras in Ancient Colchis," *Revue de l'Histoire des Religions* 109:2 (1992): 115–124.

53. For syncretism in the context of cross-cultural encounters, see Bentley, *Old World Encounters*, pp. 15–19 *et seq.*

54. H. A. Manandian, *The Trade and Cities of Armenia in Relation to Ancient World Trade*, Nina G. Garsoïan, trans. (Lisbon: Livraria Bertrand, 1965). For a later period, see Vaxtang Goiladze, *Abreshumis didi savachro gza da sak'art'velo* (T'bilisi: n.p., 1997).

55. Recently, Keith Hitchins has repeated a myth well entrenched in scholarship: "By making Christianity the state religion, [the eastern Georgian kings and elite] erected what became an *insurmountable barrier* to Persian influence in the region" (emphasis added), "Georgia" in *Encyclopedia Iranica*, p. 464. Notwithstanding, Iranian-like cultural, social, and political forms persisted for several centuries and that cultural exchanges with the Iranians also continued. Iranian-like descriptions and contexts replete in the oldest Georgian historical literature, produced around the year 800, are a vivid testimony to this enduring connection. See Stephen H. Rapp, "Imagining History at the Crossroads" and "From *Bumberazi* to *Basileus*: Writing Cultural Synthesis and Dynastic Change in Medieval Georgia (K'art'li)," in Antony Eastmond, ed., *Eastern Approaches to Byzantium* (Aldershot: Ashgate/Variorum, 2001), pp. 101–116, and *Studies in Medieval Georgian Historiography: Early Texts and Eurasian Contexts*, Corpus Scriptorum Christianorum Orientalium, vol. 601, subsidia, vol. 113 (Louvain: Peeters, 2003). Even from the point of view of contemporary Georgia, Hitchins's comment is not entirely valid. From the late fifth century, however, we have increasing indications (especially in Georgian-language hagiographical literature) that some local clerics actively sought to obliterate obvious connections with Iran.

56. Even in the Christian period the term *goliat'i*, "goliath," was used as a heroic epithet despite the obvious relationship to the biblical Goliath, the ultimate giant. It is worth noting that Muslims regarded Goliath as a hero. The same kind of imagery was also prevalent in neighboring Armenia and northern Caucasia.

57. Followers of the definition of Christ (relating to his humanity and divinity and their interrelationship) hammered out at Chalcedon self-identified as "Orthodox," a term commonly and oftentimes uncritically employed in scholarly literature. The split of the Monophysites/anti-Chalcedonians/non-Chalcedonians and Chalcedonians/Orthodox constitutes the major division with Eastern Christendom, the received labels reflecting the Orthodox view. For the schism involving the Armenians and Byzantines, see the essential study by Nina G. Garsoïan, *L'Église arménienne et le grand schisme d'Orient*, Corpus Scriptorum Christianorum Orientalium, vol. 574, subsidia, vol. 100 (Louvain: Peeters, 1999).

58. Byzantine influence upon Armenians of all confessions continued. For the tenth and eleventh centuries, and the idea of an "Armeno-Byzantine contact zone," see V. A. Arutiunova-Fidanian, *Armiano-vizantiiskaia kontaktnaia zona (X–XI vv.): rezul'taty vzaimodeistviia kul'tur* (Moscow: Nauka, 1994), with English summary, pp. 233–235.

59. Thus, the medieval Ethiopian *Kebrä Nägäst*—*The Glory of the Kings*—prominently mentions the Armenian saint Gregory "the Illuminator" (chaps. 2, 113, and 116). See E. A. W. Budge, trans., *The Queen of Sheba and Her Only Son Menyelek (I)* (London: Oxford University Press, 1932).

60. Korneli Kekelidze, *Liturgicheskie gruzinskie pamiatniki v otechestvennykh knigokhranilishchakh* (Tiflis: n.p., 1908).

61. Levan Menabde, *Centres of Ancient Georgian Culture*, D. Skvirski, trans. (T'bilisi: Ganat'leba, 1968). Compare the production of the first printed Georgian books by the Propaganda Fide in Rome in 1629. A printing press was set up in T'bilisi in 1708–1709 with the assistance of Anthim "the Georgian," the archbishop of Wallachia (in Romania) who himself was of Georgian ancestry. Despite this local press, Lang has pointed out that, by the mid-eighteenth century, three of the four centers of Georgian book production were outside Georgia (that is, Rome, Moscow, and St. Petersburg). See *The Last Years of the Georgian Monarchy, 1658–1832* (New York: Columbia University Press, 1957), p. 135. The case of the Armenians is even more instructive. For an overview of Armenian diaspora communities, see Philip D. Curtin, *Cross-Cultural Trade in World History* (Cambridge: Cambridge University Press, 1984), chap. 9, "Overland Trade of the Seventeenth Century: Armenian Carriers between Europe and East Asia," pp. 179–206. For Armenians in the Byzantine commonwealth, see Nina G. Garsoïan, "The Problem of Armenian Integration into the Byzantine Empire," in Hélène Ahrweiler and Angeliki E. Laiou, eds., *Studies on the Internal Diaspora of the Byzantine Empire* (Washington, D.C.: Dumbarton Oaks, 1998), pp. 53–124.

62. Antony Eastmond, *Royal Imagery in Medieval Georgia* (University Park: Pennsylvania State University Press, 1998). A representative example of a Byzantine-flavored Bagratid royal biography is the anonymous twelfth-century *Life of King of Kings Davit' II (C'xorebay mep'et'-mep'isa davit'isi)*, trans. by Thomson in *Rewriting Caucasian History*, pp. 309–353.

63. The continued influence of and contact with lands to the south, especially the Middle East, is plainly visible on the coinage of the Georgian Bagratids. From the twelfth century to the Mongol conquest, coins issued in the name of the Bagratids combine Christian elements with Georgian inscriptions on one side (generally designated the obverse by numismatists) and Islamic iconoclasm with Arabic inscriptions on the other (reverse). For a brief survey in English, see Stephen H. Rapp, "The Coinage of T'amar, Sovereign of Georgia in Caucasia," *Le Muséon* 106:3–4 (1993): 309–330. A more dramatic example of the continued influence and admiration for Iranians, Arabs, and Islam in Bagratid times is the Georgian national epic by Shot'a Rust'aveli, apparently a thirteenth-century figure. See Venera Urushadze, trans., *The Knight in the Panther's Skin* (T'bilisi: Sabchot'a Sak'art'velo, 1986).

64. Lewis and Wigen are aware of this issue. See *Myth of Continents*, pp. 150–154, for a discussion of Richard White's "middle ground," diasporas, cultural archipelagos, and cultural matrices.

65. Ilia Tabaghua, *Sak'art'velos-sap'ranget'is urt'iert'oba (XVIII saukunis pirveli meot'xedi)* (T'bilisi: Mec'niereba, 1972), with extensive French summary, "Les relations georgiano-françaises," pp. 374–396; and Lang, *Last Years of the Georgian Monarchy*. Orbeliani

kept a diary of his journey, but it has not yet been translated into a Western European language. Orbeliani was a Catholic convert.

66. George Bournoutian, "Eastern Armenian from the Seventeenth Century to the Russian Annexation," in Hovannisian, ed., *The Armenian People from Ancient to Modern Times*, 2:82–84.

67. W. E. D. Allen, ed., and Anthony Mango, trans., *Russian Embassies to the Georgian Kings, 1589–1605*, 2 vols. (London: Hakluyt Society/Cambridge University Press, 1970).

68. The year 1801 witnessed the annexation of the eastern Georgian kingdom of K'art'li-Kaxet'i; other Georgian and Caucasian regions followed in the ensuing decades. For the incorporation of the western Georgian lands and their identification as a "borderland zone of Caucasia" (that is, a borderland of a borderland), see Kenneth Church, "From Dynastic Principality to Imperial District: The Incorporation of Guria into the Russian Empire to 1856," Ph.D. dissertation, University of Michigan, 2001, esp. chap. 2, which draws upon Owen Lattimore, Peter Sahlins, and Cyril Toumanoff.

69. Ronald G. Suny, *The Making of the Georgian Nation*, rev. ed. (Bloomington: Indiana University Press, 1994). See also Suny, *Transcaucasia, Nationalism, and Social Change*.

70. Large-scale *connections* are, after all, one of the most prominent ways of defining the academic study of world history. See Manning, *Navigating World History;* and Jerry H. Bentley, "The New World History," in Lloyd Kramer and Sarah Maza, eds., *A Companion to Western Historical Thought* (Oxford: Blackwell, 2002), pp. 393–416. Also consider Lewis and Wigen's insightful observation: "The challenge from the historical literature, in short, is to synthesize the best of two contrasting traditions: one that recognizes the integrity and durability of cultural macroregions, and another that has developed a vocabulary for analyzing the interconnections between them" (*Myth of Continents*, p. 141).

71. Not to be confused with the "Commonwealth of Independent States."

72. Dimitri Obolensky, *The Byzantine Commonwealth: Eastern Europe, 500–1453* (New York: Praeger, 1971), p. 1.

73. Ibid., pp. 2–3.

74. Ibid., p. 2.

75. Though his focus is the eastern Mediterranean and the Near East, Fowden makes substantial reference to developments in Ethiopia, Nubia, and India.

76. Beyond the realm of his discussion is yet another possible commonwealth, that of Western/Latin Christendom. See Garth Fowden, *Empire to Commonwealth: Consequences of Monotheism in Late Antiquity* (Princeton, N.J.: Princeton University Press, 1993), pp. 8, 169.

77. Ibid., p. 163.

78. Ibid., p. 169.

79. A synthesis of Fowden's thesis and David Wilkinson's idea of "Central Civilization," which commenced with the merger of ancient Mesopotamian and Egyptian civilization around 1500 B.C., might yield positive results. See Wilkinson, "Central Civilization," in Stephen K. Sanderson, ed., *Civilizations and World Systems: Studying World-Historical Change* (Walnut Creek, Calif.: AltaMira Press, 1995), pp. 46–74. According to Wilkinson, "Central Civilization" was born in the Near East/Northeastern Africa and by the nineteenth century engulfed *all* the world's civilizations, including those he terms "Aegean" (engulfed by circa 560 B.C.) and "Indic" (by circa 1000 A.D.). In some respects, this might seem to be a culturally defined "world system" *à la* Immanuel Wallerstein. For the centrality of the Near East, see also Barry K. Gills, "Capital and Power in the Processes of World History," in Sanderson, *Civilizations and World Systems*, pp. 136–162, esp. p. 142, for his "Three Corri-

dors," that is, key trading zones in and around the Red Sea, Syria—Mesopotamia, and northern Caucasia.

80. Fowden characterizes Achaemenid Iran as a "world empire" and Sasanid Iran as an "empire." Central to these identifications is the absence of an inflexible religious monotheism.

81. Economic links also characterized the idea of commonwealth although these have yet to be satisfactorily studied on a commonwealth-wide and/or regional level.

82. From the perspective of the refined scheme, the Byzantine commonwealth may be regarded as a pivotal Afro-Eurasian crossroads. By the same token, Lewis and Wigen's model discredits the "Western Civilization" model by dividing Western Europe, the eastern Mediterranean, and Northern Africa/Near East into separate zones.

83. The point of departure for Bentley's *Old World Encounters* is the "ancient Silk Roads." As a consequence, the book downplays transregional interplay associated with Achaemenid Iran and the empire of Alexander and the subsequent Hellenistic kingdoms. Bentley's otherwise strong discussion of the Silk Roads, which he carries down to circa 1000 A.D., does not give the Byzantine commonwealth its due. In the index, Byzantium is cited once; the same holds true for Sasanid Iran. Yet one of the strengths of a recent textbook cowritten by Bentley is its substantial consideration of pre-Islamic Iran and the Byzantine commonwealth. See Bentley and Herbert Ziegler, *Traditions and Encounters: A Global Perspective on the Past*, 2nd ed., vol. 1 (Boston: McGraw-Hill, 2003).

84. See Richard N. Frye, *The Heritage of Persia* (Cleveland: World, 1963); and Lewis and Wigen, *Myth of Continents:* "At various times, the sway of Persian civilization has extended well to the east and north of its Iranian homeland" (p. 149). For the linkage of Iranian and Turkish cultures, see Robert Canfield ed., *Turko-Persia in Historical Perspective* (Cambridge: Cambridge University Press, 1991). See also V. V. Bartol'd, "Kavkaz, Turkestan, Volga," *Izvestiia kavkazskogo istoriko-arkheologicheskogo Instituta* 6 (Tiflis: n.p., 1926), pp. 1–9; and Richard C. Foltz, *Spirituality in the Land of the Noble: How Iran Shaped the World's Religions* (Oxford: Oneworld, 2004).

85. For a definition of this zone, see Fowden, *Empire to Commonwealth*, esp. pp. 160–168.

86. Some Georgian peoples are Muslim, or at least are part of the Islamic tradition. Debates have erupted in the Georgian media as to whether one must be Christian in order to be "purely" Georgian. For this and other aspects of the high degree of language-consciousness in Georgia, see Vivien Law, "Language Myths and the Discourse of Nation-Building in Georgia," in Graham Smith et al., eds., *Nation-Building in the Post-Soviet Borderlands: The Politics of National Identities* (Cambridge: Cambridge University Press, 1998), pp. 167–196.

87. Ina Baghdiantz McCabe, *The Shah's Silk for Europe's Silver: The Eurasian Trade of the Julfa Armenians in Safavid Iran and India (1530–1750)*, University of Pennsylvania Armenian Texts and Studies, vol. 15 (Atlanta: Scholars Press, 1999). The author notes, "It is difficult to speak of the Armenians as peddlers once one realizes that they were the bankers to the Safavids and had brought their organization with them. They provided enough cash to sustain the refors of 'Abbās I and Safī. . . . This cash paid for an army independent from the feudal tribes, the *ghulāmān*, all of them Caucasian converts commanded by Christian converts."

88. Caucasia, with the noteworthy exception of the Muslim Azeris (a Turkic people), is usually omitted from scholarly definitions of Central/Inner Asia. Compare David Chris-

tian, who usually—but not always—excludes Caucasia from "Inner Eurasia." See *A History of Russia, Central Asia, and Mongolia* (Oxford: Blackwell, 1998), 1:xv–xvi (and map 0.1, where Georgia is labeled and Caucasia is not!), pp. 3, 26 (for early human remains found in Georgia, the "southern borderlands" of Inner Eurasia), pp. 30, 80, 100, 123, *et seq.* Compare Lewis and Wigen, *Myth of Continents*, pp. 279–282. In numerous respects Caucasia belonged to the "Turko-Persian ecumene" as defined by Robert Canfield: "Introduction: The Turko-Persian Tradition," in *Turko-Persia in Historical Perspective* (Cambridge: Cambridge University Press, 1991), pp. 1–34. Existing scholarship on the Black Sea world tends to emphasize ancient Greek colonialism (e.g., the various works by Goch'a Tsetskhladze) and now the region's geopolitical importance, especially in terms of petroleum production and transport. For a popular account, see Neal Ascherson, *Black Sea* (New York: Hill and Wang, 1995).

89. The rehabilitation of late antiquity is usually attributed to Peter Brown. In his *The World of Late Antiquity A.D. 150–750* (London: Thames and Hudson, 1971), Brown emphasizes the Mediterranean world (later Roman Empire/Byzantium and Catholic Western Europe) and, to a much lesser extent, the early Islamic world. Within this purview, he gives special importance to the eastern Mediterranean and Mesopotamia. At best, Brown makes Caucasia a periphery of this world. As in so many other works dedicated to this period, this book restricts its engagement of pre-Islamic Iran to its rivalry with the later Roman and then Byzantine empires.

90. In Lewis and Wigen's refined scheme, the Mediterranean world is divided between three zones. Likewise, the Indian Ocean world is divided into five sectors. Compare the single unit comprising Micronesia and Polynesia.

91. Frank Clover and R. S. Humphreys, *Tradition and Innovation in Late Antiquity* (Madison: University of Wisconsin Press, 1989), p. 15. Compare the definition of late antiquity as encompassing the second to the ninth centuries by Fowden, *Empire to Commonwealth*, p. 3, and circa 150–ca. 750 by Brown, *World of Late Antiquity*.

92. Yet another transregional zone incorporating Caucasia is the "Black Sea world," though I would argue that the Black Sea is the fulcrum of an enormous premodern axis of cross-cultural interplay stretching from the Mediterranean to the Caspian (that is, central Eurasia) and to the Red Sea.

93. This is especially odd in light of Lewis and Wigen's contention (*Myth of Continents*, p. 267, note 66) that the beginning of the modern period should begin with the integration of Eurasia by the Mongols. There is merit in this position, yet it is not obviously represented in the authors' revised model.

94. For Lewis and Wigen's criticism of "a jigsaw puzzle view of the world," see *Myth of Continents*, p. 11.

95. Ibid., p. 203.

ELEVEN

Regimes of World Order
Global Integration and the Production of Difference in Twentieth-Century World History

Charles Bright and Michael Geyer

The end of the cold war has exposed the poverty of Western world historical imaginings. Two broad interpretive paradigms are available. One hails the collapse of communism as removing the last remaining barriers to the universalization of Western liberal values. As though the ideological division of the rival blocs had held the world in thrall, the failure of the second-world alternative now guarantees that democracy, individualism, and the free market will at last fulfill their promise and we will arrive at the long-heralded, oft-deferred destination of world history— or, quite literally, the end of history.[1] A second view, partly in rebuttal to this triumphalism, sees the world falling apart into contentious civilizations locked in new forms of cultural warfare.[2] The linchpin of world order, forged in cold war antagonism and the threat of nuclear annihilation, has slipped its socket and forces held in check by the period of Western hegemony now surge to the surface, exploding the patina of order and cutting across the narrative lines that, only a few decades ago, seemed to promise a "world revolution of westernization."[3] One view foresees a rather miraculous coming together of the world, while the other foresees a world of political terrorism and social disarray.

Both perspectives on the present fall comfortably within the well-established narrative conventions for telling twentieth-century history. They share a central assumption—that the past century and a half has been an era of Western dominance, during which the world and its many histories have become increasingly centered on the West, in whose narratives are to be found the secrets of the whole and the destination of world history itself. The future is either more of the same, a fulfillment of long-held promise in which liberal democracy and economic integration finally extend to the entire globe, or the opposite of what has been anticipated in the century of

Western dominance, as the putative Westernization of the world is interrupted by a proliferating renewal of difference. Either way, world history, written as the universalization of Western possibilities or as their frustration in breakdown and turmoil, has no place to go. The present is a mere coda or aftermath.

Yet, a world history of our time should amount to something more than a postscript or some terrifying rupture and new beginning. To make the present part of an ongoing history, not its aftermath or leftover, requires that we capture historically the vertiginous opposition of deepening integration and proliferating difference that together, as dialectically interconnected forces, have shaped the history of globalization and comprise the current global condition.[4] This is a history of neither the fulfillment of Western destinies nor the wreckage left behind by a Western recessional so much as the continuing elaboration of the interlinkage of the world set in motion during the era of Western ascendancy in world history. Here the danger of seeing global integration as merely an elaboration of themes of Westernization is matched by the inverse danger of treating assertions of difference as traditional, perverse, or revivalist constructions of ineluctable cultural differences, standing in the face of change or resisting the inevitable. Both miss the particularity of the present condition and misread the historically specific dynamics that created it.

The problem of a disconnected present, dangling at the end of history, arises in large part from the narrative conventions commonly used in writing the history of Western ascendancy over the past century and a half. The familiar sequence, proceeding from a "pax Britannica" to a "pax Americana," across a thirty-year interruption of world war and depression, moves us from a state-centered system of colonialism, promoting primary production and trade, organized around British (sea) power and the rules of the gold standard before 1914, to a corporate-based rationalization of world production and markets based on American (air/lift) power and investment capital after 1945. Whether this is treated as progress and improvement or simply as a passing of the torch of world leadership from one Western (Anglo-Saxon) power to another, the narrative effect of these serial movements is to reinforce the reigning themes of Western world history—the rise and fall of power systems, the recurrent fratricidal conflict among the great powers at the center, and the ever-widening, globalizing impact of the West upon the rest. Almost inevitably, such histories, whether they stress economic imperatives or geopolitical rivalries, focus on the bourgeoning power of Europe and North America: industrial production, organizational technique, communication capabilities, and military weaponry. The organization of colonial rule or the production and defense of the "free world" are seen as expressions of that propulsive power, pushing outward into and upon the world to subordinate and organize others in hegemonic systems of order. And, although there are many ways to conceptualize hegemony, a key theme of recent debates is to emphasize that hegemonic "power creates a stable international economic order and that the hegemon's decline leads to instability."[5] This again suggests the way dominant power, thrusting outward, settles upon others and imposes order. A narrative of globalization as the elaboration of, and subordination to, Western power follows all too easily.[6]

Efforts to destabilize this centered gaze began with studies in the colonial field that stressed the agency (and complicity) of the "periphery" in precipitating power extensions from the "center," and they have lately been expanded, as with chapters in this volume, in studies of globalization and world history that emphasize "global flows" and reciprocal interactivity.[7] The early modern period is one of the current "hot spots" in a new global history that explores networks of exchange, the movement of goods and ideas, and the flows of peoples, often over great distances and in broad diasporas. Work in the period of "proto-globalization" has illuminated the deep patterns of interconnectivity through which localities and elites around the world cultivated cosmopolitan tastes for luxuries and, especially, drugs (sugar, coffee, tea, chocolate, tobacco, and opium) and consumed a wider world through complex mediations and serial relays across space and over great distances.[8] This literature—like much writing on contemporary globalization—tends to presume the (relative) openness of the world and to become preoccupied with the (relative) ease and multidirectional complexity of flows moving back and forth along various "scapes" through transactions, exchanges, and markets.[9] It is perhaps less seriously concerned with the military, economic, ideational, and cultural forces that structure these global flows and create specific configurations that, if highly unstable, nevertheless delimit the range of movement and organize the actors. We certainly applaud the focus on global flows for largely displacing the central concern with economic or geopolitical propulsion and opening a deeper and more complex appreciation of the continuing interactions between metropole and periphery in an interconnected world far back in time. But we would add that design matters here: it is necessary to analyze the structured networks and webs through which interconnections are made and maintained—as well as contested and renegotiated—if we are going to attempt (dare we say it?) to narrate the directions of development that these interactions have taken over time. For it is precisely the patterning and structuring of these interactions that can give definition to a history of globalization as something other than a top-down or outward-thrusting exercise in superior power.

In this chapter we propose to study the construction of hegemony in the era of Western ascendancy, but we will treat hegemony less as a top-down project of command and obedience than as an interactive process that is made and remade by enlisting "opinion" and cultivating consent.[10] In this conception, hegemony is a practice, a complex transaction, and a continuing negotiation over the terms of domination and subordination. It is the process by which a capacity to dominate is "realized" on the ground, among real people, in place after place. Hegemony works when top-down force meets bottom-up struggles for self-assertion or renewal, and some kind of modus vivendi is achieved. It is through such fleeting and conjunctural moments of accommodation that "regimes of order" are forged. Although this term may suggest a stability, even solidity, that is unwarranted, such passages of tenuous structuring need to be understood as something distinctly more than force on the one hand and resistance on the other, and their effects need to be analyzed in terms of the continuing interplay of deepening integration and proliferating difference that characterizes the history of globalization.

Accordingly, we will proceed from two perspectives. On the one hand, we will try to grasp the key tenets of the two dominant strategies of world ordering that were deployed by Western power in the course of the long twentieth century: the British-imperial and the American-corporate regimes that congealed in the periods before World War I and after World War II. Both of these regimes of order, we would argue, expressed a new kind of power, for in mapping out rules and patterns of transnational regulation they succeeded in bending forces of local and regional self-improvement to globalizing agendas, combining resources, markets, and labor in worldwide networks and deploying cultural or ideological articulations in ways that aligned disparate efforts to purposive ends—in all, moving beyond the extension of power *over* others toward a direct and sustained organization *of* others, simultaneously and in many parts of the world. Establishing the conjunctural nature of these networks, their limits and capacities, and what was included or excluded within the resulting regimes of order are all necessary to clarify the structures that have promoted processes of a deepening global interaction in the past century.

At the same time, we will try to suggest the engagement with global ordering by those so ordered. This means examining struggles to resist encapsulation within a global compact, either by outright rejection or—what has been far more common—through efforts to make the imperial and corporate regimes more accommodating or accountable. From the point of view of understanding hegemony built on consent, it was in moments of contestation that power revealed itself—and its weaknesses—most clearly. The implicit proposition here is that in all the creative difference of "dancing with the masters" there have been discrete patterns shared across space —not as some ontological principle of resistance, but as a continuous engagement with the realities and various manifestations of prevailing power. For twentieth-century efforts to translate a capacity for global domination into sustained forms of global order implied the creation of various sorts of "social contracts" between dominant and subordinate actors that were never stable nor satisfactory and were continuously subverted or co-opted to agendas at odds with regimes of top-down control. At the same time, the capacity to dominate profoundly shaped the patterns and available modes of engagement that developed and did much to define (and delimit) the radical exit strategies of antisystems movements. Thus, the effort to realize domination "on the ground" entailed processes of contestation and compromise that made globalization far more than a centered unfolding of deepening integration and more a multilayered, multifaceted—and therefore contingent and open-ended—engagement of all with all.

IMPERIALISM AND CORPORATISM

Although we may wish to see a temporal succession, the British-imperial and American-corporate regimes of order were, in fact, markedly different in character and practice, and these distinctions may suggest ways of classifying the peculiar nature and scope of each.[11] Here we would stress a different aspect: these regimes were, in fact, coeval systems of power that emerged, together, in the last decades of the nineteenth century and were rival and competing regimes across much of the twentieth century. Seeing them as arising from the same set of circumstances and seeking to master the same conditions in the same historical period, albeit in very different ways, allows us to ground the regimes of order that expressed Western ascendancy in the context of global history.

Elsewhere we have called attention to the pivotal nature of the middle decades of the nineteenth century, especially the 1850s and 1860s.[12] In a world still consisting of disparate entities and largely autonomous power centers, a series of parallel and simultaneous, but quite unrelated, crises in the organization of power, production, and social reproduction in almost every region of the world produced generalized patterns of pervasive, endemic, and often quite deadly violence during these decades. There were, broadly speaking, some discernable patterns to the conflicts in the Americas and along the Eurasia seam, and we sought to examine these "arcs of violence" in terms of the very different kinds of social and political upheavals that flowed, on the one hand, from the devolution of the maritime empires of the Atlantic in the late eighteenth and early nineteenth centuries and, on the other, from the often surprisingly successful efforts of the great land-based empires of Eurasia to fend off internal crisis and renew their viability through projects of self-improvement and renewal. But patterns and comparisons aside, these were, in most respects, distinct and unrelated crises of regional power and stability that reflected autonomous trajectories of development and generated internal modes of coping. There was no single cause or prime mover at work, nor should we look for a neat synchronization in the timing of these crises, because they arose and developed from indigenous causes and followed their own, separate chronologies.

What made these midcentury regional crises a watershed in world history was that, in every case, they were played out in the context of deeper, more competitive interactions with other regions, driven largely (but not exclusively) by the ability of Europeans (mainly on the spot) to exploit crisis locally. This denser, more interactive plane of response meant that, in every case, solutions to regional crisis came to involve not simply efforts at restoration or conservation, but also strategies of self-improvement and self-renewal. Europeans were often actively involved in these efforts, but everyone was in motion, running as fast as they could and engaging (to adapt the Chinese phrase) the ways of the foreigner in order to go on being themselves. As Asians and Africans moved to defend autonomy, Europeans found in these essays of self-improvement the pathways and allies for further and deeper interventions. This was profoundly disruptive, of course, as Europeans picked up and amplified regional and local processes of self-mobilization, permeating and transforming them in the process. But projections of Western power were also locally articulated in strategies of self-improvement and self-mobilization and quickly absorbed into the very fabric of regional affairs, setting off ever-wider ramifications of change, much of it beyond the view, let alone the control, of Europeans. Whatever the (often unintended) effects, it is important to observe that the focus of non-Europeans was less on revamping the terms of their collaboration with European interlopers than on sustaining their own capacity to produce autonomous histories.[13]

This argument about the nature and outcomes of the midcentury crisis leaves aside the question of European motives only if we assume that the Europeans were exempt from the general global condition. But there was no exceptional state of tranquility in Europe (or in North America for that matter). The post-Napoleonic concert unraveled in the 1850s as the collision of the Russian and Ottoman Empires and the defeat of Russia in the Crimean War sparked a regime crisis in the empire and forced the Russians to abandon the role of guarantor (still critical in 1848) for conservative regimes in Central Europe. This set loose new nation-building forces across the region, but especially in Italy and Germany, and, with the failure of the Hapsburgs to contain them or the French to deflect and control them, this nationalism produced a radical realignment of the balance of power and the appearance in the center of Europe of a powerful new economic and military state that would continuously destabilize European geopolitics over the next sixty years. Moreover, the mobilization of German productive power, coupled with the emergence of a (re)United States—itself forged in the civil warfare of a midcentury regional crisis over slavery—produced a trans-Atlantic acceleration of production and a commensurate tightening of market competition, the first effects of which—a global price depression, beginning in the 1870s—intensified a general scramble for markets and quests for cost-cutting measures.[14] These changes in the European and trans-Atlantic regions—perhaps especially in the way these were registered in domestic politics—profoundly conditioned the way Europeans responded to changes generated by regional crisis elsewhere.[15] For, unlike other regional centers around the world, Europeans were uniquely positioned—and the continuing instability of continental politics and the intensification of commercial rivalry lent urgency to the instinct—to resolve its regional crisis through external projections of power.

These developments struck the British and French most directly, and not only because they were already the most prominent powers in non-European settings, poised to pursue externalizing solutions. Both were also powers on the defensive and in retreat before new regional forces. The failure of the French, under Louis Napoleon, to exploit the collapse of the European balance, as well as their defeat at the hands of the Germans in 1871, not only created an open sore at the center of Europe that oozed diplomatic and military tension, but also prompted others, including especially the Germans, to encourage French colonial adventures. If for some the colonial empire was a welcome escape from humiliations in Europe, for others it became an overseas base and essential resource that sustained the French claim to great power status and the dream of *revanche* in Europe. As for Great Britain, it has long been clear that the arrival of new, rapidly industrializing powers, especially Germany and the United States, brought an end to the mid-Victorian confidence in British primacy. The subsequent scramble for territories overseas was anything but a triumphal procession, constituting, instead, a series of fallback moves, in which the British looked increasingly to a secondary tier of developing nations overseas to absorb the goods they could no longer sell in continental European and American markets because of rising tariffs.[16] The dramatic shift in the composition of British trade with Germany (in which an exchange of industrial goods for primary produce was reversed in the two decades after 1875) was mirrored by the growing British reliance on Latin American, Dominion, and Indian markets. The challenge of the industrial newcomers in the context of a general price depression and profit squeeze drove the British to defend and consolidate global advantages and to look upon imperial preserves as a crucial asset for the future.

If, during the 1880s, this scramble to protect markets and strategic positions was done on the cheap (using charter companies and proclamations of protectorates) and amid a political rhetoric bemoaning imperial adventures, by the 1890s, a new political generation had begun to turn defensive and compensatory moves into a popular and more geopolitically modernist vision of empire as underwriting great power status in the European balance.[17] Indeed, for Rosebery, Milner, and Chamberlain, no less than for Faure and Delcasse, colonial possessions were no longer simply extensions of European power, nor certainly the fortuitous or unintended consequence of local crises on the periphery; they had become elements in a long-term plan "to look . . . to the future of the race," as one leading imperialist put it, "to consider not what we want now, but what we shall want in the future."[18] Colonies were projects to be organized and aligned in the service of national power, with all the developmentalist possibilities that were to emerge in the course of the twentieth century.[19] This "new imperialism" did not dwell upon distinctions between economic and strategic interests and was generally in accord with contemporary Marxist observers, who argued that the essential feature of imperialism in this new phase was the pivotal role of the state in securing the future of the nation.

As the British and French moved more decisively down a colonial road, pursuing a political consolidation overseas to underwrite national power, the industrial newcomers followed a different path of domestic concentration based on the direct control of home markets. Like the accelerated urge to stake out colonial claims for the future, this inward turning was in many ways an immediate response to the world price depression. In the United States, attempts to control cutthroat competition and price instability with rate pools, price fixing, and market-sharing agreements produced early and largely unsuccessful experiments in cartelization and mounting pressure on the federal government to regulate markets or permit monopoly combinations.[20] A series of import duties, culminating in the McKinley tariff of 1890, made the United States one of the best-protected domestic markets in the industrial world. In Germany, the economic crisis produced a political turn to the right and a general rejection of liberal principles in favor of tariffs and state intervention. The protectionist measures of 1879, reinforced in the 1890s and completed in 1903, shielded both agrarian interests and industry while giving a boost to cartelization, especially among large banks and heavy industry, and they fostered a peculiar state-centered interest politics built around maneuver and bargains for special concessions.[21] In both countries, a major effect of price depression was a steady targeting of investment in new industrial sectors, especially science-based industries, which offered important comparative advantages, in that their high rate of technical innovation rendered older plants and equipment obsolete and nullified the lead of established producers over newcomers.[22] The new corporate forms that crystalized by the 1890s were extremely adept at exploiting these opportunities. A high ratio of fixed to circulating capital promoted a reorganization of the factors of production and placed a premium for survival on those organizations that could gain command of the forward and backward linkages, from input supplies to market sales, and, through a greater integration and concentration of elements, achieve the economies of scale, the labor control, and the productivity gains necessary for expansion in a highly competitive world economy.

These were essentially national organizations of productive power, aimed at a more efficient management of output and better control over domestic markets. Despite many obvious differences, Germany and the United States—as well as, a bit later, Japan and even Russia—had one thing in common: they all sought to carve out independent, national paths of development, turning in upon themselves and attempting (with varying degrees of success) to mobilize national societies and to organize productive capacities in essentially Listian projects of national development aimed at overtaking Britain's industrial lead.[23] In the case of both the United States and Russia, this effort came to involve the segregation of a large, state-protected national market that, in the wake of mid-nineteenth-century social and political renovation (a civil war in the United States and the emancipation of serfs in Russia) sustained the settlement and economic organization of vast territorial hinterlands and a large increase in agricultural surpluses as a foundation for indigenous industrialization. In the case of Germany and Japan, with much smaller domestic bases to build on, the effort involved the national consolidation of state power, grounded in universal military service and state-run education, which subordinated social order to an institutionally organized and increasingly planned drive toward national efficiency and economies of scale. We have called these strategies of self-improvement "corporatist" in an effort to focus attention on the highly organized industrial core and nationalist culture of these efforts at industrial self-mobilization.[24]

In each case, efforts to mobilize national societies in institutionally controlled processes of self-transformation had serious domestic consequences, producing heightened struggles over class relations and social values that, at times, threatened to undermine or even paralyze the drive for national industrial development. Where the effort succeeded, it took the form of a reorganization and institutional concentration of society that left behind the world of shopkeepers, small entrepreneurs, traders, farmers, and petit functionaries, as well as notions of status grounded in property and civic autonomy. Instead, it attempted to solve the problems of mass participation in the context of a rapid concentration of industrial and coercive power. The strain and febrile instability of these efforts and the explosive political and social effects they generated are everywhere apparent in the comparative literature on different trajectories. Indeed, the United States appears to have been uniquely privileged, with a large domestic market that gave capital room to maneuver and a highly developed, yet fragmented, democracy that tended to absorb and deflect dissent. Leading corporate elements were able to weather the crisis of the 1890s, sidestep populist protest, and destroy organized labor, before plunging into a period of intense accumulation and consolidation leading to the great boom of the 1920s. In Russia, by contrast, where capitalist development was far less robust and the autocracy too rigid to solve the problems of social mobilization or mass participation, the concentrated drive toward a state-centered industrial transformation ended in revolution; a self-reliant, national industrialization finally emerged in the command economy and terrorist politics of Stalinism. In the case of Germany and Japan, where the absence of a large internal market reduced the freedom to maneuver and forced industries into highly competitive export drives, the enormous strain of the domestic reorganization of the nation and the struggle for mass participation tended to get channeled into fervent nationalism, culminating in military aggression. For Japan, this took the form of expansionist wars against China and Russia; for Germany, it took the form of a direct challenge to Great Britain that ended in world war. Neither the industrial boom of the United States nor the revolutionary departure of the Soviet Union provided solutions to the transformational crisis that confronted German or Japanese society during the

1920s. With the onset of the Depression, their embattled passage to high industrialization broke into wars of desperate aggression and total defeat.

In almost every respect, Great Britain followed a different course. It was not simply coincidental that the leading and most successful imperial power had, among the industrial nations, the most decentralized economy, with the most technically obsolete industrial base, and the least concentrated financial sector, which, moreover, operated quite independently of national industries. Faced with the new corporate challengers, the British had a fundamental choice—between a massive investment in the retooling of domestic plants and equipment to meet the new industrial challengers on their terms or a redoubled effort to find new markets elsewhere in the world for their traditional exports in order, in effect, to evade the challengers— and they took the latter course. It was not only the path of least resistance, in that it exported the pains of domestic readjustment and imposed it on subject people far away; it also placed control over the long-term destinies of the nation in the hands of politicians and imperial administrators, rather than industrialists and merchants, and it confirmed the primacy of commercial capital in the City of London. This was an external (or externalizing) solution to economic challenges, and it meant that pressure for state action tended to take the form of calls not for tariff protection or market regulation in the domestic economy, but for imperialism. Although essentially a defensive strategy, Britain was successful, briefly in the two decades before 1914, in using its position as the leading imperial (territorial and statist) power to shore up a system of multilateral settlements, based on free trade and the gold standard, and to maintain its role as the principal financier and liquidity supplier for world trade and investment.

In the new configurations of geopolitics at the turn of the century, then, the path of colonial expansion and imperial consolidation represented a particular trajectory for organizing economic resources and mobilizing power that, moreover, was essential for Great Britain and, to a lesser extent, France, but not for any other major power. Yet the consolidation of this imperial solution, however, registered the presence of corporate challengers that, though often mimicking the colonial annexations of Britain, pursued experiments in national organization and productivism that aimed to outflank the British. The accelerating forces of global integration, sustained by deepening economic interconnections and competitive ties, was both the context and the effect of the parallel emergence of imperial and corporate strategies, and it ensured that both would be, from the outset, world-ordering concepts.

In recognizing that conflicts among Western powers also expressed the ongoing effort to translate a Western capacity for global domination into forms of world order, we find the main coordinates of conflict that shaped twentieth-century world history—conflicts that ran along a *lateral axis* of competition in the emerging (Western) center for control over the processes of global integration—that is, struggles over who set the terms and rules by which others must play—and conflicts that ran along a *vertical axis* of proliferating contestation over the rules and terms thus established—that is, struggles over how a regional (Western) capacity for global domination was to be realized in concrete regimes of order and social contracts for governing. These two axes of conflict themselves registered the centripetal forces of Western power and the increasingly centered world that was taking shape and that progressively marginalized other, formally significant arenas of conflict and did much to suppress, for a time, low-level and local forms of violence. But the fact that these two axes of contestation were becoming so deeply imbricated with one another suggests not only that global engagement was taking on a more continuous and multidimensional character, but also that Western regimes must be treated less as the authors of globalization than as attempts to address a new global condition and to order it. That Britain—briefly, before 1914—and the United States—also briefly, after 1945—were able to deploy and defend terms for a stabilization of order is a measure of their ability, in specific historic conjunctures, using the resources of competing imperial and corporate strategies, to contain or channel conflicts along both axes simultaneously and to exercise hegemony—that is, elicit consent or acquiescence in hierarchies of subordination—on a global scale. In exploring how this was done, along both axes of conflict and with what contradictory effects, we seek to open a path of explanation for the dual and mutually reinforcing processes of globalization: the relentless, multivalent deepening of global integration and the simultaneous reproduction and proliferation of difference. In short, the effort across the past century and a half to realize Western capacities for global domination in regimes of world order has produced not only a modern world in a Western image, but also a fragmented world of multiplying modernities.

The British Regime of World Order

The imperial land grab of the late nineteenth century is commonly taken as the culmination of a long history of territorial expansion of Western power in the modern word. But while it may have brought the history of British colonialism to its zenith, it was also the first instantiation of a new globalizing epoch.[25] The rapid spread of industrialization, mainly (but not exclusively) in Europe and North America, not only increased manufacturing output, but also promoted a tremendous expansion of commodity production for export throughout the tropical and temperate zones of the world.[26] This in turn quickened world trade, in both manufactured goods within the industrial world and exchanges between the industrial and agricultural sectors. The rapid improvement of transport and communications facilities after 1860 and the growth in overseas capital investment sustained a general expansion and recomposition of world trade.[27] Closer and denser linkages between disparate parts of the world tended to erode the autonomy of regional systems of exchange and to promote a deeper penetration of Western goods and services throughout the world. An increasingly multilateral system of payments, capped by a European-centered financial structure that, after 1890, was linked to the gold standard, permitted a complex global settlement of accounts between industrial and commodity producers. This higher level of global integration, coupled with the surge of Western technical capabilities and productive capacities, meant that, really for the first time, the West acquired world-ordering capabilities.

Britain maneuvered successfully to exploit these opportunities. It is notable that the period of "high" or "new" imperialism coincided with the consolidation of the City of London as "the most powerful financial and commercial centre that the world has ever seen."[28] The invisible earnings of British services in banking, shipping, brokering, insuring, communications, and transshipment not only were important in Britain's overall balance of payments, but also made British agents and networks critical for the conduct of business worldwide and London banks and discount houses pivotal in the financing of world trade. Moreover, the general adoption of the gold standard and the central role of the Bank of England in handling exchange and interest rates made London the center of international settlements and a powerful author of rules and regulations for the global economy. Although the explosive acceleration of transport and communications and the rapid expansion of productive and technical capabilities—among them, most crucially, military power—favored the North Atlantic world generally, it was Great Britain that first tried to address the challenges of global order that arose in this context. It was able to do so because of its unique ability to link colonial empire and high finance.

Internally, this linkage was expressed in a political accommodation between the City's commitment to free trade and the use of colonial possessions to shore up the system of multilateral settlement and exchange, on the one hand, and the manufacturers of the Midlands, on the other, who were rapidly being squeezed out of the markets of the advanced industrial world of Europe and North America and whose interest in tariff protection reflected a determination to shore up Britain's position in a more competitive world and secure the geopolitical basis of British power. Externally, the British regime was built upon its growing success in harnessing the energies of subordinate producers within colonial and quasi-colonial structures of control (vertical axes of conflict) and in bending the increasingly fierce international competition to the rules and regulations of British-centered finance and banking (lateral axes of conflict). What we wish to make plain is that there was a counterintuitive connection between Britain's retreat from competition in the production and trade of the industrial core regions—especially its markets in Germany and the United States—and its continued and absolute dominance of finance and services at the heart of the world economy. And this connection was forged not in the core corridors of the North Atlantic system, but in the industrializing and nonindustrial regions of the world, where Britain's imperial position made it a preeminent economic power and its sea power secured regionally decisive projections of military strength. Positioned at the nodal or relay points between tiers of the world economy gave Great Britain unique leverage in this period.

Britain's ability to manage relations between the industrial core and the other tiers of the world economy was fashioned around its unique trading position as a major importer of foodstuffs and primary commodities, as well as manufactured goods, and its continuing capacity to dominate export markets in the developing and nonindustrial regions of the world. Britain was at the fulcrum of a system of increasing specialization and hence of growing dependency upon long-distance exchanges. Not only did better prices for primary products and relatively favorable terms of trade between agricultural and industrial sectors increase output, but improved sea communications, especially the opening of the Suez Canal, and technologies of shipment, especially steam power and refrigeration, also brought down freight rates and promoted a tremendous diversification of trade patterns. The older bilateral and triangular exchanges that had been characteristic of the Western long-distance trade from earliest times and had shaped British commerce through the mid-nineteenth century, rapidly gave way to more multitiered networks of exchange. The general migration of Britain's exports to the developing and dependent worlds overseas built up trade surpluses, while its home markets remained open to imports of all kinds, especially foodstuffs. This underwrote the huge commodity boom across the regions of European settlement in the Western Hemisphere and the Antipodes.

This uniquely positioned Britain at the critical nexus between agricultural and industrial sectors in a period of increasingly complex interaction.

Germany and the United States, enjoying trade surpluses with Great Britain, were able to use them to offset their growing trade deficits with commodity producers in the tropical world, whereas Britain, moving in the opposite direction, could do the same in reverse. By 1910, Britain ran a total balance of payments deficit with Europe and the United States of £95 million, which was largely offset by its surplus balances with India, Australia, Japan, and China.[29] In this way, the British facilitated the export drives of the new, nationally organized economies, even as the growing challenge of these newcomers drove them deeper into the regions of empire and overseas influence in search of receptive markets and saleable resources. For a brief period, Britain's slippage in, and rising deficits with, the industrial world and its shift to, and rising surpluses with, the industrializing and nonindustrial worlds produced a precarious structural balance in world trade that enabled Britain to operate at the fulcrum of multilateral settlements. Furthermore, this multilateral settlement of trade accounts limited (though it in no way eliminated) the drag of mounting trade deficits upon finance capital and invisible earnings and helped free the City's resources for deployment elsewhere.

India made this capacity for maneuver feasible. This is not to revive a "drain theory" of imperial overlordship nor to reopen debates about the value of British investment returns from India or the burden that the home charges and other transfers placed on Indian revenues. Although it is appropriate to recall that Britain utterly dominated Indian domestic markets, which remained the largest single outlet for British exports, it is to the other side of this ledger that we wish to direct attention. India remained throughout the late nineteenth and deep into the first half of the twentieth century one of the most productive societies on earth and the largest single export economy of the nonindustrial world—accounting for more than a third of the tropical world's annual exports and running substantial trade surpluses in every year between 1864 and 1920.[30] India's exports, of both primary products and manufactured goods, were also among the most diversified in the world, developing strong trade surpluses with continental Europe and the United States, while anchoring a distinct regional trade system, stretching from China and Japan to the Middle East, in which India supplied (along with Japan) a growing proportion of manufactured goods and sustained favorable balances of trade with everyone, except Java.[31] India's success, in other words, depended on the opening of the Asian and, especially, the Chinese market, with the Near East and East Africa gaining prominence in the course of the twentieth century.

The effect of this trading system on monetary policy was quite stunning. In view of its own enormous trade surpluses with the subcontinent, Britain could, of course, apply India's earnings to offset its own trade deficits with other countries, especially in the industrial core. But India's earnings regularly exceeded its deficits to Great Britain, and it was the sizeable sums left over after all the transfers and trade settlements were made—balance-of-payment surpluses running between £30 and £50 million a year by 1910 —that came to play an important role in Britain's financial operations.[32] By keeping India on a silver standard as the rest of the world went to gold and managing the specie exchange mechanisms, Britain ensured that India's annual earnings were held, as gold deposits, in London, where they became a continually replenished source of liquidity for British lenders and a critical *masse de maneuver* with which the Bank of England could defend the pound and manage the all-important interest rate. In effect, India was prevented from converting its earnings into national savings or domestic consumption during the biggest trading boom in its history, and this prohibition by the imperial overlord gave India a "special role . . . in the construction and reproduction of the international monetary and commercial system by which the City profited."[33]

By the same token, commanding Indian surplus earnings helped the Bank of England handle the other great surplus earner in world trade, the United States, whose huge calls on gold every autumn at harvest time seriously taxed the City's reserves and whose monetary policy in the 1930s eventually broke the system. For a time, however, the fact that India was not allowed to call down its gold earnings not only enabled the central bank to handle these other demands, but also made available a large and easily controlled reserve with which to do it.[34] Ultimately, the stability of the gold standard—and with it London's management of world finance and a multitiered system of trade—rested not upon the free market, but upon the unfreedom of India. Britain's ability to manage relations within the industrial core and between the industrial core and the other tiers of the world economy was fashioned, in other words, by its unique position as overlord of the only great land-based empire of the Eurasian continent to fall under direct colonial administration.

Seen from below, the colonial regime of order was built upon the counterpunctual disintegration of autonomy among subordinated peoples. Across the colonial and semicolonial world, the elements of production, power, and social reproduction whose articulation in the past had produced the capacity for autonomous histories were pulled apart, sometimes violently, often quietly, but always in ways that destroyed autonomy. Production was lifted into the channels and circuits of world trade, and while much of it remained in the hands of peasant farmers, their efforts were realigned and coordinated to global ends. But even as the economic transformation reorganized production and reoriented producers, European overlords bent every effort to separate economic change from its political consequences. Key aspects of authority, especially the control of coercion and legal sanctions, as well as ultimate political decision making, were lifted clear of indigenous society and reimposed as Western technique through the colonial state, which was charged with promoting economic activity and keeping order without spending too much money or calling too often for reinforcements from home. This state used its authority to cushion and protect "native" life against the forces of change—less out of solicitude for the quaint and the prosaic than out of concern for the integrity of indigenous power brokers and the credibility of those willing to collaborate with colonial rule. Although these were often embattled and insecure figures, anxious to shore up status and power through timely alliances with colonial authorities, white administrators usually preferred to work with them, meddling in what they found, but chary of unduly disturbing indigenous customs and social relations. Protection ensured minimal consent. In their efforts to bolster the legitimacy of those compliant elites capable of controlling peasant producers, securing rural order, and collecting taxes, colonial authorities often found themselves creating and reinforcing "tribal" or "caste" distinctions and culling up rituals, pageantries, and the regalia of mystified tradition in which to wrap their clients.[35] The effect of all this was not only to immobilize colonial societies in rituals and forms of subordination that were concocted outright or congealed from an ongoing history and frozen into timeless, therefore unchanging, practice, but also to divorce custom and culture, real or imagined, from political power—creating, on the one hand, paths of mobility for some through European schools, legal and administrative careers, police and military service and, on the other, "native worlds" beyond the pale where much went on, out of the sight of colonial masters, that was utterly marginal to the processes of global integration yet central to the organization of everyday life, social values, and human meaning.

The fragmentation of indigenous worlds and the imposition of new hierarchies of economic and political power nurtured a more plainly inscribed segregation throughout the world. If the British regime dramatically advanced interaction on a global scale, drawing peoples around the world into networks of production and exchange and into careers and livelihoods subordinated to, and structured by, the colonial order, it also established rules of classification and separation. Fundamentally, for Britain to exploit the benefits of coordination among the tiers and between the sectors of an emergent global economy, it was vital to keep the elements in exchange distinct. Increasingly the British regime of order was built around a racial division of labor and a global system of apartheid. In the last decades of the nineteenth century, rigid barriers were erected to control the movement of non-European peoples and a more visible segregation was devised in colonial and semicolonial regions to define white privilege and ensure control over racial others through apartheid, legal discrimination, and outright terror. While nonwhites remained stuck in place or their movement was carefully channeled mainly into primary and agricultural production, whites moved from agriculture to industry or were generally free to migrate around the world and colonize it. The liminal zones in rapid transition were the regions of white settlement, which were mainly in temperate climates and became major producers of agricultural surpluses, on their way to higher levels of consumption and, in some cases, industrial development. These were also the zones of the most intense racism—the dominions more than the metropole, the Pacific Rim more than the Atlantic corridor, agricultural sectors more than centers of industry.[36] The emerging (re)division of people expressed a new global division of labor separating, worldwide, agriculture from industry, capital intensive production from artisanal and secondary industrial production, as well as from extraction and handheld cultivation.

Globally organized racism meant that a sustainable social contract between imperial overlords and colonial subjects was never possible. In recent scholarship, the term most often used to describe the tenuous nature of the colonial relationship is "collaboration," which some have tried to raise to the dignity of a theory.[37] The word carries pejorative connotations, of course, and other terms—like cooperators, mediators, or intermediaries—have been proposed in an effort to strip it of associations with Quisling and Petain. However labeled, the relationship itself was a nuanced and ambiguous stance that was highly adaptable and could easily be combined with other forms of fudging, hedging, malingering, or backbiting. Again and again, once and would be "collaborators" turned into "opponents" of colonial rule. Far from being a species of native ingratitude, such defections arose from the dynamics of colonial rule itself. Indigenous elites, propped up by the colonial state but denied substantive authority and undermined by economic change, were vulnerable to ridicule and often lost their value as collaborators, but it was precisely the preservationist tactics of colonial authorities that enabled some indigenous leaders to fall back on "native" traditions, real or reinvented, and, making use of local language press, revived rituals, and appeals to cultural authenticity, to formulate opposition to alien overlords. On the other hand, Westernizing elites, products of colonial education and employees of colonial administration, found in the frustrations and racist humiliations of subordinated careers and in their association with others trapped in the same circuits of colonial service the grounds for common cause and new forms of political action.[38] Anticolonial movements were essays of experiment probing the vulnerabilities of an alien, now familiar, overlord. And whether exploring the resonances of cultural dissent or the techniques of political mobilization, they were also engaged, however inchoately, in efforts to rearticulate the conditions of autonomous histories.[39] Collaboration, by whatever name, can thus be read as a fundamentally ambiguous sign of both a deepening imbrication within an integrating world and a path to the renewal of difference.

It is often argued that anticolonial thought and action was decisively stamped by Western ideas and imaginings, and so it was, especially with respect to nationalism. But it is also the case that the antiracism and the insistent quest for equality embodied in the challenges to colonial domination were not principles widely practiced nor readily embraced in the West. The shift to a nationalist mobilization, which materialized in the course of anticolonial struggles, was decisive, not only in gaining independence and forging new nations, but also in formulating and "globalizing" a discourse of rights. In effect, nationalist fervor also succeeded in turning particularistic assertions of difference into collective claims. It was this ability of anticolonial movements to shape collective imaginings and to organize transnationally—for self-determination, for racial equality, for economic development—that was, arguably, more decisive than the dreams of nationhood in undermining the hegemony of a regime of order built upon colonial empire.

Nationalist movements and mobilizations directly challenged the combination of integration and separation that undergirded this regime of order. In struggling to control the colonial state and build new nations from former colonies, they also rejected economic subordination and developed aggressive schemes for state-induced industrialization. In claiming racial equality, they radically undercut the regimes of local and global segregation that were predicates of colonial rule. In general, they aspired to break through the exclusions embedded in the process of globalization and to partake of it as collective actors in their own right, irrespective of race and creed, and free from imposed regulatory constraints. They bent Western ideals to their advantage, often in disregard of local cultures and with the effect of exacerbating the cleavages within their own societies. But it was they, rather than the British (or, for that matter, the Americans), who made the world over into a world of nation-states, however problematic that proved to be. They made the struggle for racial equality (and occasionally for equal rights irrespective of nationality, sex, race, language, and religion) and the abolition of systems of racial discrimination a global issue.[40] They organized themselves into the single most powerful non-Western presence in the twentieth century, establishing key claims that continue to course through contemporary debates about human rights, the regulation of migration, the application of international law to national contexts, the settlement of debts, and the protection of the environment. They did not by and large form "antisystems movements"—indeed they kept system-busters both of a "bolshevik" and of a "nativist" variety at bay—but in insisting that the British regime from which they had emerged must also work to their advantage, they radically undercut it.

THE AMERICAN REGIME OF WORLD ORDER

Corporate strategies of order emerged in the last decade of the nineteenth century as competing national projects for rapid industrial development. Unlike the British colonial regime, which reflected efforts to avoid industrial retooling by finding new markets abroad for old lines of manufacture, the various forms of corporate organization that emerged in Germany, Japan, and the United States were resolutely centered on the latest technologies and product lines. They were, in essence, strategies of self-organization and self-exploitation designed to mobilize resources and labor power for maximum efficiency, feeding domestic markets and export drives in concerted bids to overtake Britain's industrial lead.

The corporate transformation was always a more implacable and uncompromising process than the colonial project. Because corporatism was first and foremost a reorganization of national societies, working upon the same cultural terrain as those being (re)organized, it was able to achieve a far more comprehensive remaking of social relations, values, and culture than imperialism could ever do. Yet for this reason its progress was always more complex, embattled, and bitter. And because it developed outward over time, from productive centers to and through entire nations, the corporate transformation took far longer to accomplish. The Fordist reorganization of production was initially aimed at controlling labor power and rendering it more productive, but it carried with it an explicit recognition that mass production depended on mass consumption, and thus it folded into ever more ramified and intensive transformations of living as well as making and came ultimately to affect politics, social reproduction, culture, and taste. Though pursued for economic reasons, this was fundamentally a social renovation involving a *structural* concentration of capital and managerial controls, coupled with the specialization of functions and their (re)combination in rationalized hierarchies of the credentialed and meretricious; a *spatial* concentration of productive facilities in gigantic plants and industrial islands, coupled with the segregation of neighborhoods and the formation of a more precisely segmented labor force; and a *temporal* concentration of work routines, linked to machine technology and an ideology of efficiency, coupled with the development of leisure and the segmentation of daily life between work place and home. New methods of work thus became bound up in new modes of living and consuming that reached far beyond the daily routines and life expectations of industrial workers, and, in their elaboration, transformed how everyone lived.

Unlike the British colonial regime, corporate projects were not about exchange, or linkages between tiers or sectors of the world economy, but all about mobilization for successful intervention in the world. They were less concerned with interrelationships and more with consolidating the forward and backward linkages of production and consumption and developing the power bases for projecting force. In the narrow sense, national corporate strategies focused on the creation of protected spaces, defended by high tariffs and powerful militaries, as corrals of resources and manpower. The exploitation of contiguous hinterlands (the American West being paradigmatic) or the conquest of neighboring *Lebensraum* was everywhere a characteristic of these projects. This meant that relations with the wider world were established, less by the coordination or organization of others, and more by an internal generation of resources and production that could then be projected externally in the form of manufactured and cultural exports, capital investment, and power.

Small was definitely not beautiful in the corporate scheme of things. The more centralized and streamlined the command structures, the more elaborate the central "system" of governance, the better. The great appeal of this regime, especially to new urban populations, was that it was propelled by hopes and aspirations to, quite literally, "construct" the perfect society, free from want and fully rationalized, healthy and strong, and in pursuit of knowledge for the mastery of a well-ordered life. Massive public investments in education, as well as the expansion of applied sciences and scientific management, were key ingredients in the vision of a prosperous and manicured society whose crises could be managed by experts in clean surgical interventions (ranging from "father knows best" to "brushfire" interventions). The idea of a life of affluence and privilege came packaged—and here the national projects differed significantly—as the technological and therapeutic mastery of life (and death) itself.

The pursuit of such promises, which typically became diluted into the trickle-down effects of mass production, also produced victims, and unlike the colonial regime, which imposed its order on subjects far away and very different, the victims of the corporate transformation partook of the same national culture and citizenship as its agents. Indeed, the consolidation of the corporate economic order threatened with extinction whole social segments—the petty capitalists, regional producers, small-town elites, and farmers—that had been the backbone of nineteenth-century industrializing society. In effect, a new, self-declared modern sphere was superimposed upon a prior (now rendered traditional, outmoded, even backward) sphere. A "modern" articulation of production, authority, and social reproduction, based on indirect (that is, mediated, constructed, and impersonal) relations emerged alongside and was increasingly laid across the everyday world of direct (that is, personal, organic, and face-to-face) relations. Yet while thoroughly colonized, the everyday "life worlds" of experience did not disappear. Indeed, corporate society was characterized by a persisting gap between its rationalized order and system of constructed experience and the lived and everyday experience of ordinary existence. The two planes became utterly interconnected, yet utterly distinct. Direct relations no longer constituted society, in the sense that it was less and less possible to control or make sense of large-scale systems on the basis of extensions and analogies from everyday experience; nevertheless, the constructed reality of the corporate system could not fully rationalize or order, let alone control, the personal and unpredictable spheres of human encounters and emotions. If the rationalizing system of a modern dispensation was increasingly central in the provisioning and ordering of ordinary existence, these life worlds remained fundamental to the reproduction of society as it was actually lived, and they repeatedly erupted into political channels to challenge the forms and practices of corporate order. Although these strains of dissent were usually harmonized with the main themes of corporate integration, thanks to the agnostic flexibility and apparent neutrality of corporate values and to the omnivorous catholicity of corporate consumerism, with its constant negations in favor of the new and the improved and its almost pornographic efforts to appropriate the realms of feeling, the springs of resistance and cultural contestation were continuously renewed throughout the century in recurrent mobilizations around lifestyle issues, religious values, and the defense of family and community.

Precisely because corporate strategies turned in upon national societies, pursuing such powerful projects of self-exploitation in the name of efficiency and productivity, the most powerful countercurrents were not economic in nature. The resistance to industrial self-mobilization—agrarian revolt, populist politics, volkish mysticism, romantic protests, and religious fundamentalism—came in the form of cultural dissent—denunciations of the soulless, impersonal city, the snares of finance capitalism, the unseen machinations of monopolies, and the rootless or godless individualism of modern life—and in the evocation of small-town or peasant life, real and imagined—of traditional values, manageable horizons, and face-to-face obligations. The preference for dreamy romanticism, racism, or religiosity over against the rationalized saneness (or sameness) of corporate society should not lead us to assume that this resistance was benighted, backward, or blankly negative.[41] For its positive project was a broadly shared determination to place something other than production—be it emperor, racial purity, cooperative society, or God—at the center of social existence and to reorganize production, authority, and social reproduction around that alternate pivot. Political mobilizations in pursuit of these goals were explosive and extremely destabilizing, especially in moments of economic crisis when the corporate project was embattled and resistance radicalized. It was the politics of this resistance in the twentieth century, more than anything else, that powered the populist hypernationalism of German and Japanese conquest in the era of world war, but also imposed the main nationalist barriers of isolationism that blocked effective projections of American power in the interwar period.

There was, in fact, a decidedly expeditionary quality to American interventions in the world through the first half of the twentieth century. Military commitments tended to be temporary; the extension of capital liquidity for European recovery in the 1920s was quickly withdrawn when more profitable opportunities arose at home; and in the Depression of the 1930s, the United States reverted to a very nationalist recovery strategy under the New Deal. What brought the United States into the Second World War and put it, if only reluctantly, into the world ordering business was the growing realization that German and Japanese expansionism in the 1930s could not be read simply as regional wars of conquest, but amounted to projects to amass the sinews necessary for global projections of power.[42] In this respect, Pearl Harbor was both a revelation and a turning point that led not only to a merciless war of revenge, but also to the anxious, preemptive development of weapons of mass destruction. Yet there was still little about Soviet power, at least until the mid-1950s, that would gainsay the plausibility of a Taftite vision, based on the budget-cutting and antistatist priorities of the Republican Right, that had the United States pulling back to its continental base and hurling massive nuclear force against the Russians if they tried to use regional power in Europe against American interests.

Postwar reconstruction was profoundly conditioned by the experience of the 1930s.[43] In grappling with the problems of destruction, dislocation, and displacement, the United States was able to forge a powerful link between a national program for sustaining growth and a global program for economic recovery. This connection, which for the first time transformed a corporatist strategy of national self-improvement into a global regime of order, was made possible by the world war itself. National mobilization brought the United States roaring out of the Depression and sealed the elements of a "social pact" between business, labor, and the state that would shape the strategies of growthmanship after the war; the decisive defeat of Germany and Japan and the widespread destruction of the industrial tier of the world left the United States, with an undamaged productive base and unparalleled currency reserves, in a position to reshape decisively the terms of global integration. In realizing the possibilities of the moment, however, American policy makers engineered two key shifts in the alignment between the American national economy and the world. On the one hand, for the first time, the United States committed massive national resources to the world system in a sustained effort to remake and revive the European and Japanese industrial cores; on the other hand, also for the first time, the United States began to open its domestic markets to the world, making them available to all in an effort to facilitate a self-reinforcing circulation of goods and capital and to promote a greater specialization in the division of labor between industrial and industrializing or nonindustrial regions. The elements of a new world order, merging British principles of free trade and multilateral settlement with a corporatist emphasis upon production and capital concentration, took shape in the linkage between American economic nationalism and the restoration of a liberal world economy.

What ultimately turned prewar essays of American power, including Wilsonianism, into permanent projections after World War II was the growing perception that as the United States mobilized its industrial might to salvage democracy and restore prosperity in the world, it found abroad legitimation for the corporate order at home.[44] In particular, the postwar recognition that the democratic conversion and rapid recovery of Germany and Japan was key both to containing the capacity of the Soviet Union to project power globally and ensuring the legitimation and self-discipline of the corporate order domestically guided policy in the early cold war. Internally, political ties forged in the New Deal and world war between corporate and investment banking, liberal intellectuals, and organized labor underwrote an external commitment to aid and military assistance that promised to make the world safe for the American way of life and to underwrite the domestic production of that life. Notably, the Truman administration overcame Congressional opposition to its long-term aid program for Western Europe by couching it in terms of containing communism, which, Soviet intentions notwithstanding, deftly linked Main Street hatred of the New Deal, labor, blacks, and state regulation to permanent projections of American power overseas and by consolidating in the name of democracy and freedom the external legitimation of the corporate sector freed it to pursue a program of domestic pacification and stabilization. The salience of the image of an industrial nation defending democracy worldwide and developing it where it did not exist turned the global arena into a powerful source of legitimacy within the United States—and assured the remaking of the nation in the image of an industrial democracy.

This link between a permanent projection of power and the requisite domestic political consensus to sustain it enabled the United States to consolidate a truly global space of mutual interests—the "empire by invitation" —which was defined by and against the brooding "threat" of Soviet communism or its Chinese communist alternative.[45] In effect the American regime stood the old geopolitical adage about the Eurasian heartland on its head: the principal targets of German and Japanese expansionism—Russia and China—were made over into the ideological outsiders whose exclusion enabled the United States to order the world. The fear of communism—and perhaps more particularly, the dread of nuclear annihilation—disciplined the lateral competition among industrial nations and muted class conflict in Western societies, both major sources of instability in the previous fifty years, and this enabled the United States to pilot a recovery that eschewed the economic nationalism and protectionism of the interwar period in favor of a more open and interdependent industrial system. West Europeans, their old rivalries frozen in the East-West standoff and their hesitant moves toward cooperation reinforced by ideological solidarities, moved quickly toward economic recovery and regional integration during the 1950s. Japan, which had suffered destruction more devastating and a capital shortage more desperate than Europe, also experienced a rapid recovery, squeezed along by the windfall of the Korean War and underwritten by American moves both to open U.S. markets to Japanese goods and to secure the raw material supplies of south Asia in the wake of the "closing" of the Chinese mainland. Growth was maintained by strong and steadily expanding demand, as European and Japanese consumption rose to match American levels and national governments deployed redistributive and countercyclical policies to sustain demand. Whereas American monetary policy was aimed at restoring convertibility, the gold standard, and stable exchanges, the huge flow of dollars overseas went mainly to sustain production and consumption, not for international settlements, and this produced in Europe and Japan a final consolidation of corporate practices — productivist pacts between management and labor, active states committed to redistribution and social welfare, and a focus on consumption as the driving force of growth.

The postwar boom required, as a first order of importance, massive infusions of capital from the United States, but it entailed, as a necessary corollary, securing raw material supplies at low cost from the rest of the world. Unlike the colonial regime, the corporate concern was not with the direct control of territory, nor with exchange relations between industrial and agricultural sectors, nor with securing the revenues of commodity producing states in the tropics, nor with using commodity trade surpluses to settled multilateral accounts. Above all was the question of securing extraction—controlling and cheapening raw material inputs as the first link in a global organization of industrial production. This lent a strong anticolonial animus to the corporate consolidation, for not only were the old imperial powers now the economic and military dependents of the United States, but the Americans were also determined to see colonial preserves opened up for general exploitation. All things being equal, finding nationalist leaders who were prepared to build postcolonial independence upon the maximization of commodity outputs of all kinds was the American priority, but the choice between underwriting continued colonial rule and fostering rapid decolonization usually turned upon the question of how to ensure the subordination of the countryside and control over peasant producers. Anticolonial movements had always faced a choice between the path of rural revolt that sought to mobilize the masses in an insurgency to overthrow the European overlords and the path of state strengthening that sought to take the colonial state from its white masters and use its centralized power in the new national interest. But in the postwar world, this choice was resolved in favor of the latter path, as American development programs for postcolonial countries were, everywhere, targeted to urban, state-based elites bent on consolidating state power and subordinating their own people. In this, the communist menace remained a powerful foil, but here the Chinese antagonist proved most relevant, as it embodied the voices of peasant unrest and rural revolt against both colonial and postcolonial regimes in the 1950s and 1960s. Both major American wars in Asia in this period arose directly from the efforts of urban, militarized elites to pacify the countryside with support from the United States that turned, in different ways, into full-blown military commitments.[46]

The containment of communism as a means of fostering the industrial recovery of the core and the resubordination and ordering of primary supply to feed the economic boom in the West comprised the main coordinates of the American regime of order. But the whole was capped and rationalized by a new, transnational organization of knowledge. Fordist technique had always involved the appropriation of knowledge(s) of production from skilled workers and its reimposition as managerial control, and during the 1920s private foundations and associations had done much to foster the "cult of the engineer." It was, however, the massive public investment in education after the war that produced a huge, interchangeable service class of state experts and corporate managers in the United States, Europe, and Japan. Academic research and intellectual production became increasingly instrumental in the formulation of global order: in the conduct of the cold war, at the level of both strategic doctrine and "brushfire" interdictions to pacify rural insurgency; in the development of applied economics, especially the Keynesian growth strategies that had become canonic by the 1960s; and in the formulation of various versions of modernization theory and its application as development projects and strategies—whether as aspects of anticommunist campaigns or of efforts to promote maximum output at lower cost. American technical and intellectual leadership, and the educational commitments that underwrote it, were as important as its economic and military power in making world order cohere and, more important, in developing and organizing the consent of subordinate participants. And the organization of knowledge continued to function as a powerful cohesive and coordinator of action even after the American economic and military capacities to organize order began to wane. The Western canon became a major pole of contestation during the 1970s and after, with the growing global critique of development strategies and Western forms of knowledge, and long after anticommunism had lost its messianic overtones and subsided into a kind of nostalgia the defense of Western knowledge against the barbarians remained a powerful preoccupation among many Western intellectuals.

Yet, however effective the lateral coordination of practices and ideas, the American regime of order was never able to shut down or contain challenges and contestation along the vertical axis of conflict. This was especially the case there because the postwar order was built not on mass participation and inclusion, but on state-strengthening strategies and repression. Again and again, collaborating elites who had bought into the terms of American order and its vision of development had to wage campaigns against internal dissidence, whether communist in fact or in fantasy, to hold societies together in the face of the accumulating strains of subordinate integration in the American world order. For the corporate regime proved far less interested than the colonial regime had been in the integrity of whole economies or in the social viability of commodity producers. A cheapening and sustained supply of raw materials was often purchased at the price of social cohesion and well-being. Indeed, throughout the postwar boom, the conditions of primary producers steadily deteriorated. The rising demand for raw materials was matched by a steady decline in the prices commanded by commodity producers. The terms of trade, which under the colonial regime had remained roughly equal, steadily moved in favor of industrial producers, hollowing out the dream that expanding commodity production could earn the necessary capital for development. And rapid technical advances in agriculture, coupled with the determination of the European community and Japan to protect their farmers, promoted realignments of demand in commodities, from foodstuffs to natural resources, the extraction of which increasingly bypassed the peasant majority of the world. In short, the main source of continuing unrest and insubordination within the American regime of order was the ramified impact of the corporate agenda itself.[47]

It was still possible in the 1950s to believe that independence in the postwar order would allow nations to make choices based on some conception of common interest and developmental goals. But the corporate consolidation cut across such aspirations with a ferocity that brought most development projects to ruin within a decade of independence. As a vehicle for cultivating and holding consent, development or modernization quickly lost its allure in the face of repeated frustration and continued repression, and American hegemony in the so-called third world came to rest on a rapidly narrowing base of clients and cronies. By the late 1960s, development strategies based on the maximization of commodity output were coming in for critical scrutiny, and various alternative models, including socialist self-reliance and revived import substitution schemes, were being explored with new theoretical sophistication and institutional support.[48] A broad, "third world" discourse of solidarity emerged from a conjuncture of forces—the Vietnam War, the civil rights movement, the Chinese "cultural revolution," and intense contestations over a new economic order—to challenge the terms of global integration under an American aegis. The defeat of American power in Vietnam coupled with the OPEC oil embargo of 1973 brought this moment to a climax. Not only were the hearts and minds of the world's people not being won over to the terms of the American regime, but the success of a producer cartel in dramatically driving up commodity prices suggested the possibility of cutting a better deal within an integrating world. The oil crisis brought the postwar economic boom to a screeching halt. Coming on the heels of the collapse of the Bretton Woods system that forced the United States to disconnect the dollar from gold and in the shadow of the Soviet approach to nuclear parity that seemed to place the whole cold war security structure—not to mention the planet itself—in jeopardy, the world recession strained the synapses of discipline that held the industrialized tier together. The momentary solidarity of the "third world" and disarray of the "first" meant that the American capacity to contain or regulate competition along both the lateral and vertical axes of conflict was suddenly and quite radically diminished.

Whether the American regime of order continued to be American—or, for that matter, remained a regime of order during the last quarter of the twentieth century—is a matter of complex debate that we will not try to pursue here. In broadcast circles over the past decade, the word "hegemon" has been frequently attached to the United States. This is because the collapse of the Soviet Union left the United States as the world's only superpower, and all the world has had to pay attention. It is not entirely clear what this excess of power means—or even how new it is—but it is apparent that the end of the cold war has loosened the disciplines that bound allies to conform and usually kept subordinate states and nonstate actors in line. It has also freed the United States to act unilaterally. To be sure, the practices and institutions of economic cooperation that flow from and foster deepening integration continue, especially in the industrial core though with less American salience. But although the United States remains an economic powerhouse, it is encumbered with huge debts and trade deficits, and its leverage has become rather perverse: because everyone depends on it as the consumer of last resort, no one is quite prepared to let the engine of their own growth go into crisis. And while American military supremacy is unparalleled and unchallenged, it is not in fact clear what the United States can do with it. In any case, tactics used in the war on terrorism and recent national security pronouncements about preemption suggest that this power now seeks less to organize consent than to command compliance.

An obvious case in point is the Middle East, long the "India" of the American regime of order. Although the characteristic elements of corporate practice—a deterritorialized control of flow and a persistent effort to cheapen raw material prices, both at the point of extraction and through a multiplication of sources of supply—were all in play, with oil, the problems of insubordination were complicated by the very success of the regime as a whole. For since the 1970s, the growing dependency of the industrial core on cheap energy has enabled the cartel of producers to control the oil market by regulating output, thus precipitating crises over access and control that remain unresolved. Economically, of course, the oil producers' bid for better terms within the system have been accommodated through various measures of negotiated price increases, alternative sources, and the transfer of "dirty" production (and its costs) to the developing world. But solutions to the geopolitical question of oil admit no such flexibility. For the claim to control oil supplies—as opposed to prices—challenged the very division of labor that undergirded the entire corporate regime, while the deep dependency of the industrial core on cheap energy created stresses in the system that continue to generate instability and conflict. The need to beat back such claims and feed such dependencies has shaped American responses to OPEC, the Iranian revolution, the Afghan invasion, and Iraq's seizure of Kuwait, and it conditions choices made in the conduct of the current war on terrorism. There is no question that, over this period, American power in the region—as a capacity to project force—has grown dramatically, both as a function of new high-tech weaponry and as a result of the collapse of the Soviet Union. But the mounting ability and inclination to act unilaterally and the determination to beat down any sign of challenge to U.S. primacy does not amount to order, and indeed, in the Middle East, arguably, American efforts have so weakened allies and stoked hostility as to make the cultivation of consent or the organization of order beyond reach.

Similarly, the oil crisis of the 1970s did much to shatter "third world" unity. The huge transfers of wealth to the oil producers created vast new reserves of capital liquidity in the hands of private (mostly Western) banks and the ensuing scramble among lenders and borrowers enabled a few countries to break out along paths of rapid, export-led industrialization, sustained by domestic repression and huge infusions of international capital, while most others, making what deals they could, often at the expense of national interests and through the complete corruption of state elites, stalled out or broke apart. The widening gaps and disparities of wealth were reinforced by corporate strategies in response to continued economic uncertainty, as they scoured the earth for cheap labor and safe havens, spreading manufacturing and assembling facilities around, selectively, and laying down new nodules of wealth and intense development beside deep poverty. As heavily polluting, petroleum-reliant industries were moved offshore, whole regions of the "first world" were evacuated, leaving belts of poverty in the deindustrialized zones of the core at the core. The greater coordination and deeper integration of industrial and financial operations, worldwide, has been carried forward in a worsening context of concentrated affluence and mass poverty. The desperation with which the peoples of the world have sought to break into the circles of affluence—whether through migration, bribery, or force —and the webs of alternating wealth and deprivation that now crisscross the world are the visible synapses of a process of global integration that fosters disorganization and fragmentation. Fears of permanent exclusion also prompt disorderly rushes at the gates; indeed, arguably, the defeat of the socialist alternative in the world was due less to American containment than to the disintegration of "third world" conditions during the 1970s and the calculation by Soviet leaders around Gorbachev in the 1980s that, in the pervading environment of *sauve qui peut*, it was prudent to jettison a moribund economic apparatus, held up mainly by oil revenues, and make a rush through the doors to the charmed circle of industrialized countries before they were slammed shut.[49]

Most do not make it. Marginal zones of unsettlement, untouched by yet unessential to globalization, multiply, bombarded with the artifacts of material production and consumption, but lacking the capacity for anything more than a perverse participation. Indeed, the story of segmentation, of narrow corridors of wealth amid deepening poverty, suggests a secret strength of corporatism itself—that, although it can include almost anyone, it can just as well do without almost anyone. Whole regions and populations are simply discarded, with no function to perform and no leverage, except perhaps to starve to death on global television; equally important, if perhaps less dramatic, corporatism can also abandon the United States, moving out along transnational circuits and jettisoning its domestic bases to operate on a global plane.[50] The result is a regime less of order than of proliferating disorder, and the reality is pressed home that the bases for organizing consent become ever narrower. Indeed, mounting evidence of environmental and planetary exhaustion render the Western project of perpetual growth itself less persuasive and the promise of universal development flatly unbelievable. The new preemptive doctrines of the United States present a unilateralism of tremendous force, but it is a capacity for violence that is designed to cow and command obedience yet displays scant capacity to organize consent and thus to sustain a regime of order. The era we have essayed here is over.

Conclusion

Both the imperial and corporate regimes of order, as expressions of Western power in the world carrying pretensions to regulate the whole, promoted processes of global integration, deepening interconnectivity, and interdependence. But as regimes of order with distinct limits and patterns of exclusion, they generated contradictions, new niches of contestation, and renewed resistance, which, far from undoing the forces of globalization, came to express the deepening conditions of globality. In this way, we have tried to argue that it is not the rise and fall of Western dominance that shapes our world, so much as the ways Western power, in seizing its fleeting opportunities and relative capabilities, tried to translate its power for domination into settled rules and regimes of order. And it is not the success or failure of these efforts that fragments our world, but rather the effect of these ordering efforts upon people around the world, who have engaged and resisted global regimes of order in the relatively brief moment that these regimes were ascendant and, by their refusal to either fully embrace or entirely reject them, have managed to bend, adapt, and rework Western efforts to order the world in ways that remade it, but not in a unified or orderly Western image.

Notes

1. The view was put most forcefully and controversially by Francis Fukuyama, "The End of History?" *National Interest* 16 (summer 1989), but it is a view that suffuses post–cold war strategic discussions and economic programs and informs some of the impatience of policy making in the "war on terror."

2. This view was most forcefully put by Samuel Huntington, *The Clash of Civilizations and the Remaking of World Order* (New York: Simon & Schuster, 1996).

3. See Theodore von Laue, *The World Revolution of Westernization: The Twentieth Century in Global Perspective* (New York: Oxford University Press, 1987), in which the world is seen as caught up in an immense and conflict-ridden engagement with the legacies of the West, not only its ideas of freedom, but its raw struggles for power.

4. Michael Geyer and Charles Bright, "For a Unified History of the World in the Twentieth Century," *Radical History Review* 39 (1987): 69–91, and "World History in a Global Age," *American Historical Review* 100:4 (1995): 1034–1060.

5. Arthur A. Stein, "The Hegemon's Dilemma: Great Britain, the United States, and the International Economic Order," *International Organization* 38:2 (1984): 355–386.

6. There are several variants of what might be called this "wave theory" of globalization, turning upon the ebb and flow of Western capabilities. It opens up a narrative of stages,

as in A. G. Hopkins's introduction to his collection *Globalization in World History* (New York: Norton, 2002), or of waves, as in Robbie Robertson, *The Three Waves of Globalization: A History of Developing Global Consciousness* (London: Zed Books, 2003); it also allows interruptions in the forward movement of globalization, when Western power proves, temporarily, unable to push the forces of integration ahead, as suggested in Kevin O'Rourke and Jeffrey Williamson's treatment of nineteenth-century progress, *Globalization and History: The Evolution of a Nineteenth Century Atlantic Economy* (Cambridge, Mass.: MIT Press, 2000), or in Harold James's analysis of the interwar depression, *The End of Globalization: Lessons from the Great Depression* (Cambridge, Mass.: Harvard University Press, 2002).

7. On colonialism, see Roland Robinson and J. A. Gallagher, with Alice Denny, *Africa and the Victorians: The Official Mind of Imperialism* (London: St. Martin's Press, 1961), and, recently, Philip Curtin, *The World and the West: The European Challenge and the Overseas Response in the Age of Empire* (New York: Cambridge University Press, 2000).

8. Christopher Bayly's helpful term, in a keynote address at the conference "Interactions: Regional Studies, Global Processes, and Historical Analysis," Washington, D.C., March 2, 2001.

9. This is the case especially in anthropology and cultural studies. See Arjun Appadurai, *Modernity at Large: Cultural Dimensions of Globalization* (St. Paul: University of Minnesota Press, 1996).

10. A seminal meditation on these distinctions—and with it a sharp critique of Weber's notions about the relationship of power and violence—is Hannah Arendt's "Reflections on Violence," *Journal of International Affairs* 23:1 (1969). We are aware that our use of the term is different from its deployment in international relations theory, which was really developed in the context of the cold war to understand the American exercise of power and then read "back" to earlier periods of equipoise, such as the Venetian-Genoese, the Dutch, and the British. Our usage has a more Gramscian nuance, though without the usual cultural turn and with an interest in politics and the negotiations of power.

11. A recent collection of papers from a 1997 conference in Windsor Great Park has stressed these differences. See Patrick Karl O'Brien and Armand Cleese, eds., *Two Hegemonies: Britain 1846–1914 and the United States, 1941–2001* (Aldershot, England: Ashgate Press, 2002).

12. Michael Geyer and Charles Bright, "Global Violence and Nationalizing Wars in Eurasia and America: The Geopolitics of War in the Mid-Nineteenth Century," *Comparative Studies in Society and History* 38:4 (1996): 619–657.

13. This point has been forcefully made about Ottoman reformers by A. T. Atmore, "The Extra-European Foundations of British Imperialism: Towards a Reassessment," in C. C. Eldridge, ed., *British Imperialism in the Nineteenth Century* (London: St. Martin's Press, 1984), pp. 108–114.

14. On the impact of the Great Depression, see S. B. Saul. *The Myth of the Great Depression, 1873–1896* (London: Macmillan, 1969), and Hans Rosenberg, *Grosse Depression und Bismarckzeit* (Berlin: de Gruyter, 1967).

15. See Tony Smith, *The Pattern of Imperialism: the United States, Great Britain and the Late-Industrializing World since 1815* (Cambridge: Cambridge University Press, 1981), who explores how great power rivalry was intensified by economic depression and domestic political competition.

16. Eric Hobsbawm's *Industry and Empire* (London: Weidenfeld & Nicolson, 1968) was an early and persuasive argument for defensive imperialism, a position further developed

in his *Age of Empire, 1875–1914* (New York: Vintage, 1989). See also W. G. Hynes, *The Economics of Empire: Britain, Africa, and the New Imperialism, 1870–1985* (London: Longman, 1979). P. J. Cain and A. G. Hopkins, *British Imperialism, 1688–2000* (London: Longman, 2001), have questioned the defensive nature of British imperialism, largely by insisting on the centrality of finance and the marginal importance of British manufacturing and export trade.

17. For a clear exposition of three stages of change in British imperialism, see James Sturgis, "Britain and the New Imperialism," in C. C. Eldridge, ed., *British Imperialism in the Nineteenth Century*, pp. 85–105.

18. Lord Rosebery, quoted in William Langer, *The Diplomacy of Imperialism* (New York: Alfred Knopf, 1941), p. 78.

19. "I regard many of our colonies as being in the condition of undeveloped estates, and estates which can never been developed without imperial insistence." Joseph Chamberlain, quoted in Michael Barratt Brown, *After Imperialism* (New York: Humanities Press, 1963), p. 103.

20. The now classic study is Alfred Chandler, *The Visible Hand: The Managerial Revolution in American Business* (Cambridge, Mass.: Harvard University Press, 1977); see also Olivier Zunz, *Making America Corporate, 1870–1920* (Chicago: University of Chicago Press, 1990), and David Noble, *America by Design: Science, Technology, and the Rise of Corporate Capitalism* (New York: Alfred Knopf, 1977).

21. The classic statement is in Eckart Kehr, *Der Primat der Innepolitk: Gesammelte Aufsatze zur preussisch-deutschen Sozialgeschichte in 19. Und 20. Jahrhundert* (Berlin: W. de Gruyter, 1965). See also Wolfgang Mommsen, *Imperial Germany, 1867–1918* (London: Arnold, 1995); Karl Erich Born, *Wirtschafts-und Socialgeschichte des deutschen Kaiserreichs, 1867/71–1918* (Stuttgart: Steiner, 1985); and Geoff Eley, *Reshaping the German Right: Radical Nationalism and Political Change after Bismarck* (New Haven, Conn.: Yale University Press, 1980).

22. David C. Mowery and Nathan Rosenberg, *Technology and the Pursuit of Economic Growth* (New York: Cambridge University Press, 1989); Thomas Hughes, *American Genesis: A Century of Invention and Technological Enthusiasm* (New York: Viking, 1989); and Fritz Ringer, "The German Academic Community," in Alexandra Oleson and John Voss, eds., *The Organization of Knowledge in Modern America, 1860–1920* (Baltimore: Johns Hopkins University Press, 1979).

23. On the Listian, nationalist development model, see Roman Szporluk, *Communism and Nationalism: Karl Marx versus Friedrich List* (New York: Oxford University Press, 1988).

24. The sticky problem of definitions, we leave to one side for now. See Philippe Schmitter, "Still the Century of Corporatism" *Review of Politics* 36 (January 1974); see also Peter J. Katzenstein's useful discussion of common attributes (central planning, close links between state and business, skepticism of markets, and possibilities of coercion) in *Small States in World Markets* (Ithaca, N.Y.: Cornell University Press, 1985) and John Zysman, *Governments, Markets and Growth: Financial Systems and the Politics of Industrial Change* (Ithaca, N.Y.: Cornell University Press, 1983).

25. The debate over "free trade imperialism" in the early and mid-nineteenth century is an old one. See Christopher Bayly, *The Imperial Meridan: the British Empire and the World, 1780–1830* (London: Longman, 1989); Oliver MacDonagh, "The Imperialism of Free Trade," *Economic History Review* 14 (1962): 489–501; and D. C. M. Platt's series of inter-

ventions, "The Imperialism of Free Trade: Some Reservations," *Economic History Review* 21 (1968): 296–306; "Further Objections to an 'Imperialism of Free Trade,' 1830–1860," *Economic History Review* 26 (1973): 77–91; and "The National Economy and British Imperial Expansion before 1914," *Journal of Imperial and Commonwealth History* 2 (1973): 3–14.

26. The output and transport of food products is of especial interest. Here the most rapid growth—and the target of major agricultural investment—was in an "intermediate" zone of white settlement—the wheat belts of Canada and the United States, the cattle ranching of Argentina, and the meat and grand production of Australia and New Zealand. These areas, which were the principal source of food imports for Britain (and Germany), are discussed by Donald Denoon, *Settler Capitalism: the Dynamics of Dependent Development in the Southern Hemisphere* (Oxford: Clarendon Press, 1983), and Avner Offer, *The First World War: An Agrarian Interpretation* (New York: Oxford University Press, 1989).

27. Estimates of trade and investment are in Albert Imlah, *Economic Elements of the Pax Britannica: Studies in British Foreign Trade in the Nineteenth Century* (Cambridge, Mass.: Harvard University Press, 1958).

28. See the prologue of David Kynaston, *The City of London.* Vol. 2: *Golden Years, 1890–1914* (London: Catto & Windus, 1994).

29. S. B. Saul, *Studies in British Overseas Trade, 1870–1914* (Liverpool: Liverpool University Press, 1960).

30. K. T. Shah, *Trade, Tariffs, and Transport in India* (Bombay: National Book Depot, 1923); an item-by-item breakdown of Indian exports is in C. N. Vakil and S. C. Bose, *Growth of Trade and Industry in Modern India* (Calcutta: Longmas, Green, 1931).

31. On economic diversification, see B. R. Tomlinson, *The Political Economy of the Raj, 1914–1947* (London: Macmillan, 1979). On the development of international trade, see A. J. II. Lantam, *The International Economy and the Undeveloped World, 1865–1914* (London: Macmillan, 1978), table 13, p. 76.

32. The mechanisms are spelled out with great clarity in Marcello de Cecco, *Money and Empire: The International Gold Standard, 1890–1914* (Oxford: Blackwell, 1974); A. P. Kaminsky, "'Lombard Street' and India: Currency Problems in the Late Nineteenth Century," *Indian Economic and Social History Review* 17 (1980): 307–327.

33. Geoffrey Ingham, *Capitalism Divided? The City and Industry in British Social Development* (London: Macmillan, 1984), p. 123.

34. As de Cecco makes clear (p. 70), the problem of commanding Indian residual surpluses was directly related to efforts to prevent the Indian government from calling down gold.

35. See Eric Hobsbawm and Terence Ranger, eds., *The Invention of Tradition* (Cambridge: Cambridge University Press, 1983), and, on caste in India, Nicholas Dirks, *Castes of Mind: Colonialism and the Making of Modern India* (Princeton, N.J.: Princeton University Press, 2001).

36. Among many others, see Jane Dailey, Glenda Gilmore, Bryant Simon, eds., *Jumpin' Jim Crow: Southern Politics from Civil War to Civil Rights* (Princeton, N.J.: Princeton University Press, 2000); A. Markus, *Fear and Hatred: Purifying Australia and California, 1850–1901* (Sydney: Hale & Iremonger, 1979); C. A. Price, *The Great White Walls Are Built: Restrictive Immigration to North America and Australasia* (Canberra: Australian Institute of International Affairs, 1974).

37. Ronald Robinson, "The Non-European Foundations of European Imperialism:

Sketch for a Theory of Collaboration," in E. R. J. Owen and R. B. Sutcliffe, eds., *Studies in the Theory of Imperialism* (London: Longman, 1972).

38. Here, of course, see Benedict Anderson, *Imagined Communities: Reflections on the Origins and Spread of Nationalism* (London: Verso, 1983).

39. There is a vast literature on these struggles, some focusing on religious revivalism (Michael Adas, *Prophets of Rebellion: Millenarian Protest Movements against the European Colonial Order* [Chapel Hill: University of North Carolina Press, 1979]; Bryan Wilson, *Magic and the Millennium: A Sociological Study of Religious Movements among Tribal and Third World Peoples* [London: Heinemann, 1973]; Peter Worsley, *The Trumpet Shall Sound: A Study of Cargo Cults in Melanesia* [New York: Schocken, 1968]; and Karen Fields, *Revival and Rebellion in Central Africa* [Ithaca, N.Y.: Cornell University Press, 1972]); some focusing on labor conflicts (Frederick Cooper, *From Slaves to Squatters: Plantation Labor and Agriculture in Zanzibar and Coastal Kenya, 1890–1920* [New Haven, Conn.: Yale University Press, 1979]; and Ann Stoler, *Capitalism and Confrontation in Sumatra's Plantation Belt, 1870–1979* [New Haven, Conn.: Yale University Press, 1985]); and some revolving around more essentialist analyses of peasant life (James Scott, *Everyday Forms of Peasant Resistance* [New Haven, Conn.: Yale University Press, 1984] and his work with coeditor Benedict Tria Kerkvliet, *Everyday Forms of Peasant Resistance in South East Asia* [London: Frank Cass 1986]; also Eric Stokes, *The Peasant and the Raj: Studies in Agrarian Society and Peasant Rebellion in Colonial India* [New York: Cambridge University Press, 1978]).

40. Paul Gordon Lauren, *Power and Prejudice: The Politics and Diplomacy of Racial Discrimination* (Boulder, Colo.: Westview, 1988).

41. Namely, Seymour M. Lipset and E. Raab, *The Politics of Unreason: Right-Wing Extremism in America, 1790–1970* (Chicago: University of Chicago Press, 1978).

42. Bruce M. Russett, *No Clear and Present Danger: A Skeptical View of the United States Entry into World War II* (New York: Harper & Row, 1972).

43. Most recently, Patrick J. Heardon, *Architects of Globalism: Building a New World Order during World War II* (Fayetteville: University of Arkansas Press, 2002).

44. We have developed this argument at some length in Bright and Geyer, "Where in the World Is America? The History of the United States in the Global Age," in Thomas Bender, ed., *Rethinking American History in a Global Age* (Berkeley: University of California Press, 2002).

45. On the domestic consensus, see "America's Cold War Consensus," in Jack Snyder, *Myths of Empire: Domestic Politics and International Ambition* (Ithaca, N.Y.: Cornell University Press, 1991). See also Geir Lundestad, "Empire by Invitation? The United States and Western Europe, 1945–1962," *Journal of Peace Research* 23 (1986): 263–277.

46. See Bruce Cumings's study of the origins of the Korean War, in which urban elites, backed by the American occupation regime and utilizing the police forces and administrative apparatus of the old Japanese colonial state, sought to bring peasant insurgency in the rice-growing south under control, *The Origins of the Korean War*. Vol. 1: *Liberation and the Emergence of Separate Regimes, 1945–47* (Princeton, N.J.: Princeton University Press, 1981), and George Kahin, *Intervention: How America Became Involved in Vietnam* (New York: Alfred Knopf, 1987).

47. There is a growing literature on the development project, including Philip McMichael, *Development and Social Change: A Global Perspective* (Thousand Oaks, Calif.: Pine Forge Press, 2000); Arturo Escobar, *Encountering Development: The Making and*

Unmaking of the Third World (Princeton, N.J.: Princeton University Press, 1999); and Frederick Cooper and Randall Packard, eds., *International Development and the Social Sciences: Essays on the History and Politics of Knowledge* (Berkeley: University of California Press, 1997).

48. Raul Prebisch was the father of this largely Latin American current. See *The Economics of Development of Latin America and its Principal Problems* (New York: Praeger, 1950). His work with UNCTAD was paralleled by radical academics, including Andre Gunder Frank, *Capitalism and Underdevelopment in Latin America* (New York: Monthly Review Press, 1969), and Celso Furtado, *The Economic Development of Latin America* (New York: Cambridge University Press, 1970). See also the collection in Mary Ann Tetreault and Charles Abel, eds., *Dependency Theory and the Return of High Politics* (New York: Greenwood Press, 1986), and Carlos Waisman, *Reversal of Development in Argentina: Postwar Counterrevolutionary Policies and Their Structural Consquences* (Princeton, N.J.: Princeton University Press, 1987).

49. As argued by Stephen Kotkin, *Armageddon Averted: The Soviet Collapse, 1970–2000* (New York: Oxford University Press, 2001).

50. The debate over the formation of a transnational civil society has only begun. A good introductory contrast may be found in Leslie Sklair, *The Transnational Capitalist Class* (London: Blackwell, 2001), and William Robinson, *Transnational Conflicts: Central America, Social Change and Globalization* (London: Verso, 2003). Other interventions include Alejandro Colas, *International Civil Society* (Cambridge: Polity Press, 2002), and Mary Kaldor, *Global Civil Society: An Answer to War* (Cambridge: Polity Press, 2003).

Contributors

C. A. BAYLY is Vere Harmsworth Professor of Imperial and Naval History at the University of Cambridge. He has published on Indian, imperial, and world history. His recent publications include *Empire and Information: Intelligence Gathering and Social Communication in India, 1780 to 1870* (1996) and *The Birth of the Modern World: Global Connections and Comparisons, 1780 to 1914* (2003).

SVEN BECKERT is professor of history at Harvard University, where he teaches nineteenth-century U.S. history. He is the author of *The Monied Metropolis: New York City and the Consolidation of the American Bourgeoisie* (2001) and is currently writing a global history of cotton.

JERRY H. BENTLEY is professor of history at the University of Hawai'i and editor of the *Journal of World History*. He has written widely on cross-cultural interactions in world history and also on historiographical issues raised by world history. His publications include *Old World Encounters: Cross-Cultural Contacts and Exchanges in Pre-Modern Times* (1993).

RENATE BRIDENTHAL is professor of history (emerita) at Brooklyn College, the City University of New York. She coedited and contributed to *Becoming Visible: Women in European History* (1977, 1987, 1998), *When Biology Became Destiny: Women in Weimar and Nazi Germany* (1984), and *Heimat Abroad: The Boundaries of Germanness* (2005).

CHARLES BRIGHT is professor of history in the Residential College, University of Michigan. He works on the history of globalization in collaboration with Michael Geyer and teaches American political history, prison history, and the history of Detroit. His most recent book is *The Powers that Punish: Prison and Politics in the Era of the "Big House," 1920–1955* (1996).

MICHAEL GEYER is Samuel N. Harper Professor of History at the University of Chicago. His main areas of interest are German and European history, the history and theory of human rights and humanitarianism, and world history and globalization. With Charles Bright, he is currently completing a book-length study titled *Global Condition in the Long Twentieth Century.*

ALAN L. KARRAS teaches world history, Caribbean history, and classical political economy in the International and Area Studies Teaching Program at the University of California at Berkeley. He is the author of *Sojourners in the Sun: Scots Migrants in Jamaica and the Chesapeake, 1740–1800* (1993), and the coeditor, with John R. McNeill, of *Atlantic American Societies: From Columbus through Abolition, 1492–1888* (1992).

ADAM MCKEOWN is associate professor of history at Columbia University. He has published *Chinese Migrant Networks and Cultural Change: Peru, Chicago, Hawaii, 1900–1936* (2001), and he is currently writing a new book titled *Establishing International Identities: Asian Migration and Global Governmentality, 1868–1934.*

COLIN PALMER is Dodge Professor of History at Princeton University. He is the author of numerous studies of the Atlantic slave trade and is currently writing a book titled *Eric Williams and the Making of the Modern Caribbean.*

STEPHEN H. RAPP, JR., is associate professor of history at Georgia State University and the founding director of the Program in World History and Cultures. He served as general editor of *Kartlis cxovreba: The Georgian Annals and Their Armenian Adaptation* (1998), and his *Studies in Medieval Georgian Historiography: Early Texts and Eurasian Contexts* (2003) is the first installment of a projected trilogy.

CAROLINE REEVES is assistant professor of history at Williams College. Her field of expertise is Chinese history of the late Qing and Republican periods. She is particularly interested in the history of international organizations in China.

JOHN O. VOLL is professor of Islamic history and director of the Center for Muslim-Christian Understanding at Georgetown University. He is past president of the Middle East Studies Association and has published numerous books and articles on Islamic movements and Sufi brotherhoods.

KÄREN WIGEN is associate professor of history at Stanford University, where she teaches Japanese history and the history of early modern mapping. She is the author of *The Making of a Japanese Periphery* (1995) and coauthor, with Martin W. Lewis, of *The Myth of Continents: A Critique of Metageography* (1997). Her research interests include the historical geography of East Asia, regional economies and rhetorics, and geographies of the imagination.

ANAND A. YANG is Golub Professor of International Studies and director of the Jackson School of International Studies at the University of Washington. His publications include *The Limited Raj: Agrarian Relations in Colonial India, Saran District, 1793–1920* (1989), *Bazaar India: Peasants, Traders, Markets and the Colonial State in Gangetic Bihar, 1765–1947* (1998), and an edited volume titled *Crime and Criminality in British India* (1986).

Index

regime: colonial, 229; American/corporate, 205–206, 228–230, 233; British/imperial, 205–206, 233
religion, 20, 23, 27, 30–31, 40, 45, 104, 184, 221; cosmic, 15–17, 40
rights: human, 221; theories of individual and state, 23
Ritter, Carl, 159

Safavid: dynasty, 188; empire, 175, 181; state, 35
Sanson, Nicolas, 154–155
Sasanid: dynasty, 174, 178–179, 185, 187–188; empire, 185
section 6 certificates, 114–115, 118–121, 124–125, 127, 129
segregation, 219–220, 222
Shamil, Imam, 42
Sino-Japanese War of 1894–1895, 74
Sirhindi, Ahmad, 37, 41, 44
slavery, 8, 16–17, 52, 54–56, 59–60, 94–96, 102–103, 105
slaves, 49, 54, 94–96
smuggling, 9, 116, 136–142
Spear, Chloe, 102
Spilhaus, Athelstan, 160
Sufi (mystic): brotherhoods, 31–32, 37, 39, 41; devotional traditions and organizations, 30–32, 35, 42; jihads, 42; orders, 36–37, 40, 43–44; teachers, 32–33, 36, 41
sugar, 54, 104, 139–140, 143–144, 204
sultans, 35
surveillance, 117; domestic, 112–113; individuals, 110; political, 25; state, 24

tariffs, 52, 57, 60, 138, 213; barriers, 57; McKinley tariff of 1890, 210; policies, 51
tariqah, 32, 33–35, 37, 38, 42–44

tea, 17–18, 204
tobacco, 17–18, 54, 204
Torpey, John, *Invention of the Passport*, 25, 110
trade, 9, 139–140, 145, 178, 203, 209, 215–216, 229; cotton, 52–53; free, 24, 59, 146; illegal, 144; illicit, 141, 143; international, 21, 119, 138; slave, 96, 101, 103; triangular, 156; world, 17, 212, 214, 217–218
Tradition and Innovation in Late Antiquity, 189
Transcaucasian Federation, 181
transnational networks, 117, 156, 161

Valladolid, Mexico, 48–51, 58, 61
visa, 9, 109–111, 112–114, 118, 120, 124, 128
Vivekananda, Swami, 27

Walker, David, *David Walker's Appeal in Four Articles*, 96, 99
Wheatley, Phillis, 96, 102
Wigen, Kären, 169–172, 175, 177, 180, 182–183, 186–187, 190–191
Williams, George Washington, 103
Williams, Rev. Peter, 99–100
world court, 78
world history, 67, 152, 157, 159, 161–164, 202–204, 207, 213
World Parliament of Religions of 1893, 25, 27

Yang Ru, 74–85
Young Robert, *Ethiopian Manifesto*, 96

Zhang Zhidong, 72, 76
Zheng Zaoru, 116
Zongli Yamen, 81–82, 85
Zoroastrianism, 174, 177–178, 185

Production Notes for BENTLEY / INTERACTIONS:
TRANSREGIONAL PERSPECTIVES ON
WORLD HISTORY

Cover and interior designed by Elsa Carl
with text in Caslon and display in Tiepolo

Composition by Josie Herr

Printing and binding by The Maple-Vail Book
Manufacturing Group.